# THE
# REAL ONES
## FOUR
## GENERATIONS OF
## THE FIRST FAMILY
## OF

by
### Elizabeth Candler Graham
and
### Ralph Roberts

Published by Barricade Books, Inc., 1530 Palisade Avenue, Fort Lee, NJ 07024
Distributed by Publishers Group West, 4065 Hollis, Emeryville, CA 94608

Copyright ©1992 Elizabeth Candler Graham and Ralph Roberts

Interior Design and Electronic Page Assembly: WorldComm®

Printed in the United States of America

Library of Congress Cataloging-in-Publication Data

Graham, Elizabeth Candler
    The Real ones: four generations of the first family of Coca-Cola / Elizabeth Candler Graham and Ralph Roberts
ISBN 0-942637-62-3 : $21.95
        1. Coca-Cola Company—History. 2. Candler, Asa Griggs, 1851—1929—Family. 3. Candler family. I. Roberts, Ralph. II. Title.
HD9349,S634C6336 1992
338.7'66362'0973—dc20                                    92-18778
                                                         CIP


0 9 8 7 6 5 4 3 2 1

The name *Coca-Cola*, the *Coca-Cola* logo, and the word *Coke* are all registered tradmarks of The Coca-Cola Company.

# Contents

## Dedication

This book is for my mother, Nancy Candler Nutter, who has been a living example of all the good things our family has represented over the years.

# **Preface**

This book is the story of a family that struck *black gold* more than a century ago, creating a dynasty that is still enjoying its benefits.

Black gold is not oil and not coal, those have to be wrested from the ground with hard labor and expensive equipment. No, this black gold is cold and delicious. This black gold is tart, yet sweet, and goes down a parched throat on a hot summer's day like nothing else. This black gold is Coca-Cola, made from inexpensive renewable ingredients, with no digging required.

Asa G. Candler — a hard-working Georgia Methodist in the pharmaceutical trade — acquired the formula for Coca-Cola some one hundred years ago for a paltry twenty-three hundred dollars. Dabbling with it, changing it by choice and at the insistence of the federal government, Candler parlayed his modest investment into one of the world's largest companies — if not its most famous one.

Along the way, his family, The Real Ones, would experience triumphs, tragedies, internecine battling, scandals, and great joys. Its ranks would be filled with hard-working, studious men and women whose primary aim in life was to enrich their company and community. And it would have its share of rogues and rascals.

What follows is an exclusive inside look at Coca-Cola

and the magnificent, powerful, and dynamic Real Ones of
Asa's generation and the generations that followed — the
good as well as the bad. Family members relate events here
as only they could know. Finally, the full story of Coca-Cola
and the Candler family can be and is being told in this one
hundredth anniversary year of The Coca-Cola Company's
incorporation.

Elizabeth Candler Graham
and
Ralph Roberts

Asheville, North Carolina
July, 1992

# Acknowledgments

It's funny how some things come into being. This book actually started
out as a quest to track down a few family photographs to complete a
scrapbook project. As it progressed, I discovered few photographs, but so
many delightful family legends and stories. At some point, it became
obvious that these little glimpses into a bygone era should be saved. It could
not have been done without the tremendous help and encouragement of
many people. I had no idea when I started what fun was in store for me and
how many people would want to help. Not only was the Candler clan
enthusiastic, but I soon found that folks connected in any way with The
Coca-Cola Company or Emory University were also happy to participate.

I am indebted to all my delightful kith and kin who not only shared their
memories, but also their scrapbooks, letters, and homes. There is a wit, a
frankness, and a charm that pervades the entire clan. Getting to know them
all has been a treat and I am grateful to each of the following for sharing so
much with me: Catherine Candler Warren, Laura Candler Chambers,
Caroline McKinny Clark, Eugenia Candler Wilson, and the late John
Holtzendorff Wilson, Louise Hancock Owens, Caroline Candler Hunt,
Frances Candler Shumway, John Slaughter Candler II and Dorothy Warthen
Candler, Henry Charles Heinz, Jr. and Martha Hurt Heinz, Laura McCarty
Candler, Marion "Bootsie" Candler Ruffner and Edward Harry Ruffner,
Thomas Homer Thompson, Jr., Mettelen Thompson Moore, Nancy Candler
Nutter and Charles Nisbett Nutter, Edgar Chambers III and Jackie Shattles
Chambers, Asa Griggs Candler V and June Rackley Candler, Mary Ripley
Warren and William Chester Warren III, Dorothy "DeDe" Candler Hamilton,

Samuel Ozburn Candler and Betsy Denny Candler, Robert Samuel Chambers, Mary Ann Edmondson Bresee, Helen Candler Griffith, the late Robert Philip Hare IV, John Howard Candler, Jr., Robert Anderson Edmondson III, Rachel Hamlin Still and Samuel David Still, Robert Hewlett Elliott, Jr., Alton Bertow Roberts, Jr., Ann Candler, Laura Hare Norton, Elizabeth Edwina Chambers, Edgar Chambers IV, Clark Ellison Candler, and Louisa Miller.

A good bit of information came from stories told to me years ago by people now missed, but never forgotten: the late Thesis "Sis" Fowler Little and the late Lucy Candler Thompson who, over the years, shared their memories and stories. The late Samuel "Slim" Green who took such pride in his connection with the Candlers, in his job, and in telling his stories to us children.

Most particularly, there is a special gratitude for the many facts and stories which came to me from the late Florence Stephenson Candler who always said that she had married and lived with a Candler and therefore could talk about them if she wanted to—which meant no one else could, especially newspaper people!

In addition to family and friends, many other people enthusiastically contributed to this effort and deserve a special note of thanks:

The Honorable Senator Herman E. Talmadge who shared his thoughts and memories with me.

Franklin Garrett of the Atlanta Historical Society who gave to me of his time and his incredible memory along with Ann Salter and her staff.

The Archives Department of The Coca-Cola Company was most gracious in allowing me access to all of their information, and I wish to express my deep appreciation to both Philip Mooney and Laura Jester for their help and assistance.

The staff with Emory University's Special Collections Department, Robert W. Woodruff Library was extremely helpful in my search for information. A special thanks to Ellen Nemhauser, Barbara Mann, Kathy Knox, and Ginger Cain for their patience and their suggestions for other sources.

I would also like to thank Dr. Judson "Jake" C. Ward of Emory University, Mellie C. Davis of Oxford College, Emory University, Tom Oertling of Galveston, Texas, Susan Taylor of Salem College, and Robin Lee and Albert W. Stubbs with Hatcher, Stubbs, P.A. of Columbus, Ga.; all of these folks helped track down little details that were necessary, but hard to find.

Jody Smith with the Clerk's Office Fulton County Courthouse, Sheila Dodd, Theresa Morrow, and Danise Wilson with the DeKalb County Clerk of Superior Court's office.

My good friend, the late Russell Cartwright Davis, Jr. whose enthusiasm and encouragement when he was in so much pain, meant more than he will ever know.

Kathryn L. Hall for her many hours of dedicated work on this, from transcribing tapes to organizing material; it has been a learning experience for our token "Yankee."

Nancy Dillingham for helping to read and edit the material.

A very special thanks and hug to those who literally handed me keys to their homes and said "make yourself at home": Sam and Rachel Still, my "favorite" brother-in-law, John Joseph "Jake" Duffy and sister, Caroline Nutter Duffy, my brother David Candler Nutter, and "favorite" sister-in-law, Susan Thomas Nutter and my aunt and uncle, June and Asa Candler. They also made phone calls and generated a great deal of enthusiasm within the family, as did my aunt, Nena Griffith.

To four of my cousins who expressed their encouragement — it meant a great deal: Nancy Griffith Hooff, Asa Griggs Candler VI, Richard Brandon Candler, and William Rackley Candler (who really went out of his way on several occasions).

To Ralph Roberts, for his valuable assistance as coauthor of this book.

To those wonderful people at Barricade: Carol Stuart, Jon Gilbert, and Sandy Stuart, and our agent, Richard Curtis.

And, finally, two people who gave so much to this book: My mother, Nancy Candler Nutter, who has threatened to write such a book for years. She gave so much of her time, and helped write, read, and review the material; her insight was of tremendous value.

Last, but perhaps most important, my dear friend, Frank Wilson Puett. This book was his idea. He insisted my hobby of family history should be more than a few file folders. He convinced Ralph that it would be a good project for him as well, he watched over my various eccentric enterprises leaving me free to travel where necessary, he was our sounding board, he gave us a "country boy's" interpretation and explanation of much of the material, and he encouraged us both when we would get tired of the project. He has been the best kind of friend, just as his kinsman, Cornelius Dysart, was for Elizabeth Anthony Candler in a previous generation.

# Section One:

# The First Generation of Coca-Cola

# The Backyard Beginning

It was once disparagingly described as "99-percent sugar and water." But it is that other one percent that makes it The Real Thing, that sweetness, that bitterness, the hint of this taste, the suggestion of another, the fizzy tickle across the tongue, and the refreshing glide down the throat. Now that's Coke.

Coca-Cola.

Coke has become a universal product. You don't need to speak the language. Ask for a Coke on the sands of the Mideast, the pampas of Argentina, among the lush foliage of a Polynesian island, or under a "Red Rising Star of the East" flag in China, people will know what you want.

For a century now, millions of soda fountain clerks and machines have mixed one ounce of Coca-Cola syrup with six-and-a-half ounces of carbonated water, and millions upon millions of people have plunked down their nickels, pesetas, francs, birrs, rupees, and rials for the pause that refreshes.

Coca-Cola has become a billion-dollar business, but it all started modestly on a May day in 1886, behind the house of one John S. Pemberton of Atlanta, Georgia.

Pemberton was a druggist, who like so many others of the day dubbed himself "Doctor," although no evidence of a formal medical degree has ever been found. He had fought with Pemberton's Cavalry and served as a captain with

3

General Joe Wheeler during the War for Southern Independence. At the end of the war, Pemberton, like the rest of his
fellow Georgians, was working hard to rebuild his life in the
defeated Confederacy — that proud country that had existed
all too briefly and was now occupied by blue-clad foreign
troops. Only slowly did Georgia and the South come reluctantly back into the Union, and some foot dragging continues even today.

For four years, Pemberton stayed in his hometown of
Columbus, Georgia, but by 1869, the aggressive vibrancy of
the rebuilding Atlanta enticed him north. There, he set up
in business as a druggist and pharmaceutical chemist. By
1870, he had joined with other businessmen to form
Pemberton, Wilson, Taylor and Company. Pemberton was
an idea man, a creative wizard more at home mixing up
amazing panaceas to cure the ills of humanity than he was
with profit-and-loss statements and ledger books. It was
always to be others who reaped the rewards of his creations,
but that would not stop Pemberton from trying.

During the next fifteen years, Pemberton went through
several business affiliations, the major one being the company of Pemberton, Iverson and Dennison. In 1885, he
established the J.S. Pemberton Company and, not long
afterwards, the Pemberton Chemical Company. By that
time, many of his medicines were quite well-known across
the South. They included Extract of Styllinger (a medicine
for the blood), Gingerine, Globe of Flower Cough Syrup,
Indian Queen Hair Dye, and Triplex Liver Pills. These were
the booming days of patent medicines and snake-oil salesmen, before the federal Food and Drug Administration came
along to insist on testing and truth. As long as the paying
public could be made to believe that a product cured insom-
nia, grew hair, loosened the bowels, and shut up mothers-in-
law, all was fair in the free market.

Somewhere in this concocting of liver pills and hair dye,
Pemberton got the idea for a new tonic. The actual moment
and method of the creation of Pemberton's Tonic, as it
appropriately was first called, has been clouded, colored,
and flavored by legend and word-of-mouth retelling after
retelling, with elaborations and embellishments added as

the teller saw fit. In later years, generations of publicity and advertising people further reworked and polished the legend for the sake of the bottom line.

E.J. Kahn, Jr., in his book *The Big Drink*, writes that the syrup for Pemberton's Tonic was based on Pemberton's French Wine Coca, patented in 1886 and sold as "an ideal nerve and tonic stimulant." Kahn states that Pemberton had simply taken out the wine, substituting "a pinch of caffeine," and added a few ingredients including an extract of cola and other oils. It is believed that Pemberton was trying to create a cure for headaches.

What is known for sure is that on or just before May 8, 1886, in the backyard of 107 Marietta Street, Pemberton cooked up the first batch of syrup for his new tonic in a brass kettle. Then later on that Saturday, he took a jug of his syrup down to Jacobs' Pharmacy, which had one of Atlanta's leading soda fountains. The fountain, with its elaborate counter running for twenty-five feet along one entire side of the drugstore, was leased and managed by Willis E. Venable.

Pemberton talked Venable into mixing some of the syrup with water and trying it. The soda-fountain man liked the taste and agreed on the spot to sell it. So it was that on that day in May, someone paid his or her nickel for a glass of Pemberton's concoction and drank it there in the store.

According to Cecil Munsey, author of *The Illustrated Guide to the Collectibles of Coca-Cola*, it was decided at about this point that with Venable having signed on to market the tonic, a new name was needed for it. Within a few days, the name "Coca-Cola Elixir and Syrup" was chosen. Involved in the naming process were various members of Pemberton's company — Pemberton himself, his business partner, Edward W. Holland, David D. Doe, and company secretary and bookkeeper Frank M. Robinson.

It was Robinson who hit upon putting together the words "coca" and "cola," two of the tonic's ingredients. He liked their alliterative, easy-to-remember sound. He also suggested that the name be written in the Spencerian script that was a popular form of penmanship then. It was from his pen that the neat and precise "Coca-Cola" signature originated. Pemberton and the others were pleased with

Robinson's ideas except for the length of the name. The words "Elixir and Syrup" were dropped, and the product became known simply as "Coca-Cola."

Later that month — on May 29, 1886 — the *Atlanta Daily Journal* had the honor of carrying the first advertisement for Coca-Cola. It was a simple ad, with "Coca-Cola" printed in plain type instead of script. The ad stated: "Coca-Cola, Delicious! Refreshing! Exhilarating! Invigorating! The New and Popular Soda Fountain Drink, containing the properties of the wonderful coca plant and the famous cola nuts. For sale by Willis Venable and Nunnally & Rawson."

As indicated by the reference to "Nunnally & Rawson," in less than a month after its introduction, more than one establishment was serving Coca-Cola. Of course, it wasn't the Coke we know today. It was flat. There was no carbonation, no fizz.

As the unconfirmed story goes, this was changed accidentally on the morning of November 15, 1886. A certain gentleman by the name of John G. Wilkes had partaken heavily of bottled spirits the previous night. Awakening with a splitting headache, he sought relief from a nearby pharmacy. Since Coca-Cola had been created and touted by Pemberton to be, among other things, a cure for headaches, it was no surprise that someone wanting quick relief would try it. Wilkes desperately seated himself at the soda fountain and called, no doubt, softly and carefully while holding his shattering skull together, for a glass of Coca-Cola. The soda fountain clerk, by mistake, mixed Coca-Cola syrup with *carbonated* water. The fizzing result was pleasing to Wilkes and brought relief to his pounding temples. Whether or not this story is true, it soon became the standard practice to mix Coca-Cola syrup with carbonated water.

Coca-Cola, however, was not an astounding sales success under Pemberton's management. In its first year, only twenty-five gallons of syrup were sold, that being enough for about 3,200 glasses. Approximately $50 was realized in sales, but $73.96 had been spent on advertising. The next year, 1887, sales rose dramatically to more than one thousand gallons. Although Pemberton was rightly convinced that he had a winner, he was in failing health and didn't have the capital to properly advertise and promote the product.

In July, 1887, Pemberton offered a friend, George S. Lowndes, two-thirds interest in the Coca-Cola formula if Lowndes would invest in the company. While Lowndes found the offer attractive, he was not interested in actually going out and selling jugs of syrup himself. He went to someone with sales experience, Willis Venable, to see if he wanted in on the deal, as well. Venable did. However, there was a problem. Venable did not have the money for his share of the purchase. Lowndes offered to lend it to him.

The resulting deal with Pemberton was a payment of twelve hundred dollars for two-thirds interest, with Venable promising to reimburse Lowndes for six hundred dollars from Coca-Cola sales profits. In the papers that were signed on July 8, 1887, the twelve hundred dollars was described as a loan to Pemberton with repayment to come from his share of profits. On July 15, a modified contract was signed changing the deal to read that Pemberton's loan was to be repaid from *total* profits.

Another stipulation of the deal was that the new partners were to take over ownership of all the items and fixtures used in the manufacture of Coca-Cola by "paying the said Pemberton therefor [sic] the original cost." In an inventory drawn up on July 27, 1887, this cost was computed to be $283.39. These assets — including advertising materials such as posters, signs, and cards — were loaded in a wagon and moved to Jacobs' Pharmacy. According to a later president of The Coca-Cola Company, although not listed on the inventory, a brass kettle, sixty tin cans, and a percolator made their way over to Jacobs', as well.

After the inventory was in place, Willis Venable took over the manufacturing of Coca-Cola in between the already time-consuming task of running his soda fountain. George Lowndes was not pleased with the result. Orders for syrup often piled up because Venable was too busy to make it. Lowndes bought out Venable, then, on December 14, 1887, turned around and sold the two-thirds to Woolfolk Walker, salesman for the Pemberton Chemical Company, and Walker's sister, Mrs. M.C. Dozier. The purchase price?

Twelve hundred dollars, Lowndes' original investment.

Walker, over the next few months, realized that he could not get the company really profitable without working capital to expand facilities and to advertise properly. He sought help from two men. One was Joseph Jacobs, who owned Jacobs' Pharmacy and on whose premises the equipment to manufacture Coca-Cola syrup was still set up. The other was a very successful druggist Walker had met while selling for Pemberton. That man was Asa Griggs Candler.

The three men joined in a new firm called Walker, Candler and Company (although Jacobs appears to have had no percentage of ownership) and on April 14, 1888, purchased Pemberton's remaining one-third of the rights to Coca-Cola for the sum of $550. Although on paper the new company bought out Pemberton, it was actually Candler who put up the money with the understanding that he would own the third. This gave Walker and his sister two-thirds interest in Coca-Cola and Candler the other third.

Then on April 17, Candler increased his share by purchasing another third from Walker and his sister, giving him a public one-third interest but, in reality two-thirds of the company. It was a complicated arrangement, similar to the earlier one where Pemberton gave away two-thirds of his company for a twelve-hundred-dollar "loan."

Pemberton, in all, received $1200 plus $550 plus the $283.39 for equipment and other inventory, or a total of $2,033.39 for the creation of Coca-Cola. Sadly, he did not even live long enough to enjoy that amount. His health continued to worsen rapidly, and he died some four months later on August 16, 1888. To honor their late associate, Asa G. Candler, as chairman of the association of Atlanta druggists, called for all the drugstores in the city to be closed during Pemberton's funeral, as they were.

Later that same month — on August 30, 1888 — Asa Candler bought the remaining ownership of Coca-Cola from Woolfolk Walker and his sister for one thousand dollars. Candler had now spent a total of twenty-three hundred dollars to obtain full and complete rights to Coca-Cola.

Asa G. Candler had already built a pharmaceutical business into one of the most successful in the South by seeing and seizing opportunities. Coca-Cola, from his vantage point, had possibilities. But after discovering the product, Candler decided that Pemberton and the other people involved in producing and selling it were not doing a very good job. Candler didn't want part of some slipshod, poorly managed operation. He wanted total control of Coca-Cola so that he could maximize its potential. He was a sharp and canny businessman with the skills and confidence to go after what he wanted.

Candler was purposely secretive in the way he handled the purchase of Coca-Cola. He was one of the leading pharmacists in Atlanta and assumed to have a lot of money. Had Pemberton known he was behind the buy offer, in all likelihood, the price would have gone up. Candler was also very clever in spreading the risk among other partners until the profit-making potential was obvious. Only then did he go for full ownership and control.

There is no question that Coca-Cola would not exist today if Asa Candler had not become involved with it. Neither Pemberton, Lowndes, Willis Venable, nor Walker and his sister had the marketing skills or the capital to achieve more than selling a few hundred gallons of syrup a year to local soda fountains. Coca-Cola was, frankly, not that special when compared to the better-established competition such as Moxie. The true genius of Asa Candler was marketing, which turned this patent medicine from a mere tonic to a soft drink that automatically gets put on grocery lists. He was to become the true Father of Coca-Cola. Still, in 1888, all this was to come.

One might wonder what Candler saw in this little-known tonic that had sold barely more than a thousand gallons in its not quite two years of existence. And while Candler was a clear-eyed businessman, the answer lay in not so much what he saw, but what he felt — constant, horrific migraine headaches.

Asa had lived with these headaches since suffering a terrible accident as a child. His mother, Martha Bernetta Beall Candler, described the mishap in a letter to his oldest sister, Florence Candler Harris, dated December 11, 1862.

> My dear daughter I know you are uneasy that you dont
> hear from us I waited some time to hear from you but mail
> quit coming. The Confederate government has taken the
> contract and now we will get the mail when it is convenient
> for them to send it. We are all well except Asa. He fell out
> of a loaded wagon and the wheel ran over his head just
> above the ears and crushed his head and left him very badly
> but stronger today. He is now we think out of danger. In his
> fever he says he wants to see you. The first word he said was
> when is my sissie coming? I shall never see my dear sister
> Harris any more. Jessie has nursed him day & night without
> number. Though he can eat & set up he cant hear. The
> nerves of his left eye were crushed so that he cant see or
> hear on that side but he can whistle yet. His escape from
> death is a miricle and only by the thoughtful kindness of
> God was he saved, for which I most humbly and cincerly
> give Him all the honor & praise & cincer thanks.

One of Pemberton's goals in formulating Coca-Cola was to present a cure for headaches. During almost all of its first decade of life, Coca-Cola was considered to be a medicine. Candler himself advertised it in the 1890s as "The Wonderful Nerve and Brain Tonic and Remarkable Therapeutic Agent."

Candler confirmed his belief in Coca-Cola as a headache tonic in an April 10, 1888, letter to his brother Warren, who was living in Nashville and would later become an influential Methodist bishop.

> You know how I suffer with headaches. Well, some
> days ago a friend suggested that I try Coca-Cola. I did &
> was relieved. Some days later I again tried & was again
> relieved. I determined to find out about it. Investigation
> showed that it was owned by parties unable to put it fairly
> before the public. I determined to put money into it & a
> better influence. I put $500 of the first and am putting a
> goodly portion of what I have of the last...

Asa was already thinking of expanding Coca-Cola's market.

"Now I don't want to make a merchant or peddler out of you," Asa went on in his letter to Warren, "but if you could either send me the name of a party who wants to engage to introduce Coca-Cola into Nashville (the best soda fountain town in the South I am told) I will make it interesting to him. It is a fine thing — certainly."

What Asa had in mind was a classic promotional ploy. He would supply two gallons of syrup gratis — enough for 256 servings when mixed with carbonated water — if the druggist would send him the names of 128 men and women. Asa then would send a ticket to the druggist's fountain to these people, entitling them to a free glass of Coca-Cola. Once they tried a glass, Asa was sure they would want more. The druggist would then have the remaining 128 servings to sell.

It was an interesting — and amusing — facet of Asa's personality that he would enlist his brother, a Methodist preacher, into selling his new product. Later, he would have another brother, a judge, drinking Coca-Cola and thus giving it at least tacit endorsement. Asa Candler used all resources to sell his product, family included. Everybody in his family worked for Coca-Cola, even if they were not on the payroll. In the case of Warren, a good preacher had to be able to sell the word of God — selling Coca-Cola should have been, at least in Asa's mind, a snap compared to that.

Brother Warren did help, as is evidenced by a letter Asa sent him on June 2, 1888. In it, he thanks Warren for his assistance with a Mr. Walker. He reports that Walker sold thirty gallons in Nashville, although he had expected him to sell one hundred. Asa wrote that they were doing "modestly well with Coca-Cola. It's only obstacle is that Pemberton is continually offering a very poor article at a less price & the public who pays for Coca-Cola & are not fulfilled commensurably decide that it is a fraud."

It would seem that Pemberton's company — if not Pemberton himself — was still marketing something similar to the Coca-Cola formula which, of course, they would have still known, or at least the version that Pemberton had sold to what became Candler's company. After Asa took over, improvements were made.

Asa Candler's great-granddaughter, Nancy, remembers her grandfather, Asa G. Candler, Jr., (called Buddie by the

family), and others in the family talking about Asa, Sr.'s
headaches and about the original formula.

"Buddie always said that he and [his brother] Howard
were sent over to Haverty's Hardware, to buy something to
mix the ingredients up in. Aunt Florence said that Asa, Sr.
changed the Pemberton formula several times to make it
taste better and to increase its shelf life. Asa believed Coca-
Cola had terrific qualities as a medical cure-all. He had
migraines and the Coca-Cola helped ease his headaches."

For several years after gaining control of Coca-Cola, Asa
Candler continued to sell it more as a medicine than a
refreshing drink. In writing to a doctor in Cartersville,
Georgia, on April 2, 1890, Candler extolled its therapeutic
qualities.

"We desire to call your attention to the Ideal Brain
Tonic, Coca-Cola, a delightful summer and winter soda
fountain beverage which has proved to be very beneficial
and agreeable in hot or cold weather at all times of the year
to those who desire a tonic stimulant...

"The medical properties of the Coca Plant and the
extract of the celebrated African Cola Nut, make it a medical
preparation of great value, which the best physicians
unhesitatingly endorse and recommend for mental and
physical exhaustion, headache, tired feeling, mental depression, etc.

"Coca-Cola has such a very marked effect in refreshing
and reviving the drooping spirits and taking away the tired
feeling and so promptly relieves the headache, that it is
constantly making good friends, who not only use it themselves but gladly recommend it to others."

Candler got into the Coca-Cola business primarily because he saw a chance to make a profit, and he stayed in it
because it became so profitable that he was eventually able
to drop all the rest of his pharmaceutical business. However,
he was first attracted to Coca-Cola because it cured his
headaches, and he continued to believe strongly in the
medicinal properties of the drink for the rest of his life even
though, for various reasons including the federal government, he would change the original formulation.

There has been much speculation over what was in that

original formula, the big question being, "Did Coca-Cola have cocaine in it?" In researching this book, and in conversations about it, that is certainly the topic that comes up most often. Such rumors have bedeviled The Coca-Cola Company, and, indeed, other soft drink manufacturers for decades.

In parts of the South even today, soft drinks are still referred to as "dopes." Then, too, there is the obvious connection between the term "coke" for cocaine and "Coke" for Coca-Cola. One must wonder if some smart public relations person years ago didn't pre-empt the damaging aspects of the word "coke" to the product by capitalizing and trademarking it, and then insisting that it was just a fondly diminutive contraction of Coca-Cola's full name. Regardless, the results have been the same. When you think of Coke, you hear the fizz. The word "coke" with a small "c" conjures up visions of crack and white powder.

Frank M. Robinson came up with the name "Coca-Cola" because Pemberton's tonic contained extracts of both the coca leaf and kola nut. The coca leaf has no relation to, and should not be confused with, the cacao seeds from which comes the cocoa beverage and chocolate. Coca leaf is grown primarily in Peru and Bolivia and is the main source of the stimulant alkaloid cocaine. Coca leaf extract which has not been de-cocainized is approximately 50 to 75 percent cocaine.

Kola nuts — which are really seeds of an African tree rather than nuts — contain the stimulant caffeine. There is no question that caffeine was in the original formula of Coca-Cola, and, still is, except for, of course, the caffeine-free versions. The big question is: "Was the coca in Coca-Cola 'de-cocainized?'" The answer is yes, and has been for decades.

But what about in the beginning? Was the early version of *Coke* also *coke*? First, it must be understood that at the end of the last century, cocaine was not recognized as a dangerous and addictive drug. The sale of products containing cocaine was perfectly legal. You could even order them from that other American icon, Sears Roebuck. The 1897 Sears catalog carried the following advertisement for Peruvian Wine of Coca:

"It sustains and refreshes both the body and the brain, and has deservedly gained its excellent reputation and great superiority over all other tonics. It is most effective and rapid in its action. It may be taken for any length of time with perfect safety without causing injury to the system, the stomach and gastric juices. On the contrary, Peruvian Wine of Coca aids digestion, removes fatigue and improves the appetite, never causing constipation. For many years past it has been thoroughly tested and has received the endorsements of hundreds of the most eminent physicians of the world, who assure us of their utmost satisfaction with the results obtained by using it in their practice. They urgently recommend its use in the treatment of Anemia, Impurity and Impoverishment of the Blood, Consumption, Weakness of the Lungs, Asthma, Nervous Debility, Loss of Appetite, Malarial Complaints, Biliousness, Stomach Disorders, Dyspepsia, Langor and Fatigue, Obesity, Loss of Forces and Weakness caused by excesses, and similar Diseases of the Same nature...

Not a bad deal for ninety-five cents a bottle, or ten dollars a dozen.

If such a solid, respected purveyor of American virtue as Sears Roebuck was selling drugs, it is little wonder that you could purchase products based on cocaine, opium, and other substances now known to be harmful at any pharmacy in the world and certainly also in Atlanta during the latter part of the nineteenth century.

Pemberton's products prior to Coca-Cola definitely contained cocaine. By about 1881 or 1882 he was selling Ginger and Coca Tonic. In 1882, he developed French Wine Coca, which contained both alcohol and cocaine. This was not a new idea. Robert L. Hester in *The Coca-Cola Cocaine Connection* reports that a similar product to French Wine Coca, Mariani Wine, had been manufactured in Paris since the 1860s, hence Pemberton's derivative name of French Wine Coca.

Pemberton, however, did not simply copy Mariani Wine, he added his own unique and innovative twist — extract of the kola nut to put in caffeine. The resulting popular product had both cocaine and caffeine in a wine base. It must have packed some wallop, and even at the high price of a dollar a bottle, it sold well.

In an interview published in 1885 in the *Atlanta Constitution*, a reporter described Pemberton, with little journalistic objectivity, as "a well known chemist ... regarded by all scientists in America as probably without a superior in this country, and he has made a study of coca for years. There is no doubt that he knows more of coca than any other American."

Pemberton is quoted, "I wish it was in my power to substitute the coca and compel all who are addicted to the use of opium, morphine, alcohol, tobacco, or other narcotic stimulants to live on the coca plant or any of its true preparations. I could confer no greater blessing on the human race."

Given his beliefs, there was no incentive for Pemberton to "de-cocainize" the coca leaves used in his products, including the last tonic he developed, which was to become Coca-Cola. There is no question that Coca-Cola's immediate predecessor, French Wine of Coca, contained at least three ingredients considered to be stimulants — cocaine, caffeine, and alcohol (the latter is really a depressant, but that's not the way it was perceived at the time).

It looked like Pemberton had a winner with his French Wine Coca. Early sales were good. Then Fulton County, in which much of Atlanta is located, saw the light of the temperance movement and enacted one of the first prohibition laws in the United States. It was only in effect for one year, but that was long enough for Pemberton to decide he needed another, nonalcoholic product on which to fall back. That's when he developed the original Coca-Cola formula. He took out the offending alcohol, but left in the cocaine and caffeine since there was no hue and cry over them.

He wanted to retain the coca and kola ingredients — the two strongest stimulants then known — and hit on putting them in a syrup base instead of the wine base. His marketing strategy, which was later so dramatically carried to success by Asa Candler, was to sell his tonic as a sweet-tasting alternative to alcoholic tonics at soda fountains.

When the prohibition was over, sales of French Wine Coca resumed. It stayed on the market until at least 1893, five years after Pemberton's death, when it finally fell victim to poor marketing and business practices.

It might seem that the proven seller French Wine Coca would have been the more logical product for Asa Candler to go after. It would have, except for one thing. Candler was a staunch Methodist, and Methodists look upon alcohol as the devil's temptation. Candler would not have knowingly involved himself with demon spirits. On the other hand, cocaine, cloaked in the ignorance of the times, received little consideration from him or anyone else.

By the 1890s, whether or not Coca-Cola contained cocaine, its advertising certainly sounded as if it did. The wording used in selling Peruvian Wine of Coca in that Sears Roebuck catalog ad is very similar to an advertising letter Candler sent out in 1891:

> The medicinal properties of the Coca Plant and the extract of the celebrated African Cola (sic) Nut, make it a medicinal preparation of great value, which the best physicians unhesitatingly endorse and recommend for mental and physical exhaustion, headache, tired feeling, mental depression, etc.
>
> Coca-Cola has such a very marked effect in refreshing and reviving the drooping spirits, and taking away the tired feeling, and so promptly relieves the headache, that it is constantly making good friends, who not only use it themselves, but gladly recommend it to others.

As is known, the Indians of the Andes Mountains in Peru and Bolivia chew the coca leaf to gain extra energy and ward off the effects of altitude sickness. The stimulative effects of the coca leaf and of its cocaine component are still accepted as beneficial there, just as they were in late–nineteenth century America.

Again, regardless of whether Coca-Cola actually contained cocaine, word-of-mouth advertising at the time imputed that it did. In the light of cocaine's supposedly safe relief of "mental and physical exhaustion, headache, tired feeling, mental depression," and so on, cocaine was a strong selling point for a soda fountain drink. So, at the very least, this was claimed by some for Coca-Cola.

Several Candler family members have agreed that part of Asa Candler's character would not have balked at people *thinking* there was cocaine in Coca-Cola, even if there was not. If you were placing orders for Coca-Cola syrup from him, and raving on about how great it was because of the wonderful cocaine it contained, he would graciously take your money and not argue otherwise.

By the turn of the century, however, the harmful effects of cocaine and other addictive narcotics were coming into public awareness. Coca-Cola may not have contained cocaine, but other colas did. Because of Candler's incredible marketing success, Coke came to symbolize soft drinks in general, and it was guilty by association. Doctors and others began recounting horror stories of "Coca-Cola addicts," such as this one by a Dr. Purse of Atlanta in 1900:

> ...a young boy, his age I have forgotten, I think 13, 14 or 15 years of age, and who had been in the habit of drinking from ten to twelve glasses of Coca Cola [*sic*] a day. He was employed by a messenger service here and lost his job and thereby lost the means of procuring his Coca Cola. He came to my office the day after in a very nervous almost collapsed condition.

Classic symptoms of drug withdrawal, indeed. A presidential commission soon afterwards issued a paper entitled "Danger of Soft Drinks Containing Habit-Forming Drugs." In it, rightly or wrongly, Coca-Cola again took the heat for the excesses of all soft drinks.

"We restrict the use of coffee and tea in children and delicate nervous individuals," the presidential commission said, "and yet these same persons frequent the soda fountains, regale themselves with soft drinks, quite unconscious of their contents, experience the stimulating and refreshing effects and soon fall victims to the habit, so that even 'Coca-Cola' fiends have come into prominence."

Okay, other soft drinks of this era contained cocaine, but did Coca-Cola itself? Its manufacture most definitely called for large amounts of the coca leaves. In a letter dated August 1, 1902, Asa Candler sent an order for ingredients to his son Howard in New York. (He often used numbers for items to insure secrecy):

> Dear Son, I have yours of the 30th. It's No. 4, we need, I return my letter of 28th, confirmed. Atlanta will need this article as soon as it is possible to get it here. Please have it attended to.
>    Please have Messrs. Parke Davis & Co., ship 1000 lbs. Dried Kola Nuts to Atlanta, Ga. via S.A. Line.
>    I enclose a letter from E.J. Barry, quoting Coca Leaves, please have him ship 2000 lbs., as per sample and price to Atlanta, Ga., via S.A. Line. Return enclosed letters.

Candler family members tend to think that Asa Candler was too religious a man to have sold drugs considered harmful and addictive — even if they were legal. Once the furor over cocaine in soft drinks erupted, he studied the subject. In his collected papers at Emory University is a copy of the book *Peru History of Coca: the Divine Plant of the Incas* by W. Golden Mortimer, M.D. It was presented to Candler, according to the inscription, by Eugene Schaeffer, president of Schaeffer Alkaloid Works, Maywood, New Jersey, manufacturers of alkaloid caffeine from tea leaves. After about 1911, according to Howard Candler, this firm prepared the flavor extract derived from coca leaves and kola nuts, using the formula furnished it by The Coca-Cola Company under a protective contract. One member of the current generation of the Candler family is in a unique position to give an informed opinion on how much, if any, cocaine was ever in Coca-Cola.

Edgar Chambers IV has a Ph.D. in food science and has achieved success in the soft drink industry like his great-great-grandfather, although he worked for a competitor, 7-Up. Among his many other accomplishments, Dr. Chambers receives the credit for developing Diet 7-Up with NutraSweet.

"Even today," Edgar said, "I have, in my laboratory, a jar of coca leaf extract. Coca leaf extract has no cocaine in it. In the past, you couldn't get it that way. Years ago, you couldn't run to a place and say, 'Well, give me some of that coca leaf extract.' You made your own. My guess is, and this is purely a guess, as long as it was a patent medicine, Coca-Cola probably was not de-cocainized. In the early stages of making it a beverage, I think it very likely that de-cocainized coca leaves were used. And it obviously has been ever since. My personal opinion is, I don't think that cocaine ever existed in the product that was sold with carbonated water.

"The other thing you have to remember, too, is that during that time frame, in the late 1800s, people thought that simple seltzer water was an invigorating, refreshing drink because it was carbonated. 'This is a fizzy water. There's something exciting and invigorating about it.' A revisit of the yuppie Perrier water, I guess. I think Asa was enough of a marketing genius to figure that out. I think he was too much of a religious man to sell drugs."

Chambers went on to say that the extraction process has been known for a long time. "I think that Coca-Cola had none in it intentionally. Did it have trace amounts in it? Very likely. Simply because the extraction process was not very good back then.

"I can remember Grandmother, maybe she told you this story, about someone trying to impress Asa Sr. once, and saying, 'You know Mr. Candler, I drink six of your Coca-Colas every day of my life.' Asa looked at the man and said, 'Well then, you are a bigger fool than I am.'"

Another Candler family member, who actually has a copy of the original formula in a safety deposit box, said, "It does call for coca leaves that have been used in some other way, I suppose in the actual manufacture of the sort of cocaine that was used in that day for medicinal purposes."

Which brings us back to the question — did Coke or didn't Coke, does Coke or doesn't Coke contain cocaine? In all likelihood, Asa Candler — with his Methodist-born distaste for excess — reduced the cocaine content when he was reformulating it to improve shelf life and taste. However, it would seem logical that Coca-Cola continued to have small or, at best, trace amounts of cocaine until 1906 or so when a federal administrator began his vigorous, almost evangelical enforcement of the new Pure Food and Drug laws.

Finally, no process is or can ever be 100 percent efficient. There is still cocaine in Coca-Cola and all the other colas using coca leaf extract, albeit in, as chemists term it, "untraceable amounts."

So that's the answer. Technically there is coke in Coke, an infinitesimal trace that's perfectly safe, but still there.

What else is in Coca-Cola?

Well, that's a *secret* and a better protected one than any of the Pentagon's. A mystique has arisen over the years about the Coca-Cola formula since only a relatively few people have ever been allowed to participate in the actual mixing of Coca-Cola and, of those, most only put in ingredients by number, such as so much of No. 4, so much of No. 5, and so on. They did not know what these substances actually were, and especially not that most secret of ingredients, 7X.

The magic formula, jealously guarded as it is, has added a great deal of romance to Coca-Cola over the years. There has been much speculation about its various components, and competitors have spent untold amounts trying to duplicate it. The original and still secret formula for making Coca-Cola rests in an "unobtrusive" safety deposit box at the Trust Company of Georgia in Atlanta. As a collectible, it is worth a few thousand dollars perhaps, but to the Coca-Cola Company it has been and continues to be worth literally billions of dollars!

*Fortune* magazine (in a famous July, 1931, article) went to some lengths to determine and expose the magic formula. *Fortune* was one of the respected but sometimes brash publications of Henry Robinson Luce, who also founded *Time* and *Life*. Taking on something as big as Coca-Cola was exactly Luce's cup of, well, in this case, of Coca-Cola.

The article contended first that Coca-Cola was 99 percent sugar and water. The other one-percent, it said, was made up of caramel; fruit flavors (including lavender, fluid extract of guarana, lime juice, and various citrus oils); phosphoric acid; caffeine from tea, coffee, or chocolate; "Merchandise No. 5," which was three parts de-cocainized coca leaves and one part kola nut; and a secret ingredient known only as "7X."

It is true that Coca-Cola, at least as it was made in the

past, had a lot of water and sugar. In a standard "batch" of 5,000 gallons of syrup, there was *28,000 pounds of sugar!* But, then, no one ever said Coke was not fattening. Today, sweeteners other than sugar are used.

Many others have speculated and attempted to duplicate Coca-Cola's formula and still do. Various "outsider" chemists doing analyses of The Real Thing have claimed the detection of such ingredients as cinnamon, nutmeg, vanilla, and glycerin.

How close have they been to the true formula? Well, among other things, the *Fortune* article left out the vanilla — Asa Candler preferred the Madagascar variety. We have no intention of revealing the full formula here — it is, after all, now the proprietary property of The Coca-Cola Company, and its attorneys have teeth that are both big and sharp in such cases. Yet, when the Candler family sold the controlling interest in the company in the early 1920s certain family members kept copies of the formula — or at least of the one in use at that time. This, knowing Candlers as we know those wonderful Candlers, was probably an insurance policy of sorts, just in case the Woodruffs failed to make a go of it, and the rights to the formula reverted to the family. And we would not be surprised if that's not the reason there are still a few copies of the formula squirreled away in safety deposit boxes, although it is by now pretty obvious that the new owners of Coca-Cola have done rather well for themselves over the last seventy years. Be that as it may, we have talked to people who actually have the fabled secret formula.

It is something of a paradox in this age of heightened consumer awareness that millions of Americans blithely drink can upon can and bottle upon bottle of a beverage filled with unidentified ingredients. And further, if you quite reasonably asked the company what it contained, you would only get the answer, "It's a secret!" And if you persisted and did manage to find out in some way, they would sue you if you revealed that formula.

The Coca-Cola Company will continue fighting to keep their valuable and highly proprietary Magic Formula secret. However, in recent years, consumer pressure has caused the federal government to require stricter and stricter listing of ingredients on food products. Take a can of Classic Coke today and look at the small vertical print on its side. You find The Coca-Cola Company reluctantly revealing that Coke contains:

> Carbonated water, high fructose corn syrup and/or sucrose, caramel color, phosphoric acid, natural flavors, caffeine.

The words *natural flavors* mean a lot. These include the "coca" and the "cola," and all the other ingredients that really make the product what it is. Among these is that most secret of substances, "7X." Coca-Cola (and other companies making food and beverage products with proprietary formulas) have battled for decades against totally divulging their component parts — so far they continue to win. Buy any candy bar and the wrapper tells you exactly what is in it but not so that delicious and refreshing soft drink.

What is the most secret of secret ingredients, the holy "7X"?

Many of Asa Candler's grandchildren and great-grandchildren had been told as kids that Coca-Cola did contain cocoa. They all liked chocolate and cocoa and attributed Coca-Cola's good taste to that ingredient. Could cocoa be the famous "secret ingredient" of Coca-Cola? One person telling this story was Asa Candler's daughter, Lucy, who most likely did know the formula.

We, of course, can neither confirm nor deny this.

Coca-Cola, regardless of what is or is not in it and despite its caramel color, became a true Golden Elixir for Asa Candler and his kin. But along with the great fortune it brought this complex and compelling family, it brought misfortune and tragedy. Some of the Candlers went on to success in other fields of endeavor — especially real estate — but none were ever able to completely separate themselves from the fizzy little drink, The Real Thing, that made them "The Real Ones."

It was the strength of Asa Candler's character, convictions, and shrewdness that molded and forged his family's destiny. What was to follow began with him.

# Asa
# Candler

$A$sa Griggs Candler came into the world just before midnight on December 30, 1851, at the end of what had been a typical winter's day in Georgia — cold, damp, windy, gray, and overcast.

Born at home, as almost everyone was in those days, his parents, Samuel Charles Candler and Martha Beall Candler, were delighted to greet their eighth child and fifth son.

By the time of Asa's birth, his father was a well-established merchant and property owner in Carroll County, but had traveled a hard road through the wilds of western Georgia to get there.

Sam's early youth had been scarred by the apparent suicide of his father, Daniel Candler. Daniel, who owned a tavern as well as a farm, had been known to take a very strong interest in regional politics and to become very emotional over some issues. According to family legends, usually whispered, if repeated at all, Daniel fought several duels over political differences. His last opponent had been a friend until their falling out. The duel ended in the friend's death. Daniel immediately plunged into a deep depression. He went home, got into bed, and refused all food and drink. He died of starvation. The year was 1816. Samuel was seven.

Following Daniel's death, his wife, Sarah Slaughter Candler, had to find some way to survive. Options were limited to a woman with young children. So she did what many women in similar circumstances did, she remarried. Her new husband was D. S. Chapman of Baldwin County. Sarah and Mr. Chapman proceeded to have four daughters of their own, making for very crowded conditions in the new household. It seemed best for Samuel Charles to live with his aunt and uncle, Mary Candler Few and her husband, Ignatius Few. Sarah rationalized that her son would have greater educational opportunities and cultural advantages.

It didn't turn out as she expected. As one of his great-granddaughters would later say, Sam landed in a "Godless environment." It seems that Ignatius Few had a mistress down the road and seven illegitimate children. Mary Candler Few was trying to get a divorce, which wasn't legal in Georgia at the time. There was no religious training and certainly a poor moral example was being set.

After awhile, Sam was moved to his first cousin's home, Ignatius Alphonso Few, who had a law practice in Augusta. Sam's cousin was the exact opposite of his parents. A graduate of Princeton University, Few was a cultured, educated, and deeply religious man. He would later give up his law career to become a Methodist minister and before his death, founded Emory College. Despite Few's influence, Sam found little use for churchgoing in the years to come.

Sam's first job led him to Georgia's wild frontier on the border of the Cherokee lands. He arrived in Carroll County in 1830 to work for an English mining concern. It is said that Sam Candler named the little village he was to live in, Villa Rica. He only stayed in Carroll County for eighteen months before moving into what would become Cherokee County. This was Indian land from which the Cherokee would be tragically removed in a few short years.

Sam probably went in search of gold; he found opportunities instead. He soon became sheriff of the county, while his brother was the local magistrate. This proved very convenient when Sam took a shine to a cute, fiery, and independent thirteen year old named Martha Bernetta Beall. Martha and Sam fell for each other and decided to marry, much to the consternation of her parents, Noble Peyton and Justianna Hooper Beall. Noble wanted to stop the marriage and looked into what could be done if the couple eloped, as he feared they might if he opposed them.

Unfortunately for the concerned father, in Georgia, if an underaged girl eloped, her parents could get the marriage annulled by contacting the magistrate and having him require the sheriff to bring the couple back. Noble Beall had a real problem: a headstrong teenager and a moonstruck sheriff. After considering his options, the father finally gave his permission for the marriage.

Because they shared the same birthday, albeit ten years apart, the couple had planned to marry on December 6. However, it fell on a Friday in 1833 and marrying on a Friday was considered bad luck—so they put the wedding off until the eighth. The ceremony took place at the Beall home. Reputedly among the witnesses were two Cherokee chiefs, Walking Stick and Toothpick. The couple received two gifts from Martha's father: a slave girl named Mary and a little pony named Picayune.

The newlyweds were not to stay in Cherokee County for long. Relations with the Cherokees were worsening, as Sam was in the position to know, having been appointed Georgia's agent for enforcing statutes that pertained to Indian affairs. Given his knowledge of the situation's explosiveness, Sam moved his family back to Villa Rica in the mid-1830s.

While the home they set up would be comparable to those of their neighbors, their home life would reflect a greater than common interest in education and culture. Sam and Martha had a piano and a library in addition to the usual furnishings found in homes of the area.

The three-hundred-acre farm was on a ridge, from which streams flowed in both directions. The house faced south and was shaded by "a magnificent oak and hickory forest," as someone at the time described it, and was built with the needs of the family as the paramount consideration. Its type and construction was similar to many others in the South at that time.

A long, wide hallway divided the frame building into two main sections. The hallway was like a breezeway with wide porches at each end, across the rear and front of the house. All the rooms of the house opened onto the hall.

Designed as it was, more rooms could be added, if needed, by attaching them at either end of the hall and moving the porch a little further out into the yard. Built slightly off the ground, there was a wonderful secret play place underneath for the children. During winter, the chickens would make their nests down there near the warmth of the hearthstone.

The dining room, located at the rear of one section of the house, doubled as the family sitting room. Since it was easier to heat just one room, it became the center of family activities in the winter months. This was particularly true of the Candler house which had a detached kitchen building to guard against fire.

After the move to Villa Rica, Sam began acquiring more slaves to help on the farm.

Slave ownership was not unusual in the South; however, in the Upcountry, the average white landowner had a small farm averaging two hundred acres or less with little need for much slave labor. Of those who owned slaves, few had more than five. That Sam Candler owned twelve and managed an additional nineteen by 1860 is indicative of his personal wealth and his approach to business. In addition to his farm, Sam ran a local country store which did very well. He also went into a real estate partnership with a group of other men, buying and subdividing land for sale.

For all of Sam's relative prosperity, life on a red-clay farm in Georgia during the 1850s was not easy and quite different from that on the large plantations, as popularized by such epics as Margaret Mitchell's *Gone With the Wind.* The mechanics of sheer survival was always the most important consideration. Farm children — barefoot through the long, hot Georgia summers — had few outlets for their energies and personal expression except chores and the simple pleasures of rural life. This seems to have been a virtue, however, in that it more deeply ingrained the basic truths of life and more strongly developed the character of Asa and his siblings than might have happened in an easier, more cosmopolitan setting.

Sam Candler's boys learned the lessons of life not only by doing their chores around the farm but by following and observing their father as he ran the store, walked off property lines, and debated and negotiated deals (both financial and political). Sam Candler had strong beliefs on all moral questions, which he steadily and successfully instilled in his sons. He taught them not only business methods but the importance of honesty in dealing and the rewards of diligent, loyal, and faithful labor. He allowed the boys no money for personal use, except what they earned for themselves. He taught them to know that work on the farm and manual service in any honorable pursuit would not only command the respect of all decent people but would give them a vigor of mind and body, and success in later life. They also learned about management and handling people by observing how their father got his workers both at the store and on the farm to do what he wanted.

A friend of the family, who knew them while Asa was still young, wrote this about Sam Candler: "There was never a man with better knowledge of how to raise children than Sam Candler, who raised a houseful and kept them all at work. From Milton (the oldest) to the bishop (Warren) and to John, the judge, he kept them busy. They had time to learn and they could find play in work. Even on Saturdays, when other boys would be idle, the Candler boys were busy doing something. Sam and Martha expected their children to do their fair share of jobs that were necessary to run the home and the farm. As they grew older, he included responsibilities at the store, giving them a wide view of the world of commerce."

In fact, this attitude continues into the present generation of the Candler family. It doesn't matter how much money you have, or how much money your daddy has, you are still expected to work.

Martha Candler, described in her 1899 obituary as a "little fire-eater," wielded great influence over her children as well.

She came to her marriage with a rudimentary education in terms of books, but she was well-schooled in running a large farm, overseeing the slaves, keeping house, and raising well-disciplined children. She and Sam appear to have been well-suited, much in love, and committed to the same values with one major exception. Martha Beall Candler was a deeply religious woman. It irked her no end that Sam did not share her strong, unquestioning belief. Because of Sam's attitude, Martha made a stronger effort to infuse her children with her firm faith in God.

Worship was at the center of her homelife. God's word was an integral part of their everyday existence. While Sam taught his children the value of money by never giving them any but by always giving them the opportunity to earn it, Martha gave them the value of a faith that withstood all earthly sorrows and disappointments.

When Sam brought Martha to Villa Rica, it was a wild and rough frontier town, not unlike Dodge City of later and greater renown. Martha set her mind and her jaw to bringing civilization to the wayward village and was one of the women in the community who could be counted on to help organize a local school and participate in church activities. Her opinions on appropriate behavior were well-known as was her reputation as a firebrand.

With eleven children, it was good that Sam and Martha were strong people. There were eight boys and three girls — Milton, Ezekial, William Beall, Noble (who was retarded), Asa, Warren Akin, John Slaughter, Samuel Charles (Charlie), Florence, Lizzie, and Jessie.

Asa was named in honor of Asa W. Griggs, who had been a tutor of the older children. At the time, Griggs was a young medical student but later became a prominent Georgia physician and a professor in the Atlanta Medical College, now the School of Medicine of Emory University. Naming a baby for a prominent or respected individual was a common custom. It reflected the parents' hopes that their child would aspire to the example set by the person for whom they were named. By the choice of his name, Sam and Martha were picking a career path for this boy at birth.

Asa wasn't an easy child. He was fidgety, hyperactive, and always on the go and into things. The fact that he was quick-witted made him all that more difficult to raise. By the time he was born, Martha was an older mother and had her hands full with Noble's retardation.

Asa was also something of a fun-loving imp. He was described as being "a tease without tormenting; he was mischievous without malice; he was a prankster without hurting — all in fun."

He never outgrew his delight in making mischief. Even as an adult he would play harmless jokes on unsuspecting victims.

His younger brother Charlie, who had a genuine fear of cats, was one target of Asa's practical jokes. The two youngsters slept together in the room adjoining their parents'. After everyone was in bed and asleep, Asa would crawl under the bed and imitate the meow and spit of an excited cat, which he could do quite well. This always threw Charlie into a state of frightened excitement, and he would go running into the next room in search of his mother. Then their father would have to get up to comfort and quiet Charlie and usually took occasion to administer appropriate punishment to the prankster.

Asa wasn't the only one who got into trouble as a child. Warren, who was to become a bishop, was no angel, as his granddaughter, Caroline Candler Hunt, recalls hearing.

"He and the slave's little boy went rabbit hunting. How they hunted the rabbits was they set the pasture on fire, and then there was a hollow tree and all the rabbits ran to the hollow tree. Grandpa came along after they had set the pasture on fire, and he burned Warren's bottom. He didn't put up with foolishness like that!"

Then there was the story Caroline Candler Hunt remembers about a foible of her great-uncle William Beall.

"Uncle Will was very vain and very stylish in his day. This was before the war, because Cal [a slave] was still working for Grandma. [Will] had bought himself one of these Southern Colonel pure white suits to wear to town. He had gotten on his horse and ridden off, and Cal came running in and said, "Oh, miss, oh, miss, somebody go catch Mr. Willie but quick — he's gone to town in his underwear!"

The year 1860 brought to a head the seething antagonisms between North and South. And Sam Candler's political position and views placed him in an odd position. He was a delegate to that year's national Democratic convention, which was to meet and choose a candidate. Like so many of the "backwoods" yeoman farmers, he was opposed to secession. He owned slaves himself and had a strong belief in self-determination and rights of property, but Sam was a realist. He knew that war would bring devastation. He was a strong negotiator and understood that talking was a much better way to solve differences than fighting. This was, perhaps, a legacy from his father's tragic and young death.

Sam Candler, a supporter of Stephen Douglas, spoke against secession at the convention. He was one of the few delegates who did, and as a result of his position, he was burned in effigy in Macon when the news made the papers there. War was coming and Sam Candler went home to try and ready his family for the troubles that were on the way.

During this same time period, Asa's eldest brother, Milton had finished at the University of Georgia and had been teaching school and running a small weekly newspaper. He, like his father, would maintain a "unionist" stand politically and editorially until the war began. By 1862, both Milton and Brother Zeke would leave their families and take up the uniform and the cause of the Confederacy.

When war broke out, in addition to worrying about kin at the front, Martha had to run her large household and deal with shortages brought on by the effective Union blockade. The war also dried up the labor supply and severely curtailed normal workings of commerce. Soon, merely staying alive overshadowed all else.

The war forced the closing of Sam's store in Villa Rica, which meant he was at home to oversee the farm and exert a more direct influence on his younger children. However, it rapidly fell to Martha to manage the farm and the slaves as well as her children because Sam fell into a debilitating depression. In a letter to Asa's sister Florence on December 13, 1861, Martha described the troubled times.

> ...we are all glad also to her that Col Harris yourself & children will be to see us soon. It seems a long time since you were here. We are all very lonesome and low spirited, so a little can vary the scene. Your Pa & Jessie appear to suffer the most from melancholy. I do not have time from nursing my crops left to enjoy anything even if I could get

it. I am sorry for Jessie. She is the best child... Your Uncle
Zeke's wife & son came to be here Christmas. Your
grandma is yet unable to move. I recon Jessie wrote you
how she got hurt by falling out of her door and put her hip
out of place 3 weeks ago. She is a great deal of trouble and
suffers a lot. Your Pa & children go over every day ...
Everything is in such distressed circumstances that no one
is able to hire negros. Our hands are doing nothing except
cut wood, cook & sleep & eat & grumble. We have done
getting our crop in & and have sown wheat rye & corn and
have nothing to do now.

Your Pa says he intends to gin his own cotton & keep
it until times gets so he can sell it. I received a letter from
my dear parents this week they were all well but very much
distressed Bro Fred left with the army for Columbus,
Kentucky, the 3 inst. Bro Sam is quite sick & has been for
3 months or he would have gone too as he volunteered last
summer. He went into cramps but took chills & has them.
How yet my heart burns against the hated hateful Yankees
& when I see these that are living here going quietly about
I feel as though I wanted to treat them to hanging. Fear is
all that keeps them from coming out openly for these
detested race. They are Yankees & nothing good clean or
honest ever did or ever can come out of Yankeedom ...

In another letter written to Florence on December 11,
1862 (the one in which she described Asa's accident), Martha
details further the hardships suffered at the home front.

" ... had a litter [sic] from Zeke dated the 3rd inst. he &
family were well he says sugar has rose to 25 cents a pound
so I recon we will not get any from them as it is so difficult
to get anything bought now on the RRs we havent got any
salt from Virginia or Florida yet we are boiling the dirt out
of the smokehouse your Grandma is about as you left her
She stayed with us 3 weeks & then would go home I look
every day to hear she is dead but stay there she will your Pa
makes Long Cal [a slave] stay with her all the time. Mrs.
Rembury died yesterday (Mr. Ivins sister) thers a good deal
of sickness in the neighborhood pluresy & pneumonia we
heard yesterday from Willie Dickinson he & Harris Dobbs
are both in the hospital at Linchburg ...

It is obvious from Martha's own letters as well as others of the period that life continued, as it does during wartime, with interruptions, inconveniences, and irritations. But every day was not fraught with fear or the threat of imminent destruction. Rather, the seasons changed and the farm chores continued. Asa and his brothers and sisters learned hardships along with their daily lessons of work and responsibility. And depressed though he may have been, Sam was continuing to buy out other farms and speculate in land.

Sherman's arrival in Georgia ushered in the last days of the Confederacy, and life became harrowing. Now Martha had to stand up to marauding Confederate deserters, outlaws, and Yankee soldiers. The Yankees had a warrant for Sam's arrest. Intent on catching him and probably hanging him, they came by daily and at all hours. Sam was forced to hide in swamps along with what livestock and provisions the family had managed to save. The fear the family, and Martha in particular faced, is revealed in this undated snippet of a letter that has survived.

> ...the Yanks are here nearly every day or night. They are fortifying at Ponches Springs & will destroy us this winter do try to get Milton to write to your Pa to leave here they keep us all half scared to death I want all of you to write to him if you think it best to leave here or not to do it.

Martha was still a young woman when the war broke out, reported an article in the centennial edition of the *Carroll County Times* in 1927, but she gave her oldest sons to the Confederate army and saw what little wealth she and her husband accumulated swept away. One of the most vivid pictures of her is from a story told by her son, Judge John S. Candler. He could remember sitting on the gate when he was three years old, keeping a watch for the Yankee soldiers while his mother fed Confederate soldiers in the house. Having sent off sons to fight in an army that her husband had backed with everything in the world he possessed, there she stood, feeding hungry Confederate soldiers from the larder she saw small chance of replenishing.

Judge Candler's grandson, John S. Candler II, remembered another family story from the Civil War that was in a much lighter vein.

"Warren and John were real little boys back during the war. And the Union troops came through there. One of them lifted the boys' hats and started walking off with them. Warren started to cry, but my grandfather John got mad. He went over and gave him a few choice words, and they gave him his hat back. John (who later became a judge) then turned to Warren and said, 'you see, it does do some good to do some cussing sometimes.'"

On one occasion a foraging Union soldier, it is said, put his pistol to Martha's breast and promised to "blow your soul to hell unless you tell me where the money and silver are hidden." She, with her slow, easy smile and deliberate manner retorted, "I do not think you will do anything of the sort, because I think hell is already full of Union soldiers sent there by Johnson's army between Chattanooga and Lookout Mountain." Disarmed by her response, the Union soldier laughed and went on his way.

The war's devastation took its toll on the Candlers as it did on all Southern families. They were ruined financially; they had suffered hardship; they had lost; and now they had to start over. Asa, as a child in hard times made even harder by the war, learned a self-reliance that was to serve him in good stead the rest of his life.

Cash money was something not often seen in the days after the war. Children, unlike more recent times, did not receive allowances. If they wanted money, they had to find ways in which to earn it. When he was older, Asa Candler loved to tell the story of how he made his first dollar.

"I was ploughing," he would say, "when I heard a commotion back at the house. Running across the fields, I found that my mother thought snakes had disturbed a hen that made her nest under the kitchen floor.

"Without stopping to think, I dropped to my knees and, on all fours, started under the house to see what was the trouble. Out by me ran a big mink. I scrambled from under the house and started after him.

"We had quite a race. He ran down by the barn, through

a patch of woods, and splashed into the creek. I splashed right after him, and, as he hit the water, I caught him."

"For a minute," he would smile, "I was almost sorry; there are the marks of his teeth on my arm to this day." He would then point to his right forearm.

"Well," he would go on, "I hadn't heard of people selling mink skins, but it seemed to me it might be a good idea, and I decided to try. Atlanta was thirty-six miles away, and there was no railroad, but that seemed to be the best possible market. So I sent the skin into town by wagon, and I said to myself, 'Maybe I'll get twenty-five cents!'

"I got a dollar — the first I had ever made. And the man who bought the mink skin sent word that he wanted more and would buy them for that price. I started people in the neighborhood to catching minks, and the skins we sold brought quite a sum.

"Then, I thought of another way of earning money that may surprise you. I sent to Atlanta for pins — plain, everyday pins — and sold them at a good profit in the country. Seems you couldn't make anything off pins, doesn't it? But when I went away to school, I had over one hundred dollars saved up through the sale of mink skins and speculation in pins."

The period of this story seems to have been right after the war and just before Asa went away to school in 1867. He was probably about fifteen years old at the time, but already a proven and successful entrepreneur.

While the War with all of its destruction gave the Candler children a background of poverty that would leave an indelible impression on them, religion also played an important part in shaping young Asa and his brothers and sisters. As adults, they would talk about the family prayers, country church services, and hymns sung around the piano that all the daughters could play.

Originally, religious training of the children had been Martha's bailiwick. In 1869, that would change. Sam Candler found religion. The description of Sam's conversion has been handed down the generations and is best told by the Bishop Warren's granddaughter, Caroline.

"Martha was raised a hard-shell Baptist. When Grandpa

(Sam) was not living like a Christian, because he wasn't, he would have people come and stay at the house. This was not uncommon, because there weren't a lot of hotels, and prominent people would come there to stay. He played whist with them in front of a fire. She had told him she wasn't going to have that, and one night he was doing that with some friends, and she walked in and swept all the cards into her apron and dumped them into the fire. Then she walked out of the room and never said a word.

"[When he converted] he did not join her church. He joined the Methodist church after he was forty years old. What happened was, they lived close to the Methodist church which is still standing over there in Carroll County, not far from where they lived. We have a preacher who had gone to that church as a child and knew all about this. Men and women sat on opposite sides of the church and came in different doors. This was a protracted meeting and [Martha] saw that Grandpa was very moved. She got up from her place and went over to him, and said, 'Sam, if you'll join the church, I will go with you.' Not 'I will join with,' mind you — she didn't join, she just went.

"The next morning, at breakfast, with the assembled children, he said, 'You all know that I joined the church last night. And you all know that I don't know how to pray, but I think that we should have family prayer. And we will be using the *Episcopal Book of Common Prayer.*' And that was what Papa (Bishop Warren) was raised on, the *Episcopal Book of Common Prayer* at breakfast."

It was ironic that while Martha had been the original religious force in the family, it was to be Sam who ended up being the strongest influence. Warren, after all, became a Methodist bishop. Caroline tells of a story near the end of the bishop's life.

"When Papa was real sick in the hospital, Dr. Louis Newton, who was the pastor of the Second Ponce de Leon Baptist Church and a new preacher in town, came to see him... Most young Methodist preachers stood very much in awe of the Bishop, to put it mildly. They were scared of him. They wouldn't go to see him. Dr. Newton walked in and said, 'Bishop, my name is Louie Newton, and I'm a Baptist preacher.' Dr. Newton told me that papa said, 'My mother died in that superstition.'"

Sam Candler's conversion to the Methodist faith would have a profound effect on his family. It is quite probable that Asa's commitment to the Methodist church also came that same summer. "One of Grandma's sons became a bishop," Caroline pointed out. "One became the South's greatest Christian philanthropist [Asa]. The others were, almost without exception, prominent in the lay work of churches wherever they made their homes."

The war's end and the family's reduced economic circumstances changed the course of Asa's life. His father, perhaps sensing the greatness in the boy, had wanted him to be a doctor.

Asa himself had, in his childhood, a desire toward the same end. In 1912 he told an Atlanta reporter, "Why, do you know that my ambition to become a man of medicine was so strong during my youth that I would concoct imaginary potions and doctor sick pigeons, hogs, dogs, and cattle?"

But, even as a child, he was realistic enough to realize the family's financial state and to set more reasonable goals.

"My hopes never ventured further than an apothecary shop," Asa said in that same 1912 interview, "and the prescription clerk in the drugstore near my boyhood home was greater in my estimation than the president, or the world's greatest ball player." Goal setting was becoming second nature to him.

What education Asa was to get began two days after his fifth birthday when he entered one of the best schools in the neighborhood on January 1, 1857. There was, in those days, no such thing as a public school system in Georgia or, for that matter, in most states. What schools that existed were organized by groups of people in the local community and taught usually either by young women or by young men just out of college or planning to enroll.

Young Asa continued in school until the end of 1861 — five years' of formal education — by which time he was barely ten years old. It was then that the doors of practically all the local schools in the state were closed because of the

War Between the States. Teachers and pupils who were old enough went to the front or into war service of some kind. Under the guidance of his parents, however, Asa continued to read and study at home. His studies were supervised by his father, even though he was suffering from periodic bouts of melancholia.

In January, 1867, Asa went to live with his sister Florence, who was running a school in Huntsville, Alabama. Florence, who married Colonel James Watt Harris in September 1860, had sought refuge in Alabama during the war.

Asa was only with Florence one year before she and Colonel Harris moved to Cartersville, Georgia. Asa returned to Carroll County where he worked on his father's farm and studied at night.

Asa must have enjoyed the year in Huntsville with his sister. He was always to value her opinion of him. Among the papers found in his desk after he died was a letter he had received almost a half-century after his Huntsville experience from a friend he had known while there. On the letter Asa had scribbled the dates and the number of years which had elapsed.

Before the war, Florence had attended Georgia Female College at Cassville, while her brother Asa was still a youngster. Milton, their oldest brother, had attended the University of Georgia. Brother Zeke had also completed his formal education and gone into the field of law. By the outbreak of the war, he had a practice in Mississippi, where his wife's people had considerable property.

In January, 1869, after a year of hard work on the farm (which was probably good for him physically but added little to his intellectual growth), he entered and attended for a year a small school conducted by John H. Featherstone. Asa, accompanied by his three younger brothers, Charlie, Warren, and John, attended these local classes held in the church building. Fire destroyed the church in the fall and for Asa that was the end of his formal education. Not that he stopped studying; he continued to read and study lessons at home with his father. However, it was a bitter blow to Sam Candler, who had been grooming this particular child for a career in medicine since his birth.

This loss of educational opportunity left Asa with a feeling of real deprivation. Later he would push his own children to study and would emphasize the importance of a good education and the availability of schools. Asa considered it a privilege to be able to attend school and particularly college.

Although Asa professed this great love of education, it's believed within the family that Asa did not want to continue his schooling even when given the chance. Because of the war, he had fallen behind in his studies. When he was nearly eighteen years old, the opportunity to enter Emory College for one year as a sub-freshman seems to have presented itself. Asa would later say that he elected to let Warren go instead because Warren's choice of a career was a noble one. Nice sentiment, however, Warren entered Emory as a prelaw student and only later chose to follow the call to the ministry. More likely, Asa decided against college because at his age, he was tired of elementary education and anxious to start into a field of work. Besides, Warren was a better student.

This left Asa with the question of what he was going to do. With his admiration of the medical profession and of pharmacists, it was not surprising that he would be attracted to the pharmaceutical trade. He could not afford to be a doctor just yet but, at that time, you didn't have to go to school to become a druggist. He thought it would be a good way to prepare himself for a later medical education.

On July 1, 1870, Asa apprenticed himself to two physicians, Doctors Best and Kirkpatrick, who were friends of his family in Cartersville, Georgia. The doctors operated a small drug store as an adjunct to their practice, and it was there that Asa went to work. He became a "man of all jobs" around the store and studied Latin and Greek and read medical books at night, occupying a room in the rear of the store, where he slept on a cot.

He quickly found that the study of chemistry was a source of pleasure to him and that he could get a feeling of accomplishment by applying his newly acquired textbook knowledge to the practical problems of compounding prescriptions. Originally, he had intended to learn only enough pharmacy to help him in the study of medicine. But instead, during his two and a half years in Cartersville, he obtained an excellent background of knowledge as well as both technical and practical proficiency in pharmacy, which stood him in good stead for the rest of his life.

Life in Cartersville was probably a pleasant change for Asa. He was very short — just five feet, three inches tall — but wiry, and very dexterous. He was not, however, built for hard manual labor such as he had been used to on the farm following the war. If he was not suited physically to heavy farm work, he was much better suited in terms of personality to the give and take of the marketplace. Cartersville offered a broader market to participate in and learn from, in addition to learning the specifics of the druggist trade.

In his spare time, Asa continued to be active in the local Methodist church, which was the major social outlet for young people. He also was near his sister Florence and her husband, the jovial Colonel Harris, as well as his maternal grandmother, Justiana Beall. So while this was a move away from home, he still had close family nearby for company and moral support.

Cartersville, however, was a small place and certainly the single clerk-apprentice in its tiny drugstore made little money. Asa's dissatisfaction is evident in a letter he wrote to Dr. Griggs, the man he had been named after, in 1872.

> Dr. A. W. Griggs West Point, Ga.
> Sept. 11th, 1872
>
> You will no doubt be at a loss to know from whom this is upon looking at the head of it but I hope and trust that the signature is still familiar.
>
> I am in Cartersville now; have been here some two years or more; am in a drug store as prescriptionist. I went in at first with the idea of familiarizing myself with Materia Medica practically & at the same time reading with a view of becoming a physician but have now almost given out the idea. The country has enough without they were better. Besides I think there is more money to be made as a druggist than as a physician & I know it can be done with a great deal less trouble of soul and body. I am very much pleased so far with the business. I want next year to go to

a larger establishment in a larger place, where I can get
sufficient compensation for my services. I can't get it in
Cartersville for the simple reason that the place is not of
sufficient importance to warrant a druggist to employ a
clerk to whom they must pay a good salary. I have now
been in the business over two years & I think I know
enough about it to support myself by it at least.

Dr. can't you locate me somewhere? You are so widely
known both professionally and socially that I thought
perhaps you would be the surest way through which I could
get a situation. I am not particular about the place—where
it is—will go to any place where I can do well. Can go now
if need be. Please write to me Dr. Remember me to all
please.

Hoping to hear from you I am
Very respectfully your friend
/s/ Asa G. Candler

Asa's letter to Dr. Griggs marks a major turning point in
his life. He had analyzed his possibilities and given up his
dream of becoming a physician. Just shy of his twenty-first
birthday, Asa had found a career that he enjoyed and
moreover where he could earn a rather good living. This
letter is also a written confirmation that, despite his later
protestations that he really wanted to be a doctor, he in fact
preferred the excitement of the world of business. It was a
trait inherited and learned from his father and one that
would carry into the generations to follow. Medicine was a
noble profession, but it represented hard work, long hours,
and poor pay. Pharmacy offered better working conditions,
control over one's hours, good profit, and the hope of being
one's own boss. It was a much better deal for a young man
who was already beginning to show his spirited, perhaps
even cocky, self-promoting personality.

Asa knew very well that the financial springboard
which had been available to Milton, Ezekiel, and Florence
before 1860 was gone. He had found what looked like a
promising career that he could enter with no formal education requirements and little start-up capital.

Dr. Griggs was unable to help, but Asa was determined
to take the big step anyway.

Asa's apprenticeship in Cartersville expired on June 30, 1873. He promptly resigned his lowly position at the drugstore and seven days later left for Atlanta.

While his father undoubtedly had some contacts in the capital city, Asa seems not to have used them. In later years, he told of the homemade clothes he wore and said he had exactly $1.75 in his pocket when he began to walk the city streets looking for work.

Atlanta held the promise for Asa of both security and excitement. It was reassuringly close to Villa Rica and his family. Also, his brother Milton was practicing law in Atlanta and living in the nearby small town of Decatur. Milton was fifteen years Asa's senior and had married a girl from a prominent background. Milton had served the Confederacy after having opposed secession as had his father. His marriage to Eliza Murphey had aligned him with Charles Murphey, Eliza's father, a prominent figure in state politics. Milton was established in his law practice and would have made a good reference for Asa.

Atlanta was also a lusty young city, a terminus of five main railroads, and an important center of commerce for the entire South. It was already the second largest city in Georgia, surpassed only by Savannah. In 1868, it became the state capital. Atlanta was a "comer," just as Asa was.

As a result of Sherman's torching, Atlanta was, in some ways, a very new town. The buildings were new, the trees were young, what streets and sidewalks existed were also new. This was a vigorous, growing place. It had the advantage and distinction of not being an old, elegant, antebellum city. Atlanta was not an old society place like Savannah, Augusta, or Charleston. Before the war, this had been a market town. The roads met in Atlanta, rails came to Atlanta, business was conducted here. But a cultured, polished society town, it was not.

The mix of people in 1873 consisted of Atlantans who had returned to rebuild their lives after the Yankee devastation, freed slaves, displaced whites from the rural areas, carpetbaggers looking for business opportunities or scams to run, fledgling industry owners, Confederate veterans, and Yankee soldiers. The city was coming out of the trauma of the war; it was tackling Reconstruction and beginning to win. Energized, Atlanta was a town on the brink of going somewhere. Maybe the citizens did not fully know where their city was headed, but the feeling crackled in the air — they were headed someplace and it was different from any other city in the state!

Asa Candler was going somewhere, as well. He had his eye on the future and Atlanta had her eye on the future, too. For a young man with plans, this was the place to be. If, like Asa, he had a talent for commerce, this was the right town. Together, Atlanta and Asa would stretch and grow and become dominant in their state and their region.

That $1.75 Asa had in his pocket bought a lot more then than it would now, but even with careful husbanding, it represented a cheap room for a night or two and a little food. It speaks volumes for his confidence in himself that Asa would make such a radical change in his life with so little capital. Or was it the desperation of impatience?

Regardless, Asa Candler found a job his first day in Atlanta, although it did take him well into the night to do so. He searched systematically — his only mode of transportation walking — and visited every drugstore as he came to it. He spoke with the druggists and asked for a chance to work for them. One place at which he applied was the Pemberton-Pulliam Drug Company, located off the lobby of the Kimball House. He had no way of knowing that the senior partner in this enterprise, who had no place on his staff for a still wet behind the ears young druggist from Cartersville, was to have a profound influence upon the whole course of his life and to give him the means to make so many millions of dollars. There is no evidence that Asa met "Dr." John S. Pemberton that day. On the other hand, there is no reason to suppose the owner of the relatively small establishment would not have been there. Certainly Asa would have waited a short time at least for the proprietor to return, if need be, at each place he applied, since most often only that person could do the hiring.

Finally, at nine o'clock, weary from the journey to the city and his day-long search, he found an opening. George Jefferson Howard, who owned a popular drug store around the corner from the Kimball House on Peachtree Street (almost everything in Atlanta was, is, or will be on Peachtree Street), agreed to try out the young pharmacist. Wages were not discussed; instead, Asa went to work on the spot to prove himself worthy of compensation. With this agreement with Mr. Howard, Asa worked that night until the store closed at midnight. He then spent that night and the next sleeping under the drugstore counter.

Call it the order of the universe, or what you will, it is almost incredible that Asa Candler would — on that one day, July 7, 1873, his first day in town — meet the inventor of the tonic that would one day make him fabulously wealthy and go to work for the very man whose daughter he would marry. He had only pocket change on that day but, fifty years later, was worth more than fifty million dollars. Averaged out, Asa Candler during his career in Atlanta made some three thousand dollars a day! He made more *every day* for more than fifty years than he paid for Coca-Cola in its entirety. Coming to Atlanta was a *good* move for Asa.

The long ordeal of that day, asking for work, being refused and going on to ask again and again made a lasting impression on Asa. When he was older, he would often say with considerable pride "that no boy of his would ever have to go with his hat in his hand and ask for a job." He was always able to provide agreeable and satisfactory employment for them somewhere in his own business enterprises.

George Jefferson Howard, Asa's new employer, was forty-two years old and the father of several daughters. He and his wife, Maria (pronounced Mariah) Louisa Goldsmith were originally from Augusta. Maria's father, Major Turner Goldsmith, and all her brothers served the Confederate States of America. After the war her brother John H. Goldsmith became city comptroller of Atlanta.

George Howard was well-connected in Atlanta and Augusta and lived a rather comfortable upper-class lifestyle. He and his family had had to flee Atlanta in advance of Sherman's army. The Howards lost everything; the Yankees even poured molasses into their piano and broke up the rest of the furniture to burn. Family legend has it that Maria Louisa gave birth during their flight to Augusta and lost at least one child to fever along the way. It is understandable that the Howard family had little use for Yankees.

Fortunately, the pharmacy trade was a profitable one, and Howard was able to successfully rebuild after the war.

What passed for "society" in Atlanta in those days were people who had been connected with the Confederate cause, as had the Howards. Certainly George Howard considered himself and his family a cut above his penniless clerk.

Years later, Asa would say little about his early years as a clerk at George J. Howard's shop. However, his children delighted in relating that the young druggist lived in a tiny room at the rear of the drugstore. Asa, a shorter than average man, would laugh about how the ceiling was so low he could not stand up straight. Asa could be extremely frugal, even if it was an inconvenience.

As good a story as this is, it is contradicted in letters Asa wrote to his son, Howard, in 1898. In them Asa claims to have found lodging the very week he arrived in Atlanta with no references and no credit. Which is really the truth? That he convinced George Howard he was honest and reliable enough to be entrusted to live in the little storeroom? Or, did he actually find a boarding room somewhere? It's impossible to say; however, Asa did have a tendency of modifying his stories to make a point. The storeroom anecdote may have been his way of showing his children the importance of being trustworthy.

George Howard's drugstore was open six days a week, every night until midnight. This left Sunday as a much needed day of rest; although Asa, quickly associated with a church and set about meeting people in Atlanta. He was essentially hired on probation but must have met his future father-in-law's quick approval because he rapidly became the store's chief clerk.

Unfortunately, Asa's budding career as a pharmacist in Atlanta was interrupted after only four months. On November 13, 1873, word reached him of his father's death in Villa Rica. As he had done before and as he was to do so many times in the years to come, Asa unquestioningly accepted as his responsibility the task of looking out for his mother and his younger brothers and returned to the home farm.

With the understanding of his employer, George Howard—who graciously agreed to hold his position open as long as possible—Asa left Atlanta and returned to the family farm in Carroll County to help his mother with its management and the care of his three younger brothers. Samuel Charles, Jr. was then eighteen years old, Warren Akin was sixteen, and John Slaughter twelve.

The next year Asa and his brother "Willie" spent working to ready their parents' farm for sale. It was a hard year for the entire family, most particularly his brother Noble. For Martha, adjusting to the loss of her beloved Sam, it was made even more difficult by the reaction of her retarded son, Noble. In Martha's letters written to Florence during that year, she is burdened by the fact that her handicapped child does not comprehend that his father, Sam, is dead. She writes that every night Noble says, "Pa will come tonight, we always walk at night and check on things." She and Asa would try to explain that Pa was in Heaven, but after a while, Noble would start to look again for Pa to come. Noble never grew mentally past about the age of four or five. Martha and Sam, unlike some parents, never put Noble away. It was a mark of their character that although they could have boarded him out, they loved all their children equally and without comparison. They administered love and discipline without bias but rather with an eye to ability.

Following the sale of the homestead where all except the first of her children, Milton, had been born and all had been reared, their recently widowed mother moved in 1874 to Cartersville to live with her eldest daughter, Mrs. James W. (Florence) Harris. Warren was then a student in Emory College at Oxford. In Cartersville, an opportunity was available for John to obtain better educational advantages. In a very real sense, Asa G. Candler was responsible for the education of all his brothers younger than himself. This sense of responsibility for the welfare and betterment of his relations became a permanent part of Asa's life.

During his last year at home, Asa was made a steward of the local Methodist church, a stepping stone to greater participation during the remainder of his life.

In January, 1875, having moved his mother and brother

John in the previous fall to his sister's home in Cartersville, Asa Candler returned to Atlanta and went back to work for George J. Howard in his old job as chief clerk in his drug store. For a little more than two years, Asa held this position. During that time, he must have had a wonderful opportunity to observe the workings of the wholesale and retail drug business from the inside, and his quick mind undoubtedly saw many improvements which could be made in the conduct of such an enterprise.

Still, Asa was not content. He had large ambitions and was not comfortable working for mere wages. In April, 1877, two years and four months after his return to Atlanta from Villa Rica, when he was twenty-five years old, he formed a partnership with Marcellus B. Hallman, under the firm name of Hallman and Candler, Wholesale and Retail Druggists, and for the first time became a businessman in his own right. Never thereafter was he to work for any other man. The days of apprenticeship were over—seven years as an employee had convinced him that his future lay in running his own enterprises.

Asa's plunge into entrepreneurship was only partly brought on by a desire to be his own boss. He and George Howard had a falling out over Howard's fifteen-year-old daughter, Lucy "Lizzie" Elizabeth. Asa had been charmed by her and was brashly telling customers that he planned to own the drugstore one day and marry Lizzie. To discourage the budding romance, Howard sent Lizzie and her sister, Alice, off to Salem College in Winston-Salem, N.C. This was quite a distance, bypassing some perfectly acceptable female academies in Georgia and South Carolina. However, distance and strict supervision appear to have been uppermost in Howard's mind. Salem's students in 1876 included 12 Georgians out of an enrollment of 190.

In checking Lizzie's expenditures against her sister's, it appears that she far outspent Alice when it came to note paper and stamps. Since all the students' mail was inspected by the staff, prior to being posted (probably a happy requirement for parents of romantically inclined teenage girls, like Lizzie Howard), it must be assumed she had found a way to sneak letters to Asa during her supervised trips into town!

The following fall Lizzie and her sisters were shipped off to LaGrange College, in another vain effort to discourage her infatuation with Asa. During Christmas break in 1877, Lizzie flatly refused to return to school. Instead she and Asa announced their plans to marry the following month. Her father was bitterly opposed to the marriage of his daughter to his former drug clerk. So bitter was he that he refused to give his consent and did not attend the wedding. For months afterwards, he would have no personal contact with Lizzie or her husband. His objections were simple: Lizzie was quite young and had been reared in a social atmosphere which George Howard was convinced was much above that of young Candler. The two young people were not to be swayed, however, and on January 15, 1878, they were married in the First Baptist Church of Atlanta by the Reverend D. W. Gwin.

Lucy Elizabeth would often relate to her children how she caught Asa by making up excuses to visit her father's business. She knew what she wanted and she arranged to get it.

If she was strong-willed and determined, she needed to be. Marrying into the Candler family was often like being absorbed. They were a dominating and clannish group. In fact, Lizzie quickly found herself with a new name! Because Asa had a sister called Lizzie, he chose to call his love by her first name "Lucy." The rest of the Candler clan would also call her Lucy, while to her own kin she was Lizzie.

Lucy and Asa had a typical honeymoon for the period — he took her home to Villa Rica to meet his people. Joining them on this romantic trip to Carroll County were Asa's brother, Warren, and his new bride of two months, Nettie. Fortunately they were able to find humor in this wild trip in the winter of 1878 that was filled with swollen streams, muddy country roads, and a series of misadventures.

Asa had already moved his mother and brother John to Atlanta in November 1877, and after their marriages, both he and Warren with their young brides, moved in with them. Apparently Lucy was happy enough in her new situation; however, Asa confided to his sister Florence in July that Lucy was so blue at being cut off from her family that he

wanted his sisters to all make a special effort to write to her
and encourage her and boost her spirits. Moreover, by this
time, Lucy was pregnant .

News of the expected baby prompted George Howard to
consider mending the fence with his son-in-law. Very shortly
before the baby was due, he sent the following letter, which
has remained famous within the family:

> Atlanta, Ga., Nov. 24, 1878
> Mr. A. G. Candler
>
> Sir,
> I am disposed to "bury the hatchet" and to be friendly
> in the future—if this should meet your approval you can let
> me know. Respt.
> (signed) Geo. J. Howard

He did not write or call upon Lucy; he just sent the letter
to Asa. They were both hardheaded and stubborn — both
suffering from male pride.

The arrival on December 2, 1878 of a boy baby, who was
promptly named Charles Howard Candler (and called
Howard for the rest of his life) served to break down the
barrier between the two men. In addition, the fact the child
was male seems to have been a particular point of pride not
only for Asa, but also for George Howard. It is obvious that
George J. Howard had been, to say the least, not overjoyed
at the addition of another girl to his own family when he
wrote his mother of the birth of the little baby who was
destined to become the wife of Asa Candler.

> Sept. 28, 1859
>
> Dear Mother,
> We have nothing of interest to write about except that
> Lou was safely delivered of another girl baby this morning
> and is now doing as well as could be expected.
> I have not heard from Father since you left. I expect a
> letter today Yours truly
> (signed) Geo. J. Howard

Far more touching is Asa's own description of the pride he felt upon walking to work that day after he "had seen his boy in the arms of his pretty mother." This delivery was attended by both the baby's grandmothers, as well as Lizzie's great-uncle, Dr. Goldsmith. At the time of the birth, Dr. Goldsmith remarked to Asa that "you certainly have a fine boy." Grandma Candler kissed the baby and said, "This is my boy, and Lucy said, "*No*, he is my baby." To ease the strain, Grandmother Howard interrupted saying, "He is ours." (The Candlers had a way of taking over.)

The next few years were busy and important ones for Asa Candler. He was establishing himself as a business man, learning the demands of operating an enterprise with wholesale contacts, and beginning to widen his business interests. In 1879, he made his first investment in Atlanta real estate.

The year 1879 brought the so-called "gold redemption prosperity" to Atlanta, and Hallman and Candler expanded to meet the widened challenges and opportunities. The wholesale end of the drug business was growing and fanning out from Atlanta. In 1881, Asa Candler bought out his partner, Hallman, who retired, and the business was renamed Asa G. Candler and Company.

In April, 1882, Asa sold a half interest to George Howard, his father-in-law and former employer, and the firm then became Howard and Candler. The business continued to grow with Atlanta. Asa figured out early that the profit in a drugstore did not come from mixing prescriptions but from carrying a wide assortment of goods and sundries. Greater profit could be made if the druggist made up and sold his own "house brands," as many major stores do today. In addition, Asa was constantly on the lookout for promising patent medicines, developed by others, which he could purchase the rights to and then promote. Asa knew he didn't have to be the originator, he just had to make it more presentable and market it. This was the source of his wholesale business.

Asa's other strength was he personally oversaw production. By insisting on uniform quality in all of his concoctions, he avoided the pitfalls and criticisms that plagued so many druggists of that era. One Atlanta pharmacist known to have had this problem was none other than J. S. Pemberton.

Asa became a member of the American Pharmaceutical Association at its twenty-sixth annual convention which was held in Atlanta in Concordia Hall November 26-29, 1878. In only five years, he had gone from being a jobless but determined seeker of employment in his vocation to becoming affiliated with his trade association, which indicates that his drug business had become stabilized in the city of his adoption.

One of Asa's enterprises at this time and into the 1880s was an interest in the manufacture of a popular patent medicine called Botanic Blood Balm, for which somewhat extravagant curative powers were claimed. The concoction was supposed to be a blood purifier and to cure skin diseases, rheumatism, catarrh, kidney troubles, and other ailments. It was an infusion of roots and herbs to which certain iodides were added; the iodides were what gave the balm any medicinal qualities it may have had. The infusion only gave it a disagreeable, bitter taste, which at the time was thought to be absolutely necessary to an efficacious medicine. "B.B.B." said Howard Candler, "was manufactured, bottled and packed one dozen to a box by my father in his drugstore and shipped to retail druggists throughout the country. In this case, as he was to do later with a far more famous and successful product, father used his instinctive faith in advertising to keep the medicine before the public."

In 1881, Asa purchased the rights to a perfume named Everlasting Cologne. Again, it was a great favorite with the general public because of Asa's continuous advertising. It remained a strong seller for him as long as he was in the drug business.

An article published on May 1, 1889, in the *Atlanta Journal* described Asa's business. This young man of just thirty-seven was by then the owner of possibly the largest drug business in Atlanta, the result of his energy, ability and determination. It was a business he had built with temporary help from two partners, whom he had then had the foresight to buy out.

This business occupied a thirty footfront, one hundred

and twenty foot deep, three story and basement building. The necessary equipment for the manufacture and compounding of drugs, proprietaries, and whatever else was made and distributed by Asa G. Candler and Company, was located in the basement. Boilers had been installed over crude furnaces for heating the ingredients used in the preparation for marketing of Coca-Cola, Botanic Blood Balm, and infusions of crude drugs.

Even though The Coca-Cola Company was still in its infancy, Asa was already bringing other members of the Candler family into the business. Specifically, he hired three nephews, sons of his sisters and of a brother. He considered this a wise business policy. The young men, Samuel C. Dobbs, Samuel L. Willard, and Daniel B. Candler, were known to him, they were his kinsmen, and they needed jobs. His affectionate regard for his own kin, no matter how far removed, was extraordinary even in a section of the country where family ties were strong. This affection for his "own folks" pervaded his entire life and even extended to the neighbors and friends of his family in Carroll County. George W. Little, one of his early employees, spent a quarter of a century in his service. When he went in for his initial interview, Asa, on learning Little was from Carroll County, asked who his parents were. "When I told him, that seemed to be all the reference he felt he needed."

G. W. Little, J. W. Phillips, and Daniel Bevill Candler, son of Asa's brother, Ezekiel, represented this aggressive young firm on the road regularly, and most of their travel was by means of horse and buggy in which merchandise samples were carried. They collected on accounts, in addition to selling, and sometimes carried considerable sums of money with them, since accounts were normally paid once a year and very frequently with gold.

By 1890, Asa Candler had been in Atlanta for seventeen years. He had worked hard and his $1.75 had grown into several tens of thousands. He had a beautiful wife and five children. His wholesale drug business was doing very well and — to his existing proprietary brand names of Botanic Blood Balm, Everlasting Cologne, and others — he had recently added a new name, Coca-Cola.

"While Father was far from being "well-to-do" at this time," Howard wrote, "he was, nonetheless, a substantial businessman whose notes to the amount of nearly $36,000 were cheerfully carried by the Merchants Bank and others and whose firm was doing better than $100,000 a year in business. This is not the picture of a struggling pharmacist who stumbled onto a gold mine by accident, as has been claimed by some. It is a picture of a hard working businessman who had started on the bottom rung of the ladder and had already, by 1890, made considerable progress upward. Had he not made the decision he reached in this year — had he remained a wholesale and retail druggist — he would still have unquestionably achieved considerable prosperity and provided well for his family."

As it was, Asa G. Candler, at this juncture in his career, made what must have been a very difficult decision. His business was secure and continually expanding. Any action he took now must of absolute necessity be carefully thought out and arrived at with due consideration of the consequences. That he was taking thought for the future of his wife and children is obvious from the character of the investments he had already made.

When he made his decision, Asa G. Candler acted on it with typical directness and dispatch. In 1890, he closed out his entire stock of "drugs, paints, oils, glass, varnishes, perfumery and fancy articles," amounting in value to approximately fifty thousand dollars — a very considerable sum for that time — to concentrate his efforts in the manufacture and marketing of the "delicious, refreshing, stimulating, invigorating" drink the formula for which he had bought two years before. He moved his operations, in the fall of 1891, to 42 1/2 Decatur Street, where he occupied two floors over a saloon, a pawnshop, and a secondhand clothing store. The saloon catered to what then was called the "colored" trade. Here, in these unlikely surroundings, he concentrated on selling Coca-Cola — a task that was to make him one of the richest men of his time and to carry the name and fame of Atlanta to the ends of the earth.

# The Coca-Cola Company

The early days of The Coca-Cola Company (although it did not officially have that name until 1892) are an interesting contrast to the international conglomerate that now does business in almost all countries in the world. The sun may now set on the British Empire but not on Coke's.

In the fall of 1891, Asa moved his fledgling business to 42 1/2 Decatur Street (upstairs) in Atlanta. At that time, his office force, in addition to himself, consisted of Frank M. Robinson, Miss Stella Gallagher, and a Mr. Christian, first name unknown. Asa's nephew Dan Candler and George W. Little, formerly traveling salesmen for the wholesale drug business, came over to The Coca-Cola Company as salesmen and were later joined by Samuel Candler Dobbs, another nephew. E.C. Reese, who concentrated on the sale of Botanic Blood Balm, was not connected with the wholesale business, but was employed as a traveling salesman for the Midwest. He later became manager of the Chicago branch of The Coca-Cola Company. J.B. Brooks, who traveled for the Atlanta Perfumery Company, also took orders for Coca-Cola as a sideline. (Asa later sold the Botanic Blood Balm business to Brooks.)

The manufacturing end of the Coca-Cola enterprise was run by another of Asa's nephews, Sam Willard, and by George Curtright, a black handyman. William Curtright,

George's brother, made all deliveries with a one-horse dray. Many years later, Sam's brother, Joe Willard, said, "I often reminisce over the thrill we all got when Bill Curtright got his first set of brass-mounted harness and how he spent most of his Sunday mornings polishing it."

Locomotion for the dray and muscle for the shining harness were provided by the same horse, "Ol' Bird," as he was affectionately called, that had pulled George Little's buggy on its many trips through Georgia and Alabama in the early selling days of Asa's wholesale drug company.

The company, obviously, was a small one. The staff of the home office in Atlanta, for almost the first two decades of the company's life (until about 1908), never exceeded more than thirty employees, even when Coca-Cola was doing a multi-million dollar business extending into every state in the union and several foreign countries.

Howard Candler said: "As I remember those days, in my boyhood, the company was a happy one. There was much to keep everyone busy. The business was expanding rapidly, and my father managed to instill into all those who worked with him a pride in their accomplishments and in the growth of Coca-Cola."

As a boy, Howard Candler often watched the manufacture of the Coca-Cola syrup. Syrup was the company's only stock in trade, and its manufacture was crude by comparison with today's ultra-clean, high-tech Coca-Cola bottling plants. As Howard described it, against the side wall, a square brick furnace was built on the wooden floor with a brick stack extending through the roof. A forty-gallon copper kettle was suspended from the top edge of this furnace with a platform extending around the three sides not to the wall. Sugar in barrels was rolled onto this platform by skids then dumped into the kettle containing hot water. A wooden paddle was used to hasten the solution of the sugar and to prevent the syrup from scorching. Sometimes the kettle of syrup was neglected and allowed to boil over, resulting in damage to the goods in the clothing store below. It was partly because of the constant trouble over this sort of thing that the manufacturing site was moved in 1893.

When the melting operation was finished, the syrup was

dipped, with a five-gallon copper measuring pot, from the kettle and poured into fifty-gallon barrels which were not filled, as the other ingredients necessary to complete the Coca-Cola were added personally by Asa or by Frank Robinson to each barrel of syrup after it had cooled.

Each barrel of Coca-Cola was thoroughly shaken and then drawn off into containers ranging from one pint to ten gallons in volume. The pints and quarts were retailed by druggists for home consumption, and the one-gallon earthenware jugs and five- and ten-gallon kegs delivered to soda fountains for dispensing.

Asa took selling Coca-Cola seriously. His nephew Joe Willard used to tell a story about something that occurred one Saturday afternoon in 1890. There were only two or three people still around the plant when a druggist, a few blocks down the street, sent word that he needed some Coca-Cola. Asa, receiving the request, went to the storeroom, only to find that there was none left.

He then proceeded to make up one gallon for this customer and sent it over by Bill Curtright, the delivery man. It seems almost inconceivable that he could have made up Coca-Cola in such a small amount and have maintained his quality standard for uniformity of product and flavor excellence. Yet, an oft-repeated axiom of Asa G. Candler was *"A sale of Coca-Cola lost today is not a sale that may be made tomorrow."* This prompted him to go to any lengths not to miss one.

Joe Willard also told of another time, in these early informal days, when a local druggist sent word that he wanted his barrel of Coca-Cola "to have a good head on it." Joe himself was sent to a wholesale drug house to get some soap bark foam.

"That particular barrel," he chuckled, "gave out a handsome head, indeed!"

"Saturday afternoon," wrote Howard Candler, "was traditionally the time when my Father would don his long denim gown, go out into the syrup room, as he called his laboratory, to mix the secret ingredients for the Coca-Cola formula for the next week.

"The same copper kettle in which Coca-Cola was made

was used at this time for the preparation of Botanic Blood Balm. Coca-Cola was usually manufactured on Saturdays and B.B.B. on other weekdays. In the beginning, about twelve barrels of Coca-Cola would be made per week. In the winter, because of the prevailing custom of closing up soda fountains for the cold season, Coca-Cola was manufactured only every two or three weeks. Even after the move to Ivy and Auburn, Coca-Cola was made only twice a week because it took the syrup so long to cool. B.B.B. was also made at the Ivy and Auburn factory about once a week until 1897, when others took over its manufacture and distribution and moved it to a different location."

Secondhand whiskey barrels were used for shipping Coca-Cola in those days. The barrels were gathered up by an outsider, sold to the company, and then cleaned by washing with hot water. They were then painted red. Asa insisted on clear barrels, not charred, and no gin barrels could be used because they had been paraffined. Barrels that had been glued were unusable, as well. This restricted the company to a comparatively few saloons that emptied clear, clean, white oak barrels. Later on, as the demand for Coca-Cola increased, methods were devised for removal of char, glue, and paraffin, increasing the number of acceptable barrels. Still later, the company had its own barrels made and also maintained its own cooperage manufacturing department.

The ingredients of Coca-Cola, throughout its early history, were referred to by numbers from one to nine, in order that branch factories, the first of which was established in Dallas, Texas, in 1894, could order supplies through the mail or via telegram without revealing the identity of the ingredient. Sugar was purchased and received at all plants except the two small ones at Philadelphia and Los Angeles in car lots of from 100 to 125 barrels of 350 pounds each.

Factory expansion, Howard Candler reported, never seemed to keep abreast of rapidly increasing demand for Coca-Cola. Frequently these heavy barrels of sugar had to be stacked two-high on floors designed for a much lighter load. To empty the sugar out of the barrels, their heads were carefully knocked in with a mallet or hatchet and each head (in several pieces) put into its own empty barrel. The Atlanta factory sold its empties mostly to N.P. Pratt Laboratory for packing and shipping of Epsom salts. Other plants sold them to various industries to be used as containers for packing and shipping appropriate merchandise.

"During the early years of the century, when much of my time was devoted to the manual labor of manufacturing," Howard wrote, "I became quite proficient in my ability to spin on its side an empty sugar barrel across a wide floor space to the area where it was to be stacked for future sale."

The Coca-Cola Company grew rapidly during its first decade of life in the 1890s. It was quickly expanding out of Georgia and the South and becoming an American instead of just a Southern enterprise.

"My cousin, Daniel Candler," Howard wrote, "who had worked for my father in Atlanta for several years, was sent in March, 1894, to Dallas, Texas, to open the first branch factory of The Coca-Cola Company. He remained there throughout the life of the Georgia corporation and for several years with the Delaware company.

"The following year, factories were established in Chicago and Los Angeles. The first manager at Los Angeles was Samuel Candler, son of Colonel Milton A. Candler. My next younger brother, Asa G. Candler, Jr., was the second manager of the California factory.

"A warehouse was established in Philadelphia in the spring of 1897 to facilitate deliveries in the East and, the following year, under plans developed by Samuel L. Willard, a factory was established in that city.

"At almost the same time, on December 13, 1898, the first distinctively Coca-Cola building and factory was publicly opened at 179 Edgewood Avenue in Atlanta.

"Erected by the company on its own property and to its own designs, the Edgewood Avenue building was thought to provide the last word in manufacturing facilities. In his annual report to stockholders in January, 1899, Father said (proudly referring to this new and magnificent plant), 'It is sufficient for all our needs for all time to come.' Actually, it was only a few years before these quarters were wholly inadequate. The Magnolia Street building went up in 1909 and the North Avenue factory in 1919, so that the company seemed to outgrow its quarters at almost regular ten-year intervals."

"In this new plant and building," according to Howard Candler, "the company had, for the first time, what was termed a laboratory space, located on the first floor in an otherwise useless acute angle corner of the building which, when enclosed by a fireproof partition and furnished with a sheet iron safe door with a combination lock, made a triangular shaped room. As late as 1903, the preparation of the formula was done only by my father and Mr. Robinson. They alone had the combination to the door, and except for a Negro helper, no one was permitted in this laboratory room.

"Considerable romance, naturally, was built up and maintained around the secrecy which attached to the room and what occurred there. As soon as a shipment of essential oils was received, the boxes were put behind the iron door, the lids removed by either Mr. Robinson or my father, the packages lifted from the cases by them and all labels, either on the tin cans or the bottles containing the oils, were scrupulously scratched off to avoid any possibility of discovery of the contents. My father received and opened all the mail; invoices covering these particular items of merchandise were not turned over to the bookkeepers for remittance, lest the Accounting Department discover the names and quantities of oils being purchased. He invariably discounted these bills, and when it came time to pay such invoices he simply scribbled a memorandum to his head bookkeeper, Will Mashburn, asking that he bring him a check made payable to the importer for a stipulated amount. He kept these invoices in a substantial file, under lock, the key to which he kept on his personal key ring. In the preparation of inventories at the end of the year, he furnished the inventory clerk a memorandum showing the aggregate value of all oils then in stock. As the business developed, however, and the fact became recognized that confidence could be reposed in the personnel of the organization, invoices and inventories relating to these essential oils were handled in a perfectly proper and conventional manner by the Accounting Department.

"One of the proudest moments of my life came when my

father, shortly after the turn of the century, initiated me into the mysteries of the secret flavoring formula, inducting me as it were into the 'Holy of Holies.' No written memorandum was permitted. No written formulae were shown. Containers of ingredients, from which the labels had been removed, were identified only by sight, smell and remembering where each was put on the shelf when it came in from the supplier or was made in the same locked room. To be safe, Father stood by me several times while I compounded these distinctive flavors to see that proper quantities were used of the right ingredients and in the correct order to insure the integrity of the batches and to satisfy himself that his youthful son had learned his lesson and could be depended upon. It has now been many years since I have gone through this ritual and I cannot even remember the names of some of the materials used, but I believe that if by the intoning of some magic phrase I could be transported back to that little triangular room behind the iron door and could pick up once again the little glass graduates which I used in those long-past years, I could close my eyes and do a creditable job of mixing this unique flavoring extract."

No matter how magic the formula of Coca-Cola, the product had to be sold and distributed before people would know. You can't have a smile and a Coke if your local soda fountain has never heard of the stuff.

Frank Robinson, during the early 1890s, was head of the sales force and handled advertising and marketing as well. Asa's nephews, Samuel Candler Dobbs and Daniel Candler, and longtime Candler employee, George Little, were the sales force for most of these years. While Pemberton had only sold Coca-Cola in Atlanta, Asa Candler suffered no such restriction in vision, and his salesmen, from the first, were regularly selling the syrup all over the South. There might not have been a lot of drugstores initially, but the few that carried Coca-Cola were widespread and helped get the product into the view of a lot of people.

Soda fountains were a big thing in the South back in the Gay Nineties — a place for social gatherings, courtship, and cool refreshments to beat the hot summer sun in that time of no air conditioning. But, soda fountains were also seasonal, many being open only from May 1 to November 1. The spring openings of soda fountains were major events in large and small, magnolia-scented Southern towns from Memphis to Mobile, from Savannah to Birmingham, down in old New Orleans, and up in the former capital of the Confederacy, Richmond.

Ladies and gentlemen dressed in their formal best when they visited the soda fountain to partake of sodas flavored with vanilla, chocolate, orange, lemon, pineapple, cherry, strawberry, and other flavors. The competition for the taste buds of these soda fountain customers was intense, and any fountain that could offer something new — something "delicious and refreshing" — stood a distinct advantage. And it was the province of the few salesmen of The Coca-Cola Company to convince fountain owners that people would want ice-cold glasses of Coca-Cola.

Samuel Candler Dobbs later wrote that, in 1890, The Coca-Cola Company's advertising costs equaled, if not exceeded its sales. "Our faith in Coca-Cola, however," he said, "never weakened."

Any salesman whose faith did waiver could expect to be with another company selling snake oil or Carter's Little Liver Pills, or whatever. Asa Candler would not want him working for The Coca-Cola Company.

During the year of 1891, the three dauntless salesman of The Coca-Cola Company covered the entire South — spending endless hours on rattling trains or in bouncing buggies and sleeping in cheap hotels. To help them in their mission, Frank Robinson provided hanging signs for drugstores which read "Delicious, Refreshing. Drink Coca-Cola. Five Cents at Soda Fountains"). Other advertising and promotional pieces included calendars and "Push" and "Pull" signs for doors with the Coca-Cola logo. Printed ads in newspapers and other publications were placed with growing frequency as revenues allowed. Tickets were also given out that, when taken to a soda fountain serving Coca-Cola, could be redeemed for a chilled glass of that beverage which, as was being constantly pointed out by the company's advertising, was "delicious and refreshing."

The first decade of The Coca-Cola Company's existence was a good one. As 1899 rolled around, starting off the second decade of Coca-Cola, the sales force had grown to fifteen men, and their territory was the entire country, not just the South. By then, the selling season had been lengthened, running from February 1 to November 1, and soda fountains were urged to sell Coca-Cola year-round. "There is so much territory," Asa Candler told them, "and so few of you men to work it that it seems imperative that we do a little work in a great many places."

Asa Candler and The Coca-Cola Company came up with many ways to spur their retailers into selling more product. Beginning in 1899, customers were offered a two-percent discount if they paid for an order in ten days or less. If they ordered thirty-five gallons or more of syrup, the company would pay the freight. At the end of the year, rebates of five cents a gallon were given to customers who had purchased one hundred gallons or more during the year, and also five cents for each additional hundred gallons, up to twenty-five cents a gallon.

Nor was Asa averse to selling non-soda products, although he didn't have much success at this. Coca-Cola glasses were the best seller and have been sold by the company ever since. The first glasses were not the fluted shape we are all so familiar with, but had straight sides. They did have the Coca-Cola logo, of course. Soda fountain managers were not always excited about using glasses with someone else's advertising, but sales were generally good and the glasses have been a tremendous advantage in establishing Coca-Cola's name recognition over the years.

In the 1890s, Coca-Cola chewing gum and even Coca-Cola cigars were marketed. These products did not do well at all and were soon dropped. The Coca-Cola Company was to sell *only* Coca-Cola syrup until well into the 1950s, when a successful diversification was finally managed.

Meanwhile, all sorts of premiums were devised and offered to encourage customers to buy more and more syrup. In the late 1890s, the company provide beautiful clocks with the Coca-Cola logo, fountain urns, prescription scales, prescription cabinets, and showcases. A thirty–five gallon order would earn the customer one of these premiums, which he would then display in his drugstore, giving Coca-Cola additional free advertising.

Being a Coca-Cola salesman in this era required far more than just taking orders. When a new fountain manager was sold on Coca-Cola, the salesman had to train all the people working at the fountain how to properly mix and serve Coca-Cola. He also had to check out the carbonation facilities and make sure the drink could be served chilled, otherwise it didn't taste right. He was also responsible for seeing that posters were put up around town proclaiming that a new beverage was now being served by the soda fountain. The early posters were thirty by forty inches and, at first, included the words, "Asa G. Candler, Proprietor," because he was more widely known than the product.

Asa, aided by Frank Robinson, devised and implemented a campaign of constant advertising on an unprecedented scale for a soda fountain drink — or a patent medicine for that matter — that would eventually lead to the incredible name recognition that Coke enjoys today. By 1909, the Associated Advertising Clubs of America was to proclaim Coca-Cola the "best advertised article in America."

Coca-Cola advertising was plastered everywhere and on everything. There were thousands upon thousands upon thousands of outdoor posters, painted wall and barn signs, calendars, serving and change trays, blotters, fans, bookmarks, marble paperweights, streetcar card signs, and much more. Look up in the streetcar on a hot summer's day, and you were likely see to a Coca-Cola sign. So what did you order when you exited the streetcar, pulled loose the shirt that was stuck to your skin by perspiration, and entered the cool darkness of the drugstore? Right. "Gimme a Coke. Quick."

There was so much advertising material that Coke salesmen had to be in really good shape to haul it around. Howard Candler recounts one of his experiences in 1899. He had been sent to Kansas City with orders to distribute one hundred boxes of fans with Coca-Cola advertising on them in office buildings, restaurants, hotel dining rooms, barbershops, and similar places. He strung the fans on cords and slung cords fully-festooned with fans over each shoulder. They were not light, and he could barely walk. He started at the top floor of office buildings and worked his way down, giving out fans to any who would take them. "I thus got rid of a tremendous amount of bulk advertising material, as well as practically all of my energy," he said.

Asa understood that advertising was essential to the success of Coca-Cola. There was intense competition from other types of soda fountain drinks — orange and lemon, chocolate and vanilla, strawberry and pineapple. Initially the advertising and promotion was aimed at establishing Coca-Cola as an alternative to the fruit and other flavored drinks. But, of course, success begets imitators and, in the case of Coke, there were plenty of them.

The very first imitator was the creator of Coca-Cola himself, Dr. J.S. Pemberton. In the brief time he had left to live after selling the rights to Coca-Cola, Pemberton and his associates marketed several drinks they claimed were based on the original formula. One of these was called "Yum Yum." This effort continued for some time after Pemberton's death and, although it was never successful, it certainly did little to help The Coca-Cola Company's sales and reputation.

Asa Candler mentioned this in a letter to his brother Warren dated June 2, 1888. He says that they are doing "modestly well with Coca-Cola. Its only obstacle is that Pemberton is continually offering a very poor article at a less price & the public who pays for Coca-Cola & are not fulfilled commensurably, decide that it is a fraud."

Many people claimed to have a copy of Pemberton's original formula and brought out drinks they said were based on it. (Supposedly the "copies" were being sold for prices of anywhere from one thousand dollars down to a bottle of whiskey.) The Coca-Cola Company had a major headache trying to protect its product from these fakes.

One, a French Wine of Cola (not *Coca* as was Pemberton's name for it) blatantly imitated The Coca-Cola Company's marketing techniques. Specifically, the company making French Wine of Cola would issue tickets for free drinks but would not redeem them. Soda fountain managers who were victims of the fraud were not overly receptive when ap-

proached by Coca-Cola salesmen with a similar come-on.
Other imitators included Cola Ree (advertised as an "idea
brain tonic") and King Cola, which used the same Spencerian
script for its trademark as did Coca-Cola. By 1916, *The Coca-
Cola Bottler* reported that no less than 153 imitations of
Coca-Cola had been counted. Among these were Noka-Cola,
Fig Cola, Candy Cola, Cold Cola, Gay-Ola, Coca and Cola,
and many more.

All of this was pretty much an accepted, if not condoned,
practice in all fields of endeavor in the nineteenth century.
Asa Candler, however, made one departure from the normal
practice which guaranteed The Coca-Cola Company's triumph over its imitators and the ease with which such
interlopers have so easily been crushed by the company ever
since. While most businessmen of the era drew up their own
legal papers, with all the resultant loopholes and legal
errors as might be expected, Asa always hired the best
attorneys he could afford, and he could soon afford the very
best. One of these, for years chief counsel of The Coca-Cola
Company, was his brother, John Slaughter Candler, who
also became a judge on Georgia's Supreme Court. Often the
mere threat of a lawsuit was enough for the company to win,
whether it was against an imitator or someone just claiming
to have found a bug in a bottle.

Asa Candler and all the others involved with The Coca-
Cola Company were working hard to build the company and
its product into a successful enterprise. There was no way
shoddy imitators would be allowed to undermine their
product. This began the tradition of the exceptionally fierce
copyright protection that The Coca-Cola Company still exer-
cises. Take, for example, the Coca-Cola logo on the cover of
this book. It is there by permission, otherwise it wouldn't be
there.

Joseph A. Biedenharn of Vicksburg, Mississippi, gets
credit for the next major leap in the Coca-Cola's marketing
effort. The owner of a soda fountain in that Mississippi river
town, he became upset because no one locally could fill his
order for bottled soda pop needed at a picnic for workers at
a nearby foundation. He decided to bottle his own carbon-

ated beverages right there at his soda fountain, including Coca-Cola.

Biedenharn's rationale for becoming a bottler was that he "wanted to bring Coca-Cola to country people outside the limits of the fountain. Even in the cities, the fountains were limited in number and scattered here and there. I could see that many townspeople wanted Coca-Cola, but it was not easily available.

"I know for a fact that I was the first bottler of Coca-Cola in the world, because when I began there wasn't anybody bottling at that time. The soda water bottlers ... were merely content to make soda water."

His innovation did not go unnoticed by Asa Candler, who had visited Vicksburg on several occasions. "He was awfully nice to me," Biedenharn said, "I liked him from the start. Whenever he would come to town ... we would sit on boxes in my store and pass the time of day talking about Coca-Cola and other things. Mr. Candler always left a good taste in my mouth, and I was glad to do business with him."

He didn't inform Asa of his intention to bottle Coca-Cola, but, he said, "I shipped the first two dozen cases of Coca-Cola I bottled. Mr. Candler immediately wrote back that it was fine. He made no further comment at all that I remember. You know ... he has never returned my bottles!"

Three years later, in 1897, R.H. Holmes and E.R. Barber, who owed the Valdosta Bottling Works in Valdosta, Georgia, also began bottling Coca-Cola. Barber later wrote, "The drink was well accepted by the trade and our customers requested larger shipments of Coca-Cola. However, we soon discovered that we were running into a great deal of trouble due to the fact that the rubber washer on the stopper caused a not-too-wholesome odor in the drink after it had been bottled for a period of ten days or two weeks." The problem was soon solved by replacing the rubber washer with a cork one.

Selling carbonated Coca-Cola in bottles might have been the future, but Asa Candler did not rush to embrace it. The Hutchinson stopper — the only appropriate one available for bottling — was an awkward thing consisting of a cork attached to a wire hook, which pushed the stopper down into the bottle and kept it there after it was opened. The opening process often resulted in a resounding *pop*, hence the name "soda pop."

The possibility of lawsuits might also have been on Asa's mind, since some of the early bottles tended to explode as well. It was difficult to clean the bottle with the stopper inside and refilling was very slow and tedious. So, even though Coca-Cola was available in bottles from 1894 on, The Coca-Cola Company did not officially condone the packaging.

Still, it was such an obvious way to increase sales that Asa was soon persuaded by two young lawyers from Chattanooga, Benjamin Franklin Thomas and Joseph Whitehead, who knew Asa's cousin, Sam Erwin. They prevailed upon Erwin to introduce them to Asa in 1899.

Though not overly impressed by the concept of bottling, Asa listened. The young men, staunch fans of Coca-Cola, must have been very convincing. They came away with one of the most momentous contracts in business history. It stated briefly that Thomas and Whitehead could set up bottling plants at no expense *or liability* to The Coca-Cola Company. In return, they agreed to buy Coca-Cola syrup from the company and not to substitute anything else for it. The company further agreed to sell Coca-Cola syrup *only* to them for bottling purposes, with the exception of Asa's old friend Joe Biedenharn in Mississippi and a company in New England. The company would also supply labels, advertising materials, and granted them the sole right to use the Coca-Cola trademark on bottles.

Nowhere in this contract is any money mentioned. It was a fantastic deal for the young men and made them many millions of dollars. They walked out of Asa Candler's office with, essentially, the rights to bottle Coca-Cola for almost the entire country, with no investment on their part. Years later, Whitehead said that Asa, even after their presentation, was not gung-ho. He said, "If you boys fail in the undertaking, don't come back to cry on my shoulder, because I have very little confidence in this bottling business."

Yet, that opinion would soon change. Beginning in 1900, Coca-Cola-sanctioned bottling plants began appearing all over the place. A new era of ever-faster increasing sales had begun. The soda fountain business was reinforced by Coca-Cola now being available in bottles, and that in turn caused more people to order Coke at the fountains. The visibility of the company was also increased by the employees of the local bottling plants who now carried the Coca-Cola banner. They may have been employees of independent companies, but to the public, a Coca-Cola man was a Coca-Cola man, whether his paycheck came from Atlanta or from the local bottler.

When the young men's partnership broke up, they had the whole United States to split between them. Thomas took the middle-Atlantic and Eastern states, as well as California, Oregon, and Washington, leaving Whitehead with the Southeast, Southwest, and Midwest. Most of the U.S. Coca-Cola bottling companies today got their start in some way from the efforts of those two.

It might seem that Asa did not make the world's smartest move by giving away the bottling rights to Coca-Cola. However, from his viewpoint, it was not a poor decision. Since he didn't have great confidence in bottling, it was better to let others take the risk. If they failed, he lost nothing. If they succeeded, as they did, he would make millions, as he did. Secondly, Coca-Cola had already made him a rich man. He had no incentive to add the headache of hundreds of bottling plants and thousands of additional employees. Things were nice and manageable as they were. The Coca-Cola Company was a smoothly-humming money machine. There was no need for the company to get into bottling, or anything else, for that matter. And it didn't, until the 1950s.

Essentially, Asa and most of the Candlers were simply not interested in bottling operations, with the exception of a bottling plant that Asa's son Buddie owned for a while in Galveston, Texas. Generally, however, they do not own bottling stocks and have always preferred to take their profits directly from the company, which in turn sells to the bottlers. However, The Real Ones do prefer drinking Coca-Cola in a bottle, and that's what you'll most often be served — not one of those newfangled cans.

Back to advertising, one of the very bedrock foundations of Asa Candler and The Coca-Cola Company's success. In the 1890s, the company's advertising was copious, but not focused. It was sometimes advertised as a remedy ("an ideal nerve tonic and brain food"), other times as the more familiar "delicious and refreshing" soft drink. There are those who believe that about 1900, it suddenly dawned on Asa that there were more healthy people than sick and, thus, he should be addressing the larger market. But other, more cynical souls suggest the company was forced into it by the newly-evolving standards of truth in advertising.

Up until 1904, what advertising the company did not do for itself was handled by the Massingale Advertising Agency of Atlanta. After 1904, part of the account was given to the W.C. D'Arcy agency, although that agency had taken care of Coca-Cola's streetcar card advertising even earlier. The Coca-Cola Company began with $45 worth of such ads (three months worth) in 1896, and, by 1910, had them on almost every streetcar in the United States, Canada, and Cuba. D'Arcy would retain this plum of an account for the next fifty years and give Coca-Cola advertising a new direction.

The old Massingale ads had featured elegant men and women in palatial surroundings. The calendars and signs they had produced were most certainly sophisticated works of art, but they had an 1890s flavor already outdated in the early 1900s. D'Arcy, on the other hand, had a lighter touch and started including testimonials from famous sports figures, such as baseball legend Ty Cobb and Jack Prince ("the strongest bicycle rider who ever lived"). Pretty girls on the beach or playing tennis were also used. They gave the ads a nice, human touch, showing businessmen "being refreshed" and mothers and daughters out shopping.

D'Arcy also presided over a branching out in advertising. While Coca-Cola ads and signs had already appeared all over the country, they had been placed locally. Now, beginning in 1904, The Coca-Cola Company began advertising in national magazines. In fact, it was the first Southern company to ever place a national ad.

In 1908, according to Samuel Candler Dobbs, the company had painted signs on 2.5 million square feet of the walls of American buildings, and another 10,000 in Cuba and Canada—in every major city in those three countries. There were also more than 10,000 window displays in 1908, and "festoons" or special displays to go up over soda fountains were also very popular and widely distributed. A dirigible floated over Washington, D.C., in 1909 with large Coca-Cola signs on its sides. A multitude of other forms of advertising reinforced the name of the product wherever people turned.

One of the earliest animated signs was also the idea and the property of The Coca-Cola Company. Located along the Pennsylvania Railroad line between Philadelphia and New York, this sign stood thirty-two feet high. It represented a young man pouring Coca-Cola from a crockery urn into a glass. The unique feature of the display was the real water flowing from the fountain. To achieve the effect, it was necessary to run a two-inch pipe four hundred feet to a city main, but the advertisement erected around 1908 was viewed by thousands of train passengers on one of the most heavily traveled lines in the country.

By 1909, Coca-Cola had become one of the pre-eminent advertisers in the United States. Samuel Candler Dobbs, who was by now managing the company's advertising and marketing, was elected president of the Associated Advertising Clubs of America. The more the company advertised, the more it sold. So it advertised even more.

Asa's sons, Howard and Buddie, were interested in working with their father's company as soon as they finished school. Howard, the oldest, was to go on to a long and eventful career with Coca-Cola, while Buddie soon followed other pursuits. Excerpts from a letter Asa wrote to Howard in Kansas City on May 30, 1899, discussed Howard's tasks during his first official year with the company (as a child, he had not been reimbursed as an employee). It also shows Asa's concern for his sons and the part they are to play in the company.

> Dear Son, I have yours of the 27th from St. Joseph, with enclosures as stated. I enclose Kansas City check for $51.56 which you will need there...

I observe that you are selling a great many one and two gallon lots. I appreciate that this seems often the best that can be done, if however you can avoid it do so...

Our reason for sending to you goods at Kansas City was that you might make sales to retailers whose account none of the Wholesalers would accept, in which case if these dispensers are worthy of credit you could sell, and have us bill direct, or if they were only fit to be dealt with on a cash basis, you could sell and collect for, always of course charging retailers the card price according to the quantity delivered. Another reason for shipping you direct is that on investigation at Kansas City you might find that while one Jobber was well supplied with goods, another might not have any. You could then sell and deliver to him out of your stock, reporting it just as you have been doing.

To simplify the matter, our policy is that the man detailed to work these large cities by staying continually there, say for a month or more, shall have under their personal control goods and advertising matter and thus not be dependent upon any one dealer, which condition might bias some other dealer.

If you can obtain without much expense storage room where you can place this goods and advertising matter it would not be well for you to sell the goods and deliver to a wholesaler immediately upon your arrival at Kansas City.

When you have finally finished your work at the City you can then doubtless sell out your stock to some one of the wholesalers if you still have it on hand. Your habit will be of course to keep well posted daily if possible as to the amount of stock on hand by the various wholesale men and do all the business that possibly can be done through them, letting nothing be done directly with the retailer that can be done through the Jobbing house, otherwise you will create an impression that The Coca-Cola Company wishes to alienate the dispensing and retail trade from the wholesaler in its own interest. The wholesale men will make this claim anyhow, but let us give them no excuse for doing so.

Now as to your brother: He is anxious to be sent to California as assistant at the Los Angeles Office, allowing the manager there to travel the greater part of the time, your brother doing the manufacturing, shipping, and other office work. We are very loath to have him go so far off. He must

however be given work to do beginning not later than July
1. If a Manufacturing plant is located at Kansas City,
George Reed possibly will be placed in charge, as I do not
care for either you or your brother to permanently engage
with The Coca-Cola Company.

I want you to write me very freely your opinion of how
to manage so as best to serve the future welfare of you and
your brother.

I wish you to continue medical lectures until you are
finished, doing say work for us in the interim of lectures as
you can, and at the same time carefully looking around for
permanent location where you can settle to carry on your
profession.

Affectionately, Asa G. Candler, Sr.

Things were indeed looking rosy for The Coca-Cola
Company in the late 1890s and early 1900s, although there
were a few hints of the coming storm. Asa must have truly
felt good to have his company so successful.

In January, 1900, he told the annual stockholders meeting: "Another year of successful business has just been
closed. Six days in every one of the fifty-two weeks, we may
almost say, has found every wheel turning out profitable
results... Few corporations can show a more satisfactory
financial condition. The assets are absolutely good and could
be realized on within six months or less time without a
greater loss than 10 percent."

His tone was even more optimistic in 1902: "Nineteen
hundred and one should be inscribed on the calendar of the
commercial and industrial world in 'golden type.' Beyond
discussion, it will be remembered by the employees of The
Coca-Cola Company as a year of constant labor and a year
of plenty by its shareholders. Economy and care in expend-
ing the resources of the corporation has been and will
continue to be relentlessly observed in the several depart-
ments of its management."

On January 28, 1904, he said: "The year past has been
one of expansion in all directions as to the affairs and
management of The Coca-Cola Company. In the month of
December we assembled all the salesmen of the company at

the Atlanta office, and for one week they were given instructions by lecture and practical illustrations into every detail
of the work that we wished them to perform. Some of these
men had never before been seen by the officers of the
company. They were brought into personal contact with
each other and have returned to their various fields of work
greatly enthused and pledge themselves to do better work
than ever before." Continuing, he made a statement that
typified his caution: "I advise that this report be read to the
stockholders and filed with the records of the corporation
but that no portion of it be issued to individual stockholders."

In his fourteenth report, January, 1906: "I gratefully
report to you the closing of a year's business, the most
profitable in the history of your corporation. We have grown
to be a very large concern, owning our places of business in
Atlanta, Chicago, Philadelphia, Dallas, Havana, and Toronto.
We intended to have built in Los Angeles during the year but
were not able to procure suitable land properly located for
our peculiar necessities. It is intended to be done before the
close of 1906."

In 1907, he said: "It affords me pleasure to report that we
have enjoyed a year of prosperity and continual activity,
resulting in a great deal of work having been done and a
large amount of money expended. If this were all, we would
not have occasion for congratulation. The year has fulfilled
the promising prospect which was plainly evidenced at its
opening, and we will do well if we can duplicate this result
during 1907. Then, as now, there was nothing to mar the
prospect of the future excepting the feeling that after a
number of satisfactory years we must be near the end of our
prosperity. Emboldened by the success that has crowned our
efforts during each year since we began business, we venture now to say that to a certain extent the future lies in our
own hands. Our enterprise has grown to such magnitude
that we ought not to be surprised that there are some who
feel it their duty to annoy us. Such conditions will doubtless
continue to the end of time; notwithstanding the above, we
believe that we will encounter less friction in the coming
year than we have perhaps in the past."

In 1908, he showed even more clearly some of the disadvantages accruing to the tremendous expansion which the company had shown: "When I wrote my first annual report in 1892, I thought all presidents of industrial corporations made reports in full detail to stockholders. Since then I have learned much. I now know that such reports are not often given to stockholders. I believe they are entitled to know exact conditions and how well or bad their investments are being managed, and so we will have this full report...

"We have paid more for everything needed to do business on during the year than any previous year. Still we have done well. The Secretary gives you in detail a report of advertising expenses and says, 'This is conclusive evidence that our methods and mediums of advertising have produced good results.' The Traffic Manager shows how great we have grown as distributors of one single article, 'Coca-Cola.' The Sales Manager comprehensively exhibits how carefully and well he deploys his corps of salesmen throughout the length and breadth of this great country. They sell 'Coca-Cola' everywhere that commerce profitably keeps busy the traders of America."

But no amount of optimistic projections in annual reports could turn away the rough reality that lay ahead for the Candlers and their company.

*This "Coke Boy" art was used in Coca-Cola advertisements between the World Wars.*

# The Sale of Coca-Cola

In the early 1900s, Asa G. Candler, Sr. seemed to have it all. The Coca-Cola Company was well-established in three countries, and he had a loving wife and five wonderful children. Money was no longer a problem and, in fact, he was able to begin investing in real estate and development that was to bring excellent returns later. "Candler" buildings were to become a common thing. Yet, all was soon to come to a crisis. Inside of Asa, inside his family, and even inside of Coca-Cola itself were problems that were to cause a good deal of turmoil during the first two decades of this century.

To understand Asa, it is necessary to understand his family — both those he came from and those who came from him — and to delve into his motivations in first buying, then risking all in one great gamble to build Coca-Cola from nothing to the mighty soft drink empire it had already become in the early years of the 1900s.

Asa Candler bought Coca-Cola because he believed in it. If for no other reason, it cured the recurring headaches he had suffered since his childhood accident. But, there was another, less obvious reason why Asa liked Coca-Cola — and one perhaps he, himself, did not even consciously understand. It was the Candler family's history of incapacitating and overwhelming melancholy. His grandfather had committed suicide. His father suffered long bouts of debilitating depression during the Civil War. Asa, too, would fall into the dark morass of depression. Then along came this tonic that relieved his headaches and *pepped* him up, made him feel *good* and energetic, alive, vigorous. No wonder he had to have the rights to that golden elixir, and no wonder, after securing full ownership, he got behind Coca-Cola with one of the most successful marketing campaigns in the history of consumerism.

To fully appreciate what was to follow, it must be understood that despite all this, The Coca-Cola Company was not Asa's first love in life. More important to him were his religious beliefs and his family. He did not have a total, fanatical commitment to the company that other capitalists of the era did to theirs. He envisioned one day handing the company over to his sons. He did not envision the problems that would arise and fester between his two oldest sons, Howard and Buddie .

From the first day of their marriage in 1878, the nature of his business kept Asa away from home long hours. The wholesale drug business required a lot of effort, and Asa put in that effort, doing whatever it took as he built up his successful pharmaceutical house. One of his sons was to remember that he was often not home until after 9 p.m., so Lucy kept his dinner warmed on the back of the stove.

Lucy was left at home to manage the house, which was basically a farm, on Seaboard Avenue, in the section known as Edgewood — then outside Atlanta, but now well within city limits. They had gardens and a menagerie of pigs, chickens, pigeons, a milk cow, a goat, and of course, horses. Because of his childhood on a farm, Asa felt more comfortable in a rural setting. Also, as a pharmacist with some medical training, he was well aware of the way diseases and epidemics broke out and ran rampant in the city. He felt his family would have better health in the countryside. This was a constant, unending concern of his. Even when his sons were grown and working for the company, he would admonish them in correspondence to look after their health when traveling through epidemic areas or to New York City on Coca-Cola business.

Lucy was very domestic and having four little children ranging from infant to seven years of age by 1885, she had her hands full. Howard, the eldest son, was born in December of 1878, Asa Jr. (Buddie) in August of 1880, Lucy (called Sister by the family) in April of 1883, and Walter in October of 1885. The only child to come along after the family took over Coca-Cola was William, born in January, 1890, proving Asa did get home occasionally despite the demands of The Coca-Cola Company.

Howard and Buddie, who were the children to have the greatest impact on the company, were boys with very different, contrasting personalities. Howard, the shy, retiring, model child was designated to carry on the family name and mantle by virtue of being the eldest. Buddie was outgoing, hyperactive, and in trouble most of the time.

Sister Lucy was something of a novelty, being the only daughter in the family. Buddie found himself stuck between the responsible older brother and the cute little sister, which probably explains the attention-seeking trouble he caused in childhood. By the time he was eight years old — in the same year that Asa bought the Coca-Cola Company — Buddie had become a worry for his parents. Sister Lucy would have many Buddie stories to tell in her later years.

One concerned the time Asa bought an expensive new harness with brass trim for his horse and buggy. In those days, your harness and buggy were important items, as they were your means of transportation. It wasn't a week after Asa had bought the new set of harness when he came home to find it cut up and made into a miniature set. It seems that Buddie had wanted to make a harness for his goat so it could pull a cart. When he came across Asa's shiny new harness in the barn, he thought that with judicious alterations, it would be perfect. His father, naturally, did not concur.

Buddie also liked to tease his two younger brothers, Walter and William, particularly William. He would put William down the well, walk off, and leave him there. William would scream and cry until finally Lucy would get their mother and pull him out. Of course, they knew that Buddie had done it. Asa would switch him, but Buddie wouldn't give him the satisfaction of crying. He was an unbelievably stubborn boy.

According to Sister Lucy, punishing Buddie had little effect. He was consistently mischievous and hard to handle. When a switch was taken to him for one of his misdeeds, instead of crying, he would threaten to run away and join the circus. He was just as headstrong as his father, many said — a true Candler trait.

In the fall of 1888, Buddie was sent to live with his aunt, Florence Harris, who was running a school called the West End Institute in Cartersville. Asa probably sent the boy away because his mother couldn't handle him and because Asa was gone for such long hours with his business concerns. Asa also had implicit faith in Florence's ability to straighten out Asa, Jr. After all, Asa, Sr. himself had been sent to Florence, under the guise of "better educational opportunities," for the same reason. What Asa, Sr., hadn't counted on, however, was that both Florence and her husband, Colonel Joe Harris, had mellowed with age. Buddie's recollections of his years in Cartersville seemed to center on the many pleasurable afternoons spent behind the barn with Uncle Joe learning to smoke and chew tobacco — certainly not the curriculum his parents had in mind!

For nine months out of the year, then, Buddie was away from Atlanta. He came home in the summers. This exiling of such a young boy for a good part of the year was unusual. He must have been quite a handful.

The Candler family's primary social outlet at this time was the Methodist Church and its related activities. The church was very important to this family and would continue to play a major role for decades to come. The Candlers attended the Inman Park Methodist Church, where Asa was superintendent of the Sunday School for twenty-two years.

Lucy's social life, like that of most women of her class, consisted of church work and paying afternoon visits on the neighbors. She did not involve herself in organized charity work or women's clubs, preferring to devote her time and energies to her own growing family and Inman Park Methodist Church. Lucy's letters indicate that her socializing centered mainly on visiting with her sisters, particularly her sister, Pauline, Mrs. T. J. Ripley. Aunt "Paul" was a highspirited, mischievous character who was a source of constant amusement for Lucy and her family. In addition to the Howard girls and their families, Lucy was constantly entertaining visiting Candler relatives and Methodist dignitaries. No wonder she had little interest in being "organized" by some woman's group! The children's social interactions were, however, more limited. They were only allowed cousins and certain approved children from the church as playmates. Their mother and father didn't want them to pick up bad habits.

This family tradition continued into later generations of children. As Nena Griffith, one of Buddie's grandchildren, put it, "When we were little, we weren't allowed to play with anyone but our cousins."

Another family member described later generations of Candler children in this manner: "They would call up a cousin to come over for the day. They played with their cousins, they did things with their cousins. They were very clannish, actually. Until the world changed, they had their own little world out there in Druid Hills, and even if the fathers weren't getting along, the children got together with their age groups and played."

From 1888 on, all the children were exposed to the factory. In addition to the chores the boys were expected to do around the farm and in the house, Asa had them work in the factory when he found something for them to do there. Candler children had chores to do and were held responsible for their completion.

These children became highly conversant with The Coca-Cola Company and its operations. Only Sister Lucy went there solely to meet her father — it would have been considered unladylike for a little girl to work in a factory. Lucy would visit with the office staff, write letters, or read while waiting for her father.

Howard, because he was the oldest, was expected to be his father's right-hand man, as Lucy was expected to be her mother's right arm. That's how this family, and others of the era were structured. It took a lot to survive, and all family members were expected to work and do their part in insuring the family's general welfare.

Buddie resented having to answer to Howard if Asa wasn't there only because his brother had been lucky enough to be born a year earlier than he. As both a boy and a headstrong young man, Asa Jr. had problems bowing to his brother's authority. In fact, Buddie wasn't too keen on accepting anyone's authority but his own, and for most of his life, he gloried in not having to.

In the mid-1890s, first Howard, then Buddie were sent to Emory College for their advanced education. At that time, Emory was in the little town of Oxford, east of Atlanta. Later Asa was to give a million dollars to the Methodist church for a college endowment. He didn't specifically mention Emory, but the board pretty quickly figured out what he wanted and moved it to Atlanta where it is now Emory University. Emory is one of the largest universities in the United States without a football team. Candlers thought the game a waste of time and opposed it.

While the boys were attending Emory, Asa tried to keep them in line through his letters. On October 11, 1894, he wrote to Howard and said that he expected his son to be the first in the class, but tempered that by promising to send money. However, Howard had to closely account for the money, as was borne out in a letter of a few days later. Asa pointed out that Howard's weekly budget was incorrect and told him to review it, make the necessary changes, and return it to him.

Being away at college did not relieve Howard of family or company responsibilities, but the education was still considered the most important as evidenced by a letter Asa sent him in February, 1895. Asa wrote that he has handled a company request that Howard arranged and reminded his son that studies must come first over Coca-Cola affairs. He also said that he couldn't help Howard with his "Christmas" topic (evidently a term paper) but would review it if Howard sent the manuscript.

On September 26, 1895, Asa wrote that he was sending Howard some advertising materials to distribute to fountains in Oxford. He instructed Howard to watch and report if the Oxford fountains are selling "false" Coca-Cola. He added that he hoped Howard and Buddie were well.

Asa was not unaware of the tensions between his sons and wanted them to reconcile their differences. In November, 1895 he wrote that he was thankful for his children and good health. He asked if the boys are getting along or wrangling.

"I hope you, Asa [Buddie], are not worrying & teasing Howard about society affiliations. Don't do that. Wait till I see you. I want you to make so splendid a record in college both as a gentleman & scholar as that you will be greatly desired by all Good Clubs .... Now be *good* brothers."

Unfortunately, admonishments were not enough and the trouble continued. In January, 1896, Asa wrote:

"My dear sons,

I am real blue about my boys today. Everybody tells me how smart you both are. I have given you as good opportunity as it has been possible — much better than I ever had. I try to pray for you. In spite of all this in some of your studies — notably Latin & Greek your marks are put as low as they can be in the absence of my visits. Can you do better? Buddie has 8 absences Howard 10. Why these? Buddie especially ought to get the best marks having a sound body, strong mind, been in good schools all his life. Now why can't I see better reports? Wish to know why — I am asking only that you do your best. I can give you nothing but a good education."

In February, Asa wrote to Howard about the boys' squabbles at school. He had heard Buddie's side and felt that while his younger son acted wickedly, Howard was at fault, as well. Howard was not doing his duty as the older brother. He was favoring others over Buddie, speaking badly of Buddie and allowing others to speak evilly of Buddie to him. Asa wanted Howard to protect and be devoted to his brother.

Being the oldest meant that Howard was saddled with being responsible for Buddie while they were away at Emory. As the new school year began in 1896, Asa chastised Howard for Buddie's poor grades. He wanted Howard to help Buddie with his books, be his closest friend, treat him kindly, and not ridicule him. Asa had put all his money and hopes in his children. If they didn't do their best, he claimed he wouldn't be able to bear it.

Poor Howard must have felt like he was caught in a wringer by this time. He not only had to do well for himself, he had to nursemaid his crazy, wild younger brother and make sure that *he* got good grades, while doing a little promotional work for The Coca-Cola Company on the side. It was definitely a tall order.

In October, 1896, Asa was again trying to smooth over troubles between Howard and Buddie, counseling them to exercise patience and love with each other. But, by that time, the pattern they were to follow the rest of their lives appears to have been set. Buddie and Howard would practice love and patience only for public consumption. In private they would always be the squabbling rivals of their boyhood.

With the beginning of the new century, Asa Candler was to find more troubles to occupy his attention than the feuding of his sons as The Coca-Cola Company came under attack from various fronts.

In Virginia a doctor claimed that one of his patients died because of Coca-Cola and started a movement in the Virginia legislature to have it banned. His support came, in a large part, from the strong liquor lobby. The makers of whiskey didn't want people drinking Coca-Cola and buying less whiskey.

Coca-Cola salesmen were meeting resistance elsewhere, as well, and had to contend with their product being called "dope." Rumors began to abound. According to one story, a man in North Carolina drank a single glass of Coca-Cola and fell over dead. Little wonder the federal government was casting a suspicious eye at The Real Thing. And if matters weren't bad enough, Coca-Cola imitations were showing up everywhere. Even Willis Venable's son besmirched his father's honor of having sold the first glass of Coca-Cola by incorporating the "Coca-Kola Company" in 1907.

The real Coca-Cola Company became involved in a number of lawsuits at this time trying to secure and protect their trademark as well as fighting the federal government just to stay in business. This latter fight would give Asa and the rest of the company some very anxious moments, indeed.

As to unfounded stories, such as the man keeling over in North Carolina, the company tried to do damage control and put the best public relations spin on things, just as companies do today. For example, *The Coca-Cola Bottler* (published and edited by one of Asa's nephews) — a somewhat less than objective publication in such matters — had this humorous response to the North Carolina story: "This ... reminds us of the druggist in West Philadelphia who for a number of years drank his Coca-Cola one-fourth Coca-Cola and three-fourths rye liquor, varying it with gin, rum, and other exhilarating beverages, according to the stock of his 'medicine case.' Whenever his wife would take him to task, he would tell her that he had been drinking Coca-Cola and she firmly believed that he died of the effect of too much Coca-Cola, when in reality, he died of the 'jimmies.'"

As was always the case when he needed help, Asa Candler looked first to his family. Three of his brothers were attorneys, and John Slaughter Candler was a judge on the Georgia Supreme Court. Asa enticed him to come over to The Coca-Cola Company as its General Counsel and become the legal brain behind suing imitators and defending against the government and others litigating against Coca-Cola. John was the same brother who, as a child, cussed the Yankee soldiers who stole his hat.

Martha had said of John that even though he was the baby of the family, he was as bright and as smart as the first. He was only twelve when his father died, but Asa had stepped in and made sure John had gotten a good education.

There is little question that John was decisive and pragmatic. One college vacation, he came home by train, eager to be reunited with his family. Pulling into the station, he could see his mother and sister ahead on the platform, waving to him. Without waiting for the train to stop, he swung out, lost his balance, and fell under the train. Part of one foot and part of the other leg were severed. A measure of the man's character is that John had enough presence of mind to tell the doctor to amputate his leg wherever it would be best for the attachment of a prosthesis. He didn't want to walk like a cripple. He wanted wooden legs that could function well, even if it meant amputating *more* of his leg or foot! This was the man who would be defending The Coca-Cola Company and its trademarks. With his bulldog ferocity and determination of purpose, John would serve Asa well as legal counselor in the years to come.

John was one of Georgia's youngest Circuit Court Judges ever. He was an excellent lawyer and didn't mind taking on even his own brothers, and if necessary using every advantage.

There was a court case where Milton was on one side and the Judge (as John is called in the family) was on the other. He was a young attorney then. They were making their final arguments to the jury, and Milton was getting a little excited. Milton had the unfortunate habit of blinking uncontrollably, when he was excited and addressing the jury.

When it was John's turn, he said, "Ladies and Gentlemen of the jury, as you know, the esteemed Prosecuting Attorney, my esteemed colleague Mr. Candler, is also my brother. I'm very deeply fond of and love my brother, but there's one thing I want you folks to know. My brother Milton cannot tell a lie. Whenever he tries, his eyes blink." And with that, John sat down. The jury came back and found for John.

John resigned from the Georgia Supreme Court to work full time in his own law practice, Candler, Thomson, and Hirsch, because private practice paid better. His first wife had died, leaving him with little children, and he became despondent over that (he was also cursed with the family melancholy). When Asa asked him to handle the seemingly unending Coca-Cola business, the Judge was happy to add to the coffers of his practice.

Sam Candler's descendants who went into public service shared a common ideology. They believed their obligation as a successful member of any community meant spending time in public service. The key word here is 'service.' They didn't look upon it as a career, or something you did to earn money, but rather as a way of giving back to the community. Where capable, they served through the church or in public service as the mayor, the governor, a judge, or in the congresses of the state and the nation.

The Judge's years working with Asa and The Coca-Cola Company paid off handsomely for him. John Slaughter Candler II, the Judge's grandson, found evidence of this among his grandfather's papers, which he gave to Howard for The Coca-Cola Company records. It was "a copy of the first income tax return that The Coca-Cola Company filed in 1913. Now, the first time they passed the income tax law, corporations didn't pay any tax, they simply filed an information return as to what the dividends were — because the dividends were taxable to the people that got them. And here was a corporation with $50,000 in capital that paid four $500,000 quarterly dividends in 1913.

"The Coca-Cola Company had a whole lot of downtown real estate. And in 1916, instead of paying cash to everybody, they distributed the property as a dividend. The government wanted to tax it as income but the Judge said, 'Oh, no. You can't do this. It would be unconstitutional for you to tax these past earnings.'

"The company won that case. My grandfather got an entire office building for himself. So it must have been a pretty good-sized dividend. He had only a small interest, and he still got a whole building!"

By far the most important and dangerous lawsuit to the company at this time was the case of *The United States v. 40 Barrels and 20 Kegs of Coca-Cola*. This case resulted from a seizure of an interstate shipment from The Coca-Cola Company by federal administrator Dr. Harvey W. Wiley, who had been appointed to enforce new pure food and drug laws. Dr. Wiley, with the zeal and righteousness of a bureaucratic Billy Sunday, wanted the caffeine and cocaine out of Coke.

The trial began on March 13, 1911 in Chattanooga. The Coca-Cola Company, ably championed by the Judge, won the first round. Howard Candler later reported that the case cost the company $85,157.62 — a large sum in those days. Appeals and other legal maneuvering continued until 1916, with the case going all the way up to the Supreme Court. The highest court in the land sent it back to the original lower court for proceedings to start all over again. By that time, Dr. Wiley, whose fervor had driven the government's case, no longer held his post. In 1918 the government was willing to settle out of court. No record of that settlement was ever made public, but obviously some changes were made to the Coca-Cola formula as the government wanted or the eventual settlement would never have been offered. Also the fact that the case bounced back to Chattanooga where the federal government had lost once already probably increased the desirability of a compromise.

Howard Candler, in his biography of Asa Candler published by Emory University in 1950, revealed the antipathy of the Candlers and The Coca-Cola Company to Dr. Wiley, who is often referred to as "the infamous Dr. Wiley," by them. Yet, Wiley was operating from a sense that something harmful was being offered to the public and that it was his duty to force manufacturers to clean up their products. This he did quite well, and the changes he forced in Coca-Cola are matched by those in many other products. However, with Coke, Dr. Wiley was only fifty percent successful. The cocaine went, but caffeine stayed, and it's still there in Coca-Cola Classic.

While testifying under oath in the Chattanooga trial, Howard was brought to task over the presence of cocaine but would not admit it was in the formula. In fact he went into lengthy technical detail about the early procedures when the company was de-cocainizing its own coca leaves rather than buying them already processed. The procedure sounds a good deal less than exact. Howard described it on the stand as, "...when the quantity we figured on making was run out, we would stop the process..." So, while the attempt was made to remove cocaine, the level of that drug probably varied widely from batch to batch with the person in charge of the process guessing when it was finished.

After the reign of Dr. Wiley and his successors on the case, no one dared guess any more. Procedures used by all companies became much tighter and more precise. The cocaine, except for "untraceable amounts," disappeared from Coca-Cola, and the formula was generally cleaned up.

The long-running court battles took their toll on Asa. It was one thing to exhaust yourself building up a dynamic, thriving company, a legacy for your beloved family. But it was another to expend your energy and efforts battling the Philistines who attacked and imitated the product and company into which you had poured your life's blood.

Asa had considered getting rid of the company as early as 1912, as evidenced by letters to his brother Warren. They had discussed the figure of ten million dollars as being a reasonable one for the company. But it was then just talk. In 1916 Asa found an excuse to spend less time on Coca-Cola affairs — he was elected mayor of Atlanta, taking office on January 2, 1917. The idea of divesting himself of the responsibilities of the company became all that more appealing, although in all likelihood he would have held onto to it if not for his wife Lucy's plan.

Laura Candler Chambers, Asa's granddaughter has vivid memories of Lucy.

"She was very sweet, a very sedate person, and she didn't take any foolishness. No ma'am. She didn't take a bit of foolishness. I didn't get close to her like my sister Lucy [another granddaughter — there are nine Lucy's in the family] did. Of course, Lucy was named for her. Lucy was more or less a favorite. She had another granddaughter named for her, and that was Elizabeth Owens. They were her pets. She was a sweet person, and she was the cause of grandpa doing what he did... I know she was behind it."

Lucy would call her husband "Pepaw." According to Laura, "She never did call him sweetheart or anything like that. Papa, she'd call him Papa sometimes. She never did call him Mr. Candler, she never did say Asa. She just said Papa or Pepaw. That's what the grandchildren called him too. Of course he thought she owned the moon. He called her my queen, my queen. He was so deathly in love with her. And that was the whole time they were together."

In 1917, however, Lucy knew they didn't have much time left together. She had had crippling arthritis for years and now had breast cancer. She also knew her husband well and, in the view of her impending death, she wanted to be sure that *her* children got what had been acquired or earned by her husband and herself during the marriage, not the Methodist church or some other charity and especially *not* some other woman. She knew from having been a member of the Candler family that the Candler men remarried because they couldn't bear to live alone. Asa was getting older, more easily despondent, and probably more easily manipulated by the people closest to him, which could include his brothers, church people, and a possible second wife. Lucy wanted to make sure that her children got the assets and that they were distributed equally. That's why she came up with the Christmas day giveaway.

Laura Candler Chambers, who had just turned ten, was present that December 25, 1917.

"I remember we all came into the solarium. This was at the big house on Ponce de Leon. In the center of the house is this skylight. I always thought of it as a solarium. They came in there and we were all there. I don't know what was said, but these envelopes were issued to all the children, the boys, and Aunt Lucy. As I say, I didn't know what was in them. It was that money. I know Danny (what everyone called Lucy) must have said to Papa, 'Now listen, I haven't got long to live and I want to see the children get their money, and if you give it to them now, you stipulate to all of them that this is not in the will, because you're not going to have a will.'"

What was in those envelopes was The Coca-Cola Company. Asa Candler ended up not selling the company. He gave it to his children, at his wife's insistence.

The Christmas Day of the company giveaway must have been something. It was in the last house that Asa built — a house all on one floor, designed by Lucy for herself. He built it after his beloved wife had gotten too ill to go up and down stairs. The giveaway took place in the solarium, which had a vaulted ceiling of leaded stained glass designed by Joseph Lorenz. It was the center of the house. All other rooms led off it. There was an enclosed, pink Georgia marble court designed in the Pompeiian style. This sunken area was surrounded by sixteen pink marble columns. In the center of the room was a marble fountain. All of the bedrooms opened onto this marble court, which was ringed by marble statues and served as the family room.

The house, erected in 1916, is referred to within the family as "the Lemon Pie House" to differentiate it from Callan Castle, their previous one. Lemon Pie House is still located on Ponce de Leon Avenue, in the Druid Hills section, which Asa and the boys developed. Today it is St. John's Melkite Byzantine Catholic Church.

Now, the Candler children owned The Coca-Cola Company. Howard was already president, since his father had given him the job the previous year. This left Mayor Asa Candler of Atlanta only the one job — his public one. For the first time since 1888, his word was no longer the final law for the people making and selling The Real Thing. Of course, people in Atlanta remained very polite. Asa might no longer have Coca-Cola, but he still had Atlanta and its police force.

Asa Candler was good for Atlanta. When he was sworn into office, the city of Atlanta had a deficit of $150,000. When Asa retired two years later, the city had a surplus of $43,000 in the treasury.

Two years after giving away the company, however, Asa was no longer in office. He had sunk into a deep depression and became ill following Lucy's death in 1919. This was a source of great worry, particularly to his daughter, the second Lucy. Even before her mother's death, Lucy II had been concerned that Coca-Cola Company problems were destroying Asa's physical and mental health. All he wanted to do was make syrup, and he took it personally that other people would attack his product and harass him because they said it was unsafe. He was also tired of continually defending himself against the legions of imitators.

Passing the company on to the children did not erase the problems—if anything, it created more. It was set up so that Howard was in charge, and his brothers and sisters were on the board. Just being on the board, however, was not the same as being in charge of the family "cash cow." It was Howard who handled their income and, if he didn't dole it out exactly as they wanted, the others complained. Of course, it was also Howard who was doing all the work running the company day-to-day, something that his griping siblings failed to appreciate.

In addition, Asa's nephew Samuel Candler Dobbs, who had worked for Asa from the very first, was feeling shunted aside now that the children had the company. With all this dissension, it is little wonder that an outsider might sense the time was right to strike. Enter one Ernest Woodruff.

Woodruff must have started working on Dobbs early on, enticing him with the promise of more power and say-so in running the company if there was a change in ownership.

It is believed that Dobbs then went to work on Howard, painting a captivating picture of a new board of directors with no contentious siblings.

The principals were primed when a consortium led by Ernest Woodruff offered them $15 million in cash and $10 million in preferred stock. No longer would the siblings have to have their hands out to Howard. About $5 million was paid in taxes, leaving the $10 million in cash that their father thought the company was worth, plus the preferred stock, which gave them some protection that they might get the company back. Both the cash and the preferred stock has translated over the years into hundreds of millions.

Ernest Woodruff was an early day corporate raider, but The Coca-Cola Company was not some cash-bloated fruit ready for the picking. Asa had already gutted the company himself. The formula was really the only asset left, that and the business network of independent bottlers. There were no concrete assets like stocks and bonds in other companies, or real estate. Asa, Sr. had already taken the real estate holdings out of the company by this time — some of it going as dividends to stockholders. Anything else of value was held by Asa G. Candler, Inc. or other companies he controlled.

Basically the deal gave the children a nice sum of money that freed them from being in business together. It gave them the capital and the freedom to pursue other interests that did not include their brothers or sister.

This sale of the company was the largest single financial transaction in the South up to that time.

The Candler children did not consult with their father about the sale of the company. The initial understanding was reached in April of 1919, and in July, 1919, a majority of the stockholders committed to the sale by assigning an option to purchase the capital stock to Robert C. Alston, representing the Trust Company of Georgia and its part-

The Sale of Coca-Cola 91

ners. The sale was completed in September, 1919. The children never discussed this with their father, *not one of them*. Maybe they thought he would oppose it, or maybe it would upset him. Or maybe they truly believed that "He gave it to us, it's ours to do with as we want, and we don't want to be in business together."

Asa first heard about the deal in July. He was shocked, and he never really reconciled himself to the sale. The Coca-Cola Company was no longer his, but it was still his baby.

Aunt Laura remembers the aftermath of the sale and Asa's reactions. "Oh, the boys did that. Grandpa didn't," she said when asked about selling the company. "I could have kicked their butts... The idea of them selling that company. Lordy!

"Well, of course, you can't foresee the future, and the boys, the four of them—well, Aunt Lucy, too, she had to get in on it—they decided that Grandpa was getting too old to take care of business, and the best that they could do was to sell the business and him not have that load, you know. Well, of course, that was the wrong thing. You know, you can't tell them anything, so they sold it.

"I never will forget Pepaw coming by. Mama invited him to supper, right after that happened... She was very fond of him. I don't think she understood him, but she was fond of him.

"After dinner, he turned around at the side door, I'll never forget, and great big tears rolling down his cheeks. And he said, 'Helen, I'm fixing to walk down the streets of Atlanta tomorrow, like I did when I first came. A man without a job.'

"I'm telling you, Mama, she just. It almost ruined her, him talking that way. Because that was really his baby."

But Asa Candler was not through yet. He had ten years left to live — years of great philanthropy, service, and accomplishments.

And, literally inside the product itself, was trouble. Many people were starting to complain about cola products, and the many other food and food-related products of the day. They were starting to demand to know if harmful ingredients were included, and to insist on removal of such substances. Congress and the federal government responded with the pure food and drug laws. A Federal administrator, Dr. Harvey W. Wiley, was appointed to enforce these laws. He set out to clean up what the citizens of America ate and drank, and to identify and remove the dangerous additives in food products. It was good and much needed work.

The Coca-Cola Company, already dominant in the soft drink industry, was an obvious target. If Dr. Wiley could clean them up, the smaller cola companies would fall meekly into line. A decade of lawsuits, product seizures, and almost continuous trouble followed for Asa Candler and The Coca-Cola Company. They never admitted to any harmful ingredients, and they did not lose in court, but the formula was changed. The incessant battles so exhausted Asa Candler that he decided to give control of the company over to his children in 1917. In 1919, they sold it.

So, we have these little known facts explaining why Asa Candler first risked all on Coca-Cola, then was willing to give it up after it had become such an astounding success. Asa's inborn melancholy, relieved by the pep of Coca-Cola, gave him the extra edge that allowed him to see potential in this beverage that other people who had tried it did not see or feel. Asa was a believer—he believed in this product with the conviction of a man "born again." No wonder he thrust all of his tremendous marketing wizardry behind the product to ensure Coca-Cola's success. Yet, what was in Coca-Cola in the very early days that supplied the pep — the cocaine and high caffeine content — was to give it problems in the early part of this century as cocaine came to be recognized for the harmful drug it was. Dr. Wiley was death on caffeine, too, although he never managed to have it totally eliminated as he did with other drugs.

Let's look at the family and the lawsuits in more detail. This will make it obvious why the Candler children were willing to sell the goose that was laying the golden eggs — although they did keep quite a few of the eggs.

# Asa Candler's Later Years

The last decade of Asa's life did not start off well. In 1919 he lost his beloved wife, Lucy, and his children sold The Coca-Cola Company. Two very important parts of himself were forever severed from him.

Since he had given The Coca-Cola Company — lock, stock, and secret formula — to his four sons and one daughter, no money came to him from the sale. However, there was no need to shed tears for Asa Candler, who was not exactly broke. He had taken millions out of the company in both money and real estate. Even without the soft drink empire he had built and run for almost thirty years, Asa would continue to have a marked impact on his beloved Atlanta, the South, and the world in general.

Methodists of Asa's day were taught to "work as hard as you can so you can make as much money as you can, so you can give as much as you can." Asa heeded these teachings all his life — he was a *very* good Methodist.

During this period, the Methodists, Baptists, and other religious affiliations were divided into Northern and Southern branches, a holdover from the War Between the States (as the Civil War is still called in the South today). The Methodists united relatively recently, but not the Baptists — whose strong Southern Baptist Conference is in the process of fragmenting even more. Baptists and Methodists,

93

in the South at least, traditionally did not see eye to eye.
(Some of the greatest and funniest jokes Baptist preachers
used to tell concern "those heathen Methodists.") Asa was a
devoted Methodist and his wife, Lucy, was also active.
However, Lucy drew the line when it came to what she saw
as Asa's excessive zeal for giving. This is, perhaps, one
reason she wanted to make sure the children got The Coca-
Cola Company while Asa was still alive, instead of taking a
chance that he might will part of it to the church or Emory
or any of his other "causes." Despite Lucy serving as a brake,
the Methodists did exceptionally well over the years from
the Candlers.

Asa's many philanthropies were made possible by his
wealth and were dictated by this strong Methodist faith.
Throughout his life he devoted himself to church activities,
sometimes straying slightly out of the Methodist fold. While
he was a member of Inman Park Methodist for decades and
regularly involved himself in church-sponsored activities
and charities, he also took great delight in attending reviv-
als and camp meetings with their days and nights of preaching and religious singing. These meetings would reach
points where the emotions ran high, bordering on the hys-
terical; the excitement and fever would cause Asa to shake,
his body would tense, and his eyes would glitter — a not
uncommon manifestation among fundamentalist sects in
the South today, where equal fervor and "speaking in tongues"
is still seen and heard.

His sons said Asa frequently would become physically ill
from the experience. He felt this was a sign that he and
others had been really "touched" by the Word. He strongly
supported evangelical organizations with his money and his
influence. He was drawn particularly to the preaching of
Sam Jones, Len Broughton, Wilkie Collins, and the legendary Billy Sunday. He found a release that was both emotional and physical from these services.

Asa was active as a steward in his church for most of his
life. For nearly fifty years, he served variously as a Sunday
school teacher and Sunday school superintendent. Among
his many students at Inman Park Methodist Church was a
young man named Robert Winship Woodruff, the son of

Ernest Woodruff. From his Sunday School teaching experience, Asa, with his brother Warren, developed a deeply felt
philosophy regarding education.

Asa believed that education without a strong Christian
influence would lead to a population of an educated elite
with no moral foundation. A people unable to distinguish
between right and wrong had as little value to their community as those who could neither read nor write. He was
opposed to the liberal or humanistic teaching beginning to
come out of the wealthy, industrialized Northeast. He took
the Bible literally and used it to guide his own decisions. He
expressed his views on secular and religious educations in
his speeches and his letters.

"...Education alone is not enough. We must have the
right kind of education. Bad education is infinitely worse
than no education. It has been truly said that 'Knowledge is
Power.' So it is, but power may be useful or dangerous power.
If we educate the heads of men without at the same time
purifying their hearts, we create a vast deal of perilous
power to be let loose upon an unsuspecting people to their
hurt sooner or later. Virtuous ignorance is preferable to
vicious intelligence. Education, to be socially useful, and if
it is to accomplish the highest results in the creation of
personal character, must be penetrated through and through,
saturated from its dregs to its cream, with moral purpose
and religious life."

Asa stood as a prime example of Henry Grady's "New
Southerner." Grady, a famous editor of the *Atlanta Constitution*, first used this term in a speech in 1886 in which he
preached the doctrine of the self-made man and industrial
wealth as the means of lifting the South out of its difficulties.
He was advocating that the South no longer depend on the
agrarian pursuit of "King Cotton," but beat the North at its
own game — industry.

As a successful capitalist, a millionaire many times over,
with legions of Coca-Cola salesmen rolling triumphantly
over Northern competitors on the economic fields of battle,
Asa exemplified this New South. He and his fellow Southerners had experienced the deprivation of the Civil War
years and the subjugation of Reconstruction. The South was

enslaved by discriminatory laws and policies passed by a government controlled by the wealthy Northern industrialists who had benefited from the Union victory. Many of these policies would remain in effect long after the end of Reconstruction and, in some cases, until the present day. No wonder Grady urged men like Asa Candler to beat the North at its own game.

As a conquered land, the South was dependent economically on the whims of nature and the political whims of the victor. But the Yankees had fallen in love with the concept of the "New South," and Asa Candler, whether he accepted it or not, was the very embodiment of that concept. When he took a stand, the very fact that he was Asa Candler gave weight to his position. In his businesses, Asa honed his beliefs and his strategies by building big successes upon little successes. He would apply the same techniques to his philanthropies.

An important key to understanding why Asa gave what he did and to whom is found in his relationship with his brother, Warren Akin Candler, the longtime senior bishop of the Southern Methodist church.

While Asa depended on his brother Johnnie for legal advice and counsel, he was closest to Warren, who was six years younger.

Warren, like both Asa and John, was a very complex character. Here was a man who, when put in charge of Methodist missions in Cuba, taught himself Spanish to better serve in his position. While his horizons broadened, his views remained fundamental. Warren's position as a bishop and impassioned preacher meant he wielded great influence in the Protestant South and considerable influence in Protestant circles throughout the Americas.

John Slaughter Candler II, the grandson of brother John, has memories of the Bishop (Warren was always called "the Bishop" or "Uncle Bish" in the family). "When he went into the ministry [instead of law]," John Candler said, "the Supreme Court of the United States missed one of the greatest candidates that they ever had. He taught political science at Emory, you know.

"I did a few things for the Bishop, professionally, when

he was still alive. I'd go out there, and he'd ask me about some newfangled decision of the Supreme Court. And then [he would] proceed to tell me about old precedents and how they were changing them. In other words, the political scientist is inclined to look at Supreme Court decisions based on their effect on history. He didn't. He went right into the guts of them, and he knew just as much about the legal side of the philosophy that was involved, as if he had been a lawyer himself."

While the outside world may have seen the Bishop as a firebrand evangelical and, in later years, as an old-fashioned conservative, there are more funny family stories and fond memories about this brother than any of the others.

Dede Hamilton (the Judge's great-granddaughter) recalls one her mother told her. "I have no idea if this was true, but apparently he had a driver most of the time. But one day he took off in the car on his own and wound up in a ditch. Of course, that was back when Atlanta was a much smaller town and friends, and probably ex-parishioners, stopped immediately and asked if he were hurt and could they get a doctor.

"He said, 'No. You better get a veterinarian, because I was a jackass to ever get behind the wheel of this car.'

"She also told another funny story about how he would come eat with my grandmother and his nephew. Grandmother had this wonderful rum dessert. He said, 'This is the best dessert. You must have some secret ingredients.' But nobody ever mentioned what the secret ingredient was (liquor)."

John Slaughter Candler II added: "He also would look at something and say, 'I don't know whether I'm supposed to eat it or not. I'll eat it and then see.'"

Warren married Antoinette Curtright just two months before Asa and Lucy were married. The two couples settled down to early married life in Atlanta, sharing a house with the bridegrooms' mother, Martha. Both couples' first children, born six weeks apart, were delivered at home. "Nettie," as she was called, provided Warren with the same strong partnership that Lucy gave to Asa. Warren, like Asa, would suffer from bouts of depression, and he came to depend on this tomboyish, mischievous, fun-loving wife. However, in matters of importance, Warren shared his thoughts and his heart with Asa. They frequently worked in tandem for the betterment of their community and the success of their cause, the Protestant influence on everyday life.

Warren believed in a Christ-centered life and home. Like Asa, he saw the family as the strength and the basis for a strong democracy and nation. They lived in a time of great changes. In their respective careers, they met the challenges of the modern world. But the agrarian world of their childhood would remain the ideal in their hearts and minds. They would cling to their traditional beliefs as they forged ahead.

Their personalities meshed well. They both were capable of seeing the big picture. While Warren was more of a dreamer of big dreams, Asa was the pragmatist who could put the deal together. These two men used each other as sounding boards on questions of religion, morality, personal finances, problems with relatives, the future of their religion, and the future and direction of their region. Asa by nature was a very giving person. Warren influenced the choices, the amounts, and the direction that those charities would take. The brothers developed very successful fund-raising techniques together.

The philanthropic teamwork of Asa and Warren resulted in several significant and lasting monuments. One was Atlanta's Wesley Memorial Hospital, now Emory University Hospital.

When First Methodist Church decided to sell their building and move to a new location further up Peachtree Street, Warren sought to replace it with a church that would be home to the people in the core of the town — both office workers and residents. It would be an urban church. Asa bought the church's old site.

The site must have been too tempting for Asa, as he promptly put up the Candler Building. Warren's new "institutional" church, Wesley Memorial, was built on a different location. Warren's concept was to include a church, education facility, and a hospital.

To kick off the fund-raising effort, in 1904, Asa pledged $12,500 for the hospital as a matching gift, if other Atlantans would raise the same amount. This "challenge" fund-raising method would be used by Asa and Warren many times in the future for many causes. They were sharp operators, and when they found something that worked, they used it mercilessly. Similarly, Asa had developed his marketing techniques with Botanic Blood Balm and other patent medicines decades before, then used them to create Coca-Cola's astounding success.

By 1907, Asa had pledged $50,000 toward building Wesley Memorial Church if other Methodists would raise $150,000. These subscriptions were emotional revival-like gatherings of a great number of people. Bishop Candler found this frenetic atmosphere conducive to extracting necessary pledges. This particular one proved embarrassing. They could only raise $125,000 in pledges. Without another $25,000, Asa's pledge would be lost. Then, in the last moments, Asa himself stood and pledged the missing, needed $25,000!

Asa and Warren's experiences with the Wesley Memorial enterprises, coupled with the philosophy that both men had regarding education, would lead Asa to make two investments in education. One was interesting in its purpose and location. The other would become the guiding passion and love of Asa's life outside his family.

The Methodist church had founded a mission college in Cuba in 1899. It was established by Professor Thad E. Leland of Michigan, who named the college for Warren Candler, who was responsible for Methodist work in Cuba, Mexico, and Central America. Naturally Warren took a strong interest in the development of this little school. He saw it as a beacon of light bringing to an industrious and intelligent people the chance of true democracy which he and Asa believed thrived in a Christian (read that Protestant) atmosphere. Warren had taught himself Spanish to better communicate with these congregations.

Being the pragmatist, Asa Candler had no objection to combining good works with plain old profit-making. In 1906, Asa arrived in Cuba on a business trip; Cuba was fertile ground for Coca-Cola sales. Once there, he, too, perceived the country's need for Protestant-guided education. By 1912,

Asa gave $20,000 in seed money to the school. More dona-
tions followed, and eventually Asa would contribute ten
times his original gift. The fact that Coca-Cola was selling
well in Cuba certainly did not diminish his interest in that
island nation.

Cuba was a logical target for expansion. It had been
taken by American troops during the Spanish-American
War and was United States territory until May 20, 1902,
when independence was granted. There would continue to
be heavy American involvement and investment in Cuba
until Fidel Castro took over in 1961.

In 1913, Lucy, Asa, and their friends the Withams,
traveled to Cuba for the dedication of Candler College's new
administration building. Lucy fell in love with the country;
Asa was so impressed with the island and its inhabitants
that he increased his participation in the college's financial
affairs and bought land there. The land he bought was
located on the outskirts of Havana and would be developed
as a residential section similar to Atlanta's Druid Hills. As
late as the 1930s, Asa G. Candler, Inc., would be selling
these lots.

Candler College continued to operate under the aus-
pices of the Methodist Church until 1961, when it was
nationalized by the Communist government. A little mystery remains, however. Professor Leland set up a trust for
Candler College as an honorarium for his deceased son. This
money was not to be touched until after the year 2000, when
it would have multiplied to a value in excess of $1,000,000.
What happened to that money is unknown.

A paper entitled "Georgia Methodism and Coca-Cola"
was published by the Institute for Southern Studies in
Atlanta in 1972 and distributed at the United Methodist
General Conference in April of that year. It gives a fascinat-
ing look at the close ties between the Methodist church
(specifically its Southern branch) and The Coca-Cola Company during the company's control by the Candler dynasty.

The paper speaks of Bishop Candler exhorting the
church to expand "American-Christian-Civilization" into
Latin America "with bread in one hand and the Bible in the
other."

"But as it happened," the paper continues, "Bishop Candler's hand didn't have bread; rather he introduced Cuba to his brother, Coca-Cola chief, Asa Candler. And this Candler was only too anxious to put a Coke in every empty hand. As in the States, the brothers shared the same program: winning new territory and new converts for their two personal enthusiasms — Christ and Coca-Cola."

Both imports into Cuba achieved some initial success. The first Coca-Cola bottling plant was opened in Havana in 1906. By 1913, a second plant was established in Santiago to serve the eastern end of the island, including the huge American naval base which still exists at Guantanamo Bay.

However, the process of capturing Cuba for Methodism and Coca-Cola was not a simple matter. The Bishop and his American missionaries complained about the "evil effect of centuries of Romanism." They were not referring so much to the Cuban people's poverty and lack of freedom as to their inability to read the Bible. The "dullness" of the Cubans was also mentioned, along with their lack of Church-sanctioned marriages and funerals.

Meanwhile, the other "missionaries" in Cuba — agents of The Coca-Cola Company — also had problems. One wrote back to Atlanta that "As a rule the average Cuban doesn't know and doesn't care what he is drinking, and the words 'hygienic,' 'pure materials,' and 'cleanliness' have no meaning to him; but once he learns that there is a difference, that Coca-Cola has more to it than wetness or sweetness, we have secured a steady consumer and an advocate of the drink."

Asa and Warren felt that the way to overcome all of these "problems" would require the Cubans to give up their old ways and *become like Americans.*

As the Bishop put it:

> The North American and South American continents cannot be bound together firmly by ties of commerce alone. They will become fast friends when they *think and feel alike*. Our universities, if they are richly endowed and adequately equipped, will serve this end more effectually than all the consuls and commercial agents who have been or can be engaged to accomplish it. In this matter our commercial

interests and our religious duty coincide.

That, then, was the real reason behind Candler College. However, third world countries are usually not too keen on "thinking and feeling alike" with richer countries. Not only that, but it must have truly galled Asa and Warren to be called *"Yanquis,"* since Yankees they certainly were not and would "nevah, nevah" be.

Candler College was a mere footnote compared to the institution of higher education that benefited from Asa's greatest largesse. That was Emory College.

It was founded originally as the Georgia Conference Manual Labor School by Dr. Ignatius Alphonso Few, that same first cousin who had overseen Samuel Charles Candler's rudimentary education. Two years after its opening, the school was chartered as Emory College, named for Bishop John Emory, and established in the village of Oxford, Georgia. Asa's brothers and then all four of his sons were to attend. (Today, the Candler family still sends their sons and daughters there. The coauthor of this book is an Emory graduate.)

Asa's early interest in being an Emory benefactor can be found in a letter dated April 10, 1888, to Warren, in Nashville. Asa reported that Emory College had lost its president, Dr. Hopkins, who resigned for a better paying position. Several Methodists had asked him if Warren might take the presidency. Asa was of two minds. While it would have been nice for Warren to be closer to Atlanta and the family, he had a new home and position in Nashville, and it would be a blunder to move. Asa wished he had $100,000 to give the financially troubled Emory, but didn't have a penny to spare. In following years, of course, Asa gets his wish many times over.

Asa's active involvement with Emory University began when he was elected to the Board of Trustees in 1899 and became chairman of the college's finance committee. This — to which he applied the same techniques that were serving him so ably in running The Coca-Cola Company — was to prove both an immediate and lasting boon to the university.

Asa accepted the job on July 17, 1900, and wasted no

time in setting affairs straight. His first self-imposed task was to increase the yield of the endowment, and he didn't let any grass grow under his feet. He requested all information on college-owned real estate and by August 8, 1900, was reviewing both the properties that Emory owned and the real-estate manager's reports. He decided the rental houses needed improving so that higher rents could be charged. A letter written on August 10, 1900, to Professor Harry H. Stone bears this out. (Stone was a longtime mathematics professor at Emory and, perhaps because of his ability to add and subtract, also chairman of the Finance Committee.)

"...I see that during the past seven months $105.00 has been charged out for repairs," Asa wrote. "It's mighty hard to make real estate a profitable investment for endowment funds. I am going to do my very best to improve on last year. I am giving to the matter about one-fourth of my time [he was still running The Coca-Cola Company]. Yesterday I spent nearly all day showing our vacant property to prospective investors. I hope to make sales between this and spring. I enclose a deposit ticket of $70.00. This is last coupon on the J.B. Stewart loan. They say they will pay this loan up in a week or so. Several other loans are going to be paid up during this month."

Other letters show how conscientiously Asa took this volunteer job. He oversaw foreclosures, property improvements, rentals, and sales.

There is no question that Asa worked hard while he was on the board, and that might have been the extent of his involvement with the school. Something happened in 1914, however, that pushed Asa to the pinnacle of philanthropy. That was the year that the Methodist church lost Vanderbilt University.

Vanderbilt, a Methodist-controlled institution located in Nashville, Tennessee, was home to the church's main theology school. But it had fallen prey to the lure of easy money in the form of grants from educational foundations, in this case, the Carnegie Foundation.

For years, Warren had seen a conspiracy by Northern philanthropists making donations to Southern universities. From his viewpoint, there was a noxious string attached to the gifts. To receive the money, the schools had to become secular and reduce or sever ties with their religious affiliations, which were both fundamental Protestant and Southern.

If Asa Candler's view was that education without a religious framework gave no moral foundation, Andrew Carnegie felt just the opposite. This Yankee millionaire offered one million dollars to Vanderbilt with the understanding that the Methodist Church would no longer control its administrative policies.

Carnegie was for secular, humanist education; Asa Candler was not. Like many Southerners, Asa and his fellow Southern Methodists were tired of the domination by the industrialized northeast and Carnegie's millions were seen as another intrusion by a wealthy carpetbagger. For Asa, education's purpose was to aid in building the total person. To him this included the positive development of the body, the mind, and the spirit. Without religion, without faith, the spirit would falter.

Following the loss of Vanderbilt, the Methodists looked to establish a replacement. The committee charged with overseeing this project soon decided that two such institutions were needed, one west of the Mississippi and one east of the river. For the eastern university, locations as diverse as Birmingham, Washington, Atlanta, and Hendersonville, North Carolina, were considered. Until the site could be determined, the committee decided to open a temporary theology school in Atlanta. Asa and Warren made their move.

Wesley Memorial Church offered its educational facilities for the school and the Wesley Memorial Hospital its facilities as a teaching institution. To further sweeten the offering, the Druid Hills development (owned and controlled by Asa and his children) promised to throw in seventy-five acres if Atlanta was chosen as the site of the new university.

But Asa Candler was not to be outdone by some Yankee meddler. He, too, would donate the exact same amount that Andrew Carnegie had coughed up to entice away Vanderbilt — one million dollars, a vast sum in those days, and still today not small potatoes.

On July 16, 1914, Asa Candler wrote Warren a beautiful
and inspirational letter that has become known and revered
at Emory as "the Million Dollar Letter." Here it is:

Atlanta, Ga. July 16th, 1914
Bishop Warren A. Candler,
Chairman of Educational Commission, etc.,

My Dear Brother:

Impelled by a deep sense of duty to God and an earnest
desire to do good to my fellow men I make to you as the
Chairman of the Educational Commission appointed by
General Conference of the Methodist Episcopal Church
South, held at Oklahoma City, to take in hand the repairing
of the loss inflicted upon the Church by the decision in the
case of Vanderbilt University, the communication which
follows:

While I do not possess by a vast deal what some
extravagantly imagine and confidently affirm, God has
blessed me far beyond my deserts by giving to me such a
measure of this world's goods as to constitute a sacred trust
that I must administer with conscientious fidelity with
reference to His divine will.

During all the years of my life I have endeavored to do
what good I could with the earnings of my toil, but at this
time the Church and the country are confronted by a
situation which, as I see it, requires that I do for the cause
of Christian education what I am about to set forth.

In my opinion the education which sharpens and
strengthens the mental faculties without at the same time
invigorating the moral powers and inspiring the religious
life is a curse rather than a blessing to men; creating
dangerous ambitions and arousing selfish passions faster
than it supplies restraints upon these lawless tendencies in
human nature; stimulating into activity more of the things
by which men are tempted to wrong than it quickens the
powers by which temptation is resisted with success.

I am profoundly impressed that what our country
needs is not more secularized education, but more of the
education that is fundamentally and intentionally religious.
I see no way by which such religious education can be

supplied without institutions of learning owned and controlled by the Churches. Under our political system the limitations upon the civil government in matters religious put such education beyond the reach of that power. And I cannot agree for a moment that the best type of religious education is that which some claim is propagated in an unwedded state, outside any and all Churches, by institutions which are subject to neither civil or ecclesiastical authority and which acknowledge no responsibility to the people whom it proposes to educate.

Boards of Trustees that are independent of all government must inevitably change in person and policy with the changeful years. But the Church of God is an enduring institution; it will live when individuals and secular corporations have perished. It is not easily carried about by the shifting winds of doctrine which so affect men and institutions too responsive to the transient modes of thought and custom which come and go with the seasons. Hence I desire that whatever I am able to invest in the work of education shall be administered by the Church with a definite and continuous religious purpose.

In this I do not seek a sectarian end; for I gratefully acknowledge that I have received benefits and blessings from all the Churches of our land. I rejoice in the work of all the denominations who love our Lord Jesus Christ in sincerity and seek to do good to men. But to some one Church I must commit my contribution to Christian education, and I see no reason to hesitate to trust money to that Church to which I look for spiritual guidance. To that Church at whose altars I receive the Christian gospel and sacraments and upon which surely I depend, I may safely entrust the things I possess. Its history in the work of education justifies me in believing that it will use what I entrust to it in a liberal and catholic-spirited manner; for in all of its institutions of learning it has on occasion engaged Christian men of other denominations when the needs of the work seemed to require the services of such instructors, and it has never used its schools for purposes of proselyting the sons and daughters of other Churches.

I cannot believe that the promotion of the evangelical and brotherly type of Christianity for which it stands will fail to benefit the people of my section and country without regard to denominational lines.

This type of Christianity has prevailed generally in the South, and I desire to do what I may be able to perpetuate it, believing as I do, that it makes for a wholesome conservatism politically and socially, and for a blessed civilization crowned with piety and peace.

I wish that the characteristic excellencies of our people may be made better and that the things which blemish our lives may be speedily obliterated.

To this end, as far as education can accomplish it, I offer to the Educational Commission of the Methodist Episcopal Church South, charged by the General Conference with the duty of establishing an institution of university grade east of the Mississippi River, the Sum of One Million ($1,000,000.00) Dollars, for the endowment of such an institution, the plans and methods of which are to be definitely directed to the advancement of sound learning and pure religion. To the end that the institution may be secured to the Church beyond the possibility of alienation at any time in the future I will accompany my contribution with a deed of gift explicitly so providing.

In making this contribution under these terms and with this expression of my views and purposes, I seek no controversy with any who may hold opinions with reference to educational work at variance with the sentiments above expressed. It is surely permissible that I endeavor to strengthen the things in which I steadfastly believe without giving just offense to any who are of a different mind.

I fully appreciate that One Million Dollars is insufficient to establish and maintain the University, which is needed and intended by the Church. Indeed, no amount of money alone is adequate for such a purpose. The faith, the love, the zeal and the prayers of good people must supply the force to do that which money without these cannot accomplish. But I trust all these precious things will be given, together with many other gifts, great and small, from people of large means and from people of small means, so that in due time the great institution which is proposed may be fully equipped for the blessing of men and the glory of God.

In humble trust in the Christ to whom I look for salvation, I dedicate the means with which Providence has blessed me to the up-building of the Divine Kingdom. In the confidence that my brethren and fellow-citizens of

Atlanta, of Georgia and of our Southern Methodist
connection will join with the Commission in carrying this
great enterprise to speedy and large success, I offer this
contribution to its foundation. Respectfully, Asa G. Candler.

While Asa and Warren never explicitly stated that they
wanted the new Methodist university in Atlanta or that
Emory College should be the site of the new university, and
while the million dollar gift was not contingent upon such
decisions, the church's education commission — being made
up of relatively intelligent men — quickly decided that
Atlanta would be a wonderful location and Emory's trustees
voted to join with this new university. Thus, Emory University came to be.

Once it was decided to accept the gift of seventy-five
acres, the university's trustees soon decided they needed
additional land, which Asa bought for Emory and added to
the original gift. At the time Asa made this gift, it was
deemed to be the largest such donation made by a Southerner to a Southern institution.

Emory would receive even more funds to come from Asa
over the remainder of his lifetime. He would endow the
university with more than eight million dollars in cash and
securities, in addition to real estate.

While Emory may have been dearest to Asa Candler's
heart and philosophy, his philanthropic activities and interests were wide ranging.

He was something of a white knight riding to the rescue
in times of crisis, although he was not averse to finding a way
to make a profit from his chivalry.

Take the panic of 1907, a bad year for the entire United
States.

The fall of the Knickerbocker Trust Company in New
York caused a panic that affected cities everywhere, including Atlanta. Many people lost their jobs, and there were
general hard times, although the recession was mercifully
short.

In Atlanta, the Neal Bank, which had been in business
since 1887, fell and more than nine thousand depositors
stood to lose their savings. That is until in stepped Asa

Candler, president at that time of both The Coca-Cola Company and the recently reorganized Central Bank and Trust Corporation.

On December 4, 1907, the Central Bank was made receiver for the Neal Bank. As a Christmas present to the worried Neal depositors, Asa issued the following statement:

> I have every reason to believe that every depositor in the Neal Bank will receive every dollar of his money, and that when the affairs of that institution are wound up there will be something left for the stockholders.

Although it took some time, Asa Candler was true to his word. When the Neal Bank was liquidated, all depositors were paid in full. Of course, Asa saw nothing wrong in making some money in the process. He was paid for his services, although taking only half of the customary five percent fee.

Asa did not limit his service to saving depositors' money. He also bought more than one million dollars worth of homes at the fair market value during the panic, then he and the Adair boys came up with a method of selling them to people of modest means for a very low down payment and a ten year payout at low interest. This was an early day model of the FHA program that would later be instituted by the U.S. government.

Asa believed everyone should own his own home. He was able to kill two birds with one stone — helping the city avert a major devaluation of real estate, and at the same time making it possible for some of the least able members of the community to make an investment in a home and have the sense of accomplishment and participation that such a purchase would give them. It was the icing on the cake that he could do this and still clear a tidy profit.

It was Asa to the rescue again seven years later.

The eruption of the First World War in 1914 cut off the markets for cotton, creating grave problems for the South where King Cotton still ruled the economy.

Cotton prices fell through the floor and a deep depression spread across the Southland; politicians cried for the state governments to do something. The collapse of cotton affected not only the growers, but also all the businesses associated however indirectly with the cotton business.

The gravity of the situation and the profound negative impact it would have on business in the South generally was not lost on Asa. He hit upon the idea of building a huge warehouse to provide storage space until cotton prices went back up. In the meantime, his bank, the Central Bank and Trust Corporation, would lend the farmers, at a low interest rate, six cents a pound on their cotton. No bank had ever done anything like this before. The news had an amazing, uplifting effect on the spirits of people across the region.

Next, Asa covered forty acres of Atlanta property with warehouses and, then, had the idea of building the structures of steel-reinforced concrete, with automatic sprinkler systems to protect against fire and lower insurance rates.

The total cost was just under two million dollars. Before the warehouses could be fully put to use, Asa, who by that time was mayor of Atlanta, arranged for the U.S. government to locate a quartermaster's depot at the Candler warehouses. The result was an increase in business for Atlanta, an increase in deposits in Atlanta banks, and a further cementing of Atlanta as a regional center of commerce. Asa divested himself of the warehouses in 1922 after his purposes were in motion.

Asa had been drafted by the business community as a reform candidate for mayor in 1916. The city was in such bad financial shape, many feared it would go broke without someone with Asa's business acumen at the helm. As it turned out, it was often Asa's generosity that steered Atlanta away from the rocks.

There was the problem, for instance, of the siting of an Army training camp outside Atlanta. Asa saw this as a good business opportunity for the city; however, the government had a requirement for the site that Atlanta could not meet. The city would have to provide the camp with water. The city was broke when Asa was inaugurated mayor and it was not able to come up with the funds to make this commitment. Asa himself advanced the necessary $710,000 for the work,

$360,000 in cash and the balance in guarantees. This way he secured for his city a major asset for Atlanta's depressed economy.

Asa was in many ways the "Santa Claus" mayor for Atlanta. He came to the aid of his city whenever possible.

Of course, much of Asa's philanthropy would have been impossible without his real estate investing. From his earliest years in Atlanta, Asa began to accumulate real property. He had an almost uncanny ability to spot winning parcels and to acquire them. This would be one of the great outlets for his talents and interests outside of his company and his church activities. And he would often allow them to overlap. After The Coca-Cola Company began to make enough money so that there was a surplus not needed for reinvestment, he began to buy more properties through the company.

His interest in real estate was a natural outgrowth of what his father had taught him as a child in Villa Rica. This Candler family real estate tradition has become even stronger over the years, and quite a few family members still engage in the buying, selling, and management of properties, including the coauthor of this book.

Asa's interest in real estate helped Atlanta grow. He believed that you should put money where you live, and he wanted to develop Atlanta first, then the South. He further believed that if he put out his money this way, it would come back to him — as it did, over and over.

Deep in his psyche was a feeling of having been dispossessed. His ancestors had come to America having been forced to leave their country of origin for a variety of reasons. Furthermore, in the South, they had lost a war (the Civil War was not yet forgotten and will not be for generations yet to come). Many Southerners lost everything they had. The Candlers were lucky, they were able to hold onto the land. For many immigrants — such as Martha Beall Candler's family — there was a strong sense of being pushed out. They had been forced out of Scotland and exiled to the American colonies by the English. Martha's ancestor had served his time as a virtual slave, then won his release, but he would

never see his native Scotland again. So there was a strong
sense of the power in the possession of land. It gave them
some control over their environment. Real property unlike
stocks and bonds is concrete. You can see it and use it. Asa
enjoyed the thrill of the feeling he got as his investments
multiplied in value.

He also enjoyed the sense of civic pride he got from
erecting the various Candler Buildings, the huge Cotton
Warehouse project, Atlanta's Druid Hills subdivision, the
Cuban residential developments, and just owning a great
deal of property. Candler buildings were put up not only in
Atlanta but also New York City, Kansas City, and Baltimore. He built syrup plants across the nation — in Atlanta,
Chicago, Dallas, New Orleans, New York, and Philadelphia,
and outside the U.S. in Winnipeg, Toronto, and Havana.

Asa *really* liked seeing the Candler name on buildings in
places like New York City. It was solid proof that his colored
water had infiltrated the North and the detestable North-
erners were paying for the privilege.

Still, his greatest pride was in the Atlanta Candler
Building — opened in 1906 and still standing. It is built of
Georgia Marble, terra–cotta, and three thousand tons of
structural steel. Asa imported sculptors from Europe to
carve the elaborate friezes, gargoyles, and busts. Among the
representations of famous people from history whom Asa
admired were busts of both of his parents. For years the
expression "as tall as the Candler building" was a common
expression in Atlanta. Caged elevators were such a novelty
that school children were taken on field trips to the Candler
building to ride them. The time capsule under the corner-
stone of the building contains, among other things, a Bible
and a bottle of Coca-Cola.

In addition to real estate and Coca-Cola, Asa branched
out into investments in a myriad of fields including banking,
railroads, cotton mills, and utility companies. He invested
with an eye to making a profit but also to bettering his
community as he saw fit and as he was able. Whether it be
in investing or in his charitable work, Asa put his money
where his mouth was. He did not look to or expect aid from
the government. He did not see a need and then gather a

group to lobby the government for the funding.

Asa believed that if you, as a community or as an individual, saw a need, it was your responsibility to solve that problem, just as it was your responsibility to look after yourself and your family. It was not someone else's responsibility, not the taxpayers, it was yours. He and the men he associated with worked together to provide for their community the schools, hospitals, churches, and whatever else was needed.

All of Asa's charities and self-promotions did have a negative side. Being so much in the public eye made him fair game for extortion plots.

One had an almost comical ending, the other was not so funny. Asa's handling of both was indicative of his character. In neither case, did he succumb to the blackmailers' demands.

Over the years, Asa was the recipient of unwanted and unwarranted contacts, letters, and so forth. This would irritate and depress him particularly since they usually contained criticisms, accusations, or threats.

The spring of 1909 brought a threat that could not be ignored. A letter was received by the pastor of the Inman Park Methodist Church addressed to Asa which threatened death to his family if a payment of thirty-five thousand dollars was not paid. A second note arrived, several days later, warning him to comply and not to go to the authorities.

Asa was not one to be cowed. He arranged immediately for extra security for his wife and grandchildren. He then went to the police. The chief post office investigator for Atlanta, George M. Sutton, was put in charge because of the involvement of the U.S. mail. Sutton and Asa devised a scheme to place a dummy package at the pickup point. The idea being they would nab the blackmailer when he went for the ransom. No one appeared, however, and the family continued to wait and watch. Two days had passed when Asa received a phone call demanding $1,000. Again a dummy package was prepared. Police detectives waited all night on Moreland Avenue watching for a pickup, and this time met with success.

The police collared their blackmailer only to find that it was just a young boy. Most surprising of all was the young man was a member of Asa's Sunday School class and the son of a family friend. The boy told police that his escapade was inspired by reading too many dime store novels!

Asa's family was relieved after ten days of worry, but in addition to the fear, they had been subjected by the press to a series of sensational articles which had termed this the case of the "Blackhand Letters." Asa, bitterly disappointed that a young man of the church and a member of his own study group would conceive of such a prank, did not prosecute. But his actions on this occasion would prove the norm in future attempts by other, more serious extortionists.

One such came while he was mayor. A Mrs. H.H. Hirsch, the wife of an Atlanta insurance agent, accused Asa of sexually assaulting her. She claimed that she was attacked in his office where she had gone to discuss a real estate matter. At just the opportune moment, a Mr. J.W. Cook, a real estate agent, rushed in and rescued her. This was a typical ploy of the old "Badger Game." This era must have seen many such attempts by unscrupulous couples because it was often used as a movie plot. Obviously Mrs. Hirsch and Mr. Cook had made a mistake. After they made their demand for hush money (five hundred thousand dollars for Margaret Hirsch and five thousand dollars to pay Mr. Hirsch's debts), Asa went to the police. Instead of the money, Cook and Mrs. Hirsch got guilty verdicts for attempted extortion and one thousand dollar fines. In addition, she received a year in jail and he, a year at hard labor on the chain gang.

These blackmail cases pointed up Asa's implicit belief in the justice system and his own unassailable character. He lived by his faith, and he trusted in his God. He simply could not understand that others did not live as he did. However, once duplicity was pointed out to him, he did come down as hard as he could on the malefactors.

Asa Candler had taken Lucy's death in 1919 very hard, falling into a deep despondency and becoming ill for several months. He got better, but was never quite the same. At sixty-nine, Asa was beginning to fail physically and his continued ailments would be complicated by recurring bouts of depression. He grew increasingly saddened by the deaths of his various brothers and sisters. John, William, and Warren would survive him, but all the others died before Asa. Of particular concern was his brother, Charlie (Samuel Charles Candler, Jr.). Charlie suffered from severe depression and attempted suicide on several occasions. Once the Bishop had to stop him. Charlie was finally institutionalized and died in 1911.

With the passing of each sibling, Asa continued to check on the surviving spouses and offer his help should it be needed. His trips to Decatur to visit Milton Candler's widow, Eliza Murphey Candler, were a source of news and companionship for the elderly lady. They were usually entertainment for her grandchildren as well. Milton's granddaughter, Caroline McKinney Clarke, looks back fondly on the following incident: "Uncle Asa was particularly good at calling on Grandma after my Grandfather Milton's death. I remember one day I came home and there was Uncle Asa's big black limousine, and I was very much interested in it. I was a little thing. And I noticed that there was a donkey painted on the door of the car. When Uncle Asa came out to get in the car, I said, 'Uncle Asa, why have you got a donkey painted on your car?' He replied, 'Oh, because the Candlers are descended from asses.'" (Actually, it was the family coat of arms, which has six little donkeys on it.)

Entering into his seventies, Asa was a lonely man, not as sharp as he once had been. His extended family visited him often to check on him, however, their company did not dispel his loneliness. His great niece Frances, a granddaughter of Bishop Candler, remembers his despair: "He was showing my parents around his house [the "Lemon Pie House"] and my mother said, 'Uncle Asa, you must be very proud.' And he said, 'I'm not. Everything is only ashes, just ashes.' In his later years he was very unhappy — but then the family all tended to have melancholy."

Not all the visits to Asa's mansion were of so somber a tone. Frances and her sister Caroline both recall playing in the room with the marble floor — full of animal skins, a polar bear, a leopard, and a zebra, among others. In those days, everything in Atlanta was heated with soft coal. Soot would float in the air like a miasma. Their mother (Frances Godfrey Candler) despised for them to go in that room to play, because they would be all dressed in their Sunday clothes and would come back black at the end of a visit. But that's what they loved about visiting Uncle Asa, playing on his animals.

Family members were not the only ones that were aware of Asa's loneliness. His son Buddie's secretary, Miss Florence Stephenson of Lithonia, Georgia, found herself Asa Senior's frequent companion at business meetings and functions.

Asa's great-granddaughter, Nancy Candler Nutter, said this about Florence: "... after she became my Grandfather Buddie's private secretary, he told her: 'When my father wants to do something, you quit what you were doing and do it.' And that's how she got to know the old man. She was very fond of him. He was old and lonely and so she'd drive him around. They went to Emory, wherever he wanted to go. I thought that was rather sweet."

During that period, Asa Senior still had an office at Asa G. Candler, Inc., but Buddie Candler was running the company. There wasn't much for Asa to do except occasional philanthropic activities. With all this free time, he liked to inspect the progress at the new campus of Emory, which was then being built. Invariably he would ask Florence to accompany him. He liked her; she was a good listener and accommodating. She was an attractive young woman, but she wasn't falling all over him like so many women were. She later said, "We would ride out to Emory and he'd check the footings of every building they were building. If they were going to pour the footings today, he had to be there."

Florence would bring her stenographer's pad and take some notes, but said that mostly he just wanted company. He was just a delightful old man, in her view, and he would tell her little stories — and he was very shy. Which must have made him all the more endearing since Florence claimed that all old women, every widow and old maid in America would just fall all over him.

"They wanted that money and they were chasing Mr.

Candler," she said. So part of her real duties were not just to take notes and to keep Asa company. "I was there to beat off the women."

The coauthor of this book knew Florence personally in later years and can attest that if Florence decided to beat you off, she could do it. She would walk right over you if she chose. She was a regular little bulldozer.

Florence was sporty — this girl played basketball, tennis, and golf. She was a totally new kind of women for Asa, as well as for his Buddie, a thoroughly modern lady, especially for the 1920s. She was the kind who would say, "Now Mr. Candler has a business meeting... Mrs. Johnson, Mr. Candler would love to talk to you right now, but we have some notes we have to take about these footings over here..." She could do it and let you know, "You'd better step back, lady."

Unfortunately, she wasn't strong enough to hold off the likes of Onezima de Bouchel or May Ragin or other women who did eventually get through to the old man.

Onezima de Bouchel, now there was a name meant for scandal, and scandal it caused.

Mrs. de Bouchel seemed to burst out of nowhere when news of her engagement to Asa G. Candler, Sr., hit the papers in August, 1922. Now here was a story, and the newspapers went digging gleefully for information on the bride-to-be.

At first it was reported that Onezima was a New Orleans society matron, from a distinguished family and wealthy in her own right, although at the time of the announcement, she was a resident of Reno, Nevada. This last tidbit must have whetted the appetites of the inquiring reporters, who continued digging. It was next revealed that Mrs. de Bouchel was a Catholic, a divorcee, a Creole, and a suffragette — all cardinal sins in the South, especially among Methodists.

The details got spicier as the days progressed, and the papers gloried in them. Twelve days after Mrs. de Bouchel made her announcement, Asa was quoted as saying the date and place were not correct. Meanwhile, Onezima was on a buying spree for her trousseau in San Francisco. Atlanta papers and the Candler family were suddenly deluged with letters claiming that the New Orleans woman was a fraud, a hussy, and a woman of bad character. John the Judge was dispatched to New Orleans to check the woman out. Meanwhile, Congressman Ezekial Candler, Jr., of Mississippi (Asa's nephew) was doing his own checking in Reno on the legality of her divorce and her divorce proceedings.

The wedding scheduled first for August was delayed until September. Mrs. de Bouchel was quoted as saying that Bishop Candler and other family members opposed the marriage because she was Catholic, divorced, and active in suffragette causes. (She got that right.) In following days she added that the Candler family also objected to the fact that she was not of Anglo-Saxon descent, but rather of Latin extractions.

Another few days passed, and the story broke that she was not, in fact, legally divorced, but rather was awaiting her divorce ruling. The newspapers lapped it up. Here was Asa G. Candler, pillar of Atlanta society, patriarch and head of one of the city's most distinguished families, being taken in by Onezima de Bouchel. The editors couldn't have asked for a better copy-selling story.

September passed with no wedding. In October she again made the papers by claiming that she had been defamed in writing by "persons unknown" and that Asa would not tell her who had defamed her. The charge now was that she had invited men to her room one evening in 1919 while she was attending a meeting of the United Daughters of the Confederacy. By October 10, the accusations led Asa to break the engagement.

The newspapers were filled with juicy details, speculations, and rumors. Mrs. de Bouchel vowed to force Asa Candler to clear her name or pay, stating all the while that she was never interested in his money, only his companionship. Claiming that it was the only way to clear her name, she filed suit in October 1922 against Asa for "breach of promise." Then she tried public blackmail!

On October 13, it was reported that Onezima de Bouchel believed the Candler family had stopped her wedding because Asa was going to change his will and leave his entire Coca-Cola fortune to her. (No one seemed to have bothered to tell her that he had already given the company to the family.) The kicker was that she threatened to publish Asa's love letters to her if she wasn't compensated for the humiliation and embarrassment she had endured on his behalf. The papers also reported that the society women of New Orleans were organizing to support her cause.

The Candlers declined to comment, or to give in, and she followed through on her threat to publish the love letters. They were not especially spicy. Here's a sample:

> As I wrote to you a few days ago, I will be apprehensive of some hindrance to our plans being consummated up to the last hour of August 22. I know that there has gone to New Orleans from Atlanta, a prominent Atlantan who is greatly disturbed about my marriage to you, as you have been described by these bad Atlanta papers. I love you with all my heart.

To help win the lawsuit that resulted, Asa retaliated and published *her* love letters to him. This was a fairly tepid relationship, as these excerpts, written in 1918 and 1919, indicate:

> ...I was quite, or to be truthful, considerably disappointed at your not ringing me up as I had requested ... ; however, I thoroughly understand that a man of affairs like you has not much time for little unimportant me. I would have phoned but — oh well, I will explain when I see you. When is that to be? Surely you have some business or other calling you to the City of Cities [New Orleans], and may you hear the call while I am still here... O de B. Rocquet "Mrs. Adolphe Rocquet."

> (Writing from Palm Beach, Florida) My dear Mr. Candler, Have you ever been here? If not, let me tell you it's the most beautiful spot in the world! Not even excepting my old love, California. It would be an ideal place for a winter honeymoon for anyone contemplating an early matrimonial excursion... You said in your last letter that the Atlanta business men do not seem to want to understand that you have retired. Well, the solution to that is simple, why remain in Atlanta and be annoyed...

What the press didn't know was Asa had been showing
signs of senility for some time. He was easily led, easily
influenced, and would change his mind depending on whom
he was with. Mrs. de Bouchel had figured this out early in
the courtship. They had met at the United Daughters of the
Confederacy convention in the fall of 1919, at which he was
speaking. Asa was suffering the double blows of Lucy's death
and the sale of the company. This charming, sophisticated,
and much younger lady of apparently good background paid
him attention. Romance began to flower on his part. The
exchange of letters got her attention.

During the courtship he had written to Howard that:

> ...If I take a hand in mine to steady my tottering body
> as it winds its way down the path. Know all of you that your
> mother's memory is as dear to me as to you for whom she
> lived and loved us all. Affectionately Papa

Obviously Asa was lonely and in desperate need of a
loving companion on whom he could lean. He believed he had
found it in this exciting woman, who was in her thirties. But
his tendency to vacillate on issues depending upon his
company complicated the situation. Perhaps she did not
understand how tenuous her engagement was. Certainly
she had played upon his frailty to manipulate him into the
engagement; amusingly, she was outraged to see that others, particularly his family, could do the same. Asa became
despondent for a while after the engagement was called off.

In March of 1923, he filed his answer to her suit. In it he
stated that once he became engaged to her, she pressed him
to marry her immediately without contacting his family,
and that after receiving the information about her unsavory
comportment at the Daughters of Confederacy meeting, he
ended the engagement.

The newspapers had another field day — this was all
great copy! — and as a result many everyday people, especially Methodists, felt compelled to express their views to
the Bishop and other members of the family. One woman
implored, "For the sake of the Protestant Church and the
purity of women don't allow the Bouchel woman to marry

( Above ) A poster from 1900 features Hilda Clark, a vaudeville
singer and an early endorser of *Coca-Cola*.
Courtesy of the *Coca-Cola Company* Archives.

( Right )
Walter Candler with his
favorite horse, the Duke
of Lullwater.
Courtesy of the family of Walter
Turner Candler, Sr.

( Left )
Walter Turner Candler as a
senior at Emory in 1907.
Courtesy of the Special Collections
Department, Robert W. Woodruff
Library, Emory University.

W.T.CANDLER.

( Below ) Walter's rat-catching dogs with Marion, Bootsie, ar
Walter Candler at Lullwater. Courtesy of Mr. & Mrs. Edward Harry Ruffn

Above ) Christmas, 1903. Buddie, Helen, Asa Sr., Lucy I holding
ucy III, William, Walter, William Owens, Lucy II, Charlie
ulpepper ( who was with Coca-Cola's New York office ), Flora, and
oward. Courtesy of Mrs. John Holtzendorff Wilson.

( Left ) Helen, their
youngest child Sam, and
Buddie about 1923.
From the collection of Elizabeth
Candler Graham.

( Above )  Al Langdon ( trainer ) with three of Buddie's elephants.
Courtesy of Mettelen Thompson Moore.

ight ) Florence and
ddie at the time of
ir marriage in 1927.
m the collection of Elizabeth
dler Graham.

elow ) Touring the pyramids, 1929. Edgar Chambers Jr.,
rence Candler, Laura Candler Chambers, and Buddie. From the
ction of Elizabeth Candler Graham.

( Above ) Buddie as a senior at Emory, 1899.
Courtesy of the Special Collections Department,
Robert W. Woodruff Library, Emory University.

(above) Buddie and Florence on their 25th wedding anniversary.
In the collection of Elizabeth Candler Graham.

(below) Martha, John, Lucy III, and Laura--Christmas Eve at Larcliff, 1938. Courtesy of Mettelen Thompson Moore.

( Above ) Asa V with Brother Landrum and pony.
Courtesy of Mr. & Mrs. Robert Sherill Griffith, Jr.

( Left ) Lucy Magill Candler
as a debutante.
Courtesy of Mettelen Thompson
Moore.

your brother Asa G. Candler. If she gets the chance, she will kidnap him, marry him, get his money, and murder him..."

Another writer saw it as "a Jesuit plot to get [Asa's] millions for the Catholic church. We thank God that the Jesuit failed."

One might think that the romantic and legal brouhaha in which Asa found himself with Onezima might have made him, even in his reduced mental condition, a tad bit wary of younger women murmuring sweet nothings. Apparently not. He was in the headlines again, three months after filing his answer to Mrs. de Bouchel's suit. This time it was not for anything as insignificant as an engagement. No, this time Asa went and got himself married.

In June of 1923 it was announced that Asa had taken a second wife, a May Little Ragin, who had been a stenographer in the Candler Building. She was about thirty-eight years old, as was Mrs. de Bouchel, and had twin daughters to support. Asa must have learned one thing from the de Bouchel debacle. He waited until most of his family was out of town before springing the news.

Asa and May were married at Emory University and promptly left on a two-week honeymoon in Washington, DC. His children were not happy about the marriage. May didn't suit them any better than Onezima.

The marriage didn't cause Onezima to pack her litigious tent and slink away into the night. Five hundred thousand dollars was five hundred thousand dollars, after all. Onezima had her reputation to consider. So on January 30, 1924, the infamous breach of promise suit was brought to court.

His letters to her were duly read to the court and published in the papers. The press unable to read Asa's poor handwriting went wild in printing all of his salutations as my "sweetums" when in fact he addressed her as "my sweet one." The adorations used in the letters were so very typical of the way in which he had always addressed members of his family — nicknames, effusive expressions of love and hope, coupled with his views on just what he thought the agreements he had with her included. A big deal was also made of the fact that they had met in 1919 and she had continued to encourage his suit although she did not obtain a divorce from her husband until September 1921. This gave a less than wholesome twist to their relationship.

The real kicker came when Asa's attorneys entered Onezima's letters into the record. For a woman who claimed to be wealthy and not interested in Asa's money, her veiled request for twelve thousand dollars to pay her estranged husband in an effort to speed up her divorce did not strengthen her case.

This may have influenced the jury, but what decided the case was pure legal footwork on the part of Asa's legal team. His attorney, William Thomson, got the court to agree that Georgia did not have to recognize her Nevada divorce because of a technicality. It was decided that she had not actually resided in Nevada for any purpose other than obtaining a "quickie" divorce in order to marry Mr. Candler, making it illegal in Georgia. It then stood to reason that if Mrs. de Bouchel was not legally divorced and she could not enter into an agreement to marry someone else; therefore there was no "breach of promise."

The verdict came in February 5, 1924. Asa had won, and Mrs. de Bouchel departed Atlanta, not taking the time to gather up her furniture which had been sent to Asa's home on Ponce de Leon Avenue and then stored. An auction was arranged, and the last vestiges of Mrs. de Bouchel in Atlanta were sold.

Asa's relief at winning was very short-lived. Three days later on February 8, his not-so-blushing bride May was arrested for violating the prohibition laws. Not only was she caught with liquor, but she was with two men at an apartment house having, as she said "just a little party." The men arrested with her were W. J. Stoddard, president of the National Association of Dry Cleaners and Dyers, and G. W. Keeling, owner of an Atlanta brick company.

What was a little strange was that they were arrested by none other than the chief of police, James L. Beavers. The next exciting revelation was that Asa had tipped off the chief and arranged for the arrest.

This arrest made headlines all across the country. The normally staid *New York Times* even trumpeted the story on February 10, 1924.

**TAKE MRS. CANDLER ON LIQUOR CHARGE**
Millionaire's Wife and Two Men Companions Accused by
Atlanta Police of Having a Little Party

Atlanta, Feb. 8 — Atlanta was excited tonight over the
arrest of Mrs. Mary L.R. Candler, young wife of Asa G.
Candler, Sr., millionaire soft drink manufacturer, and W.J.
Stoddard and G.W. Keeling of this city, as they were sitting
around a table today on which reposed a quart bottle which
the police said contained liquor.

The trio was taken from an apartment house in a
fashionable residence section to the police station by
James L. Beavers, Chief of Police, and Police Captain A.J.
Holcombe, who personally made the arrests. They were
released on bond of $100 each for appearance before the
City Recorder next Tuesday morning. Mrs. Candler
admitted her identity to the police chief, who said she told
him she and her friends were only "having a little party" in
the apartment, which she said, belonged to a friend of hers
who had gone to a nearby suburb for the afternoon.

"We are just having a little party. I don't see any harm
in that," Chief Beavers said Mrs. Candler told him, when
he entered with the captain. He said he told her that, as a
personal friend of her husband, he thought it was "an
outrage that you have to be arrested under such
circumstances as these," to which Mrs. Candler replied:

"There are other people in Atlanta besides members of
the Candler family, and besides, we were just having a little
party here, in which there was no harm."

Beavers soon found himself being discharged for breach
of duty and Asa's attorneys filed a suit for divorce against
May who had moved out the day after her arrest. What the
public didn't know at the time was that May had been
scheming to have Asa committed. His frailty of mind continued to worsen as did his general health. He seemed to have
had a series of small strokes since their marriage and was
moving much more slowly.

The split with May was eventually patched up on some
basis, probably financial. She remained his wife and lived in
his home until his death.

What neither she nor Onezima de Bouchel — nor any of

the other women that were chasing him — fully understood was that he had already given his money away. The vast portion of his fortune he had disposed of that memorable Christmas day in 1917.

The family's opinion of May never mellowed over the years. Asa's granddaughter Laura Candler Chambers still has little good to say of May. "She was nothing, just nothing! Do you know what amused me — it doesn't really amuse me, it makes me tired — is these men would not seek their own level to date ... There were plenty of widows out there that would have loved to have gone out with Asa Candler. No, he had to pick this thing that nobody had ever heard of. Don't you know, she had twins. Made Martha and Helen so mad, they could die, because everyone would say, 'Oh, the Candler twins...' Well, they had been the Candler twins for 'centuries,' and then people come along and talk about those other girls being the Candler twins."

After Asa died, May Candler was ostracized from the family. "I think Florence saw her once or twice," Laura said. "Not in a social way, she just saw her. Nobody was going to be chummy with her. She was just nobody."

Although Laura doubted her grandfather provided for his second wife in his will, he did leave May a quarter of a million dollars. She did not come off quite as badly as some in the family might have wished.

By the latter half of the 1920s, Asa's health was starting its final decline. He had another severe stroke in September of 1926, after which he entered Emory University's hospital, which had benefited from his benevolence for so many years. He never fully regained his mobility. For a while he could move, take food, but eventually lapsed to the point that he did not recognize his own family. It was a tragic end for a man who had been so energetic that both his mother and his wife would describe him as "fidgety." He had accomplished so much, overcome so many obstacles, but old age and its vagaries defeated him at last.

Asa's youngest grandchild, Marion "Bootsie" Candler Ruffner, remembers his final days. "That was my eighth birthday in the year grandpa died. I remember it vividly, very vividly. I remember going to Emory Hospital and seeing him on that bed. He was as white as the sheet. Papa (Asa's son, Walter) was just in a state of shock. 'My precious Papa's going to die,' he said. Papa just did not handle things like that well."

For the three years prior to his death, Asa Candler spent most of his time in the hospital, with increasingly diminishing faculties.

Bootsie said that her father would go up there every week and take her with him. "We'd go see my Grandpa and he'd be laying in that bed, just staring at the ceiling. We always went, religiously."

Granddaughter Eugenia Candler Wilson said, "He was the same every day. ... May would come to the hospital. The nurse would call up Walter and say, 'the coast is clear, she's come and gone.' Lucy would make a little pot of jam. I made a pot of soup or some custard or something. He liked that. We'd take it to him in the hospital."

Asa died on the afternoon of March 12, 1929. He was seventy-eight years old. But even in death, he left specific instructions and surprises.

Buddie was in Europe when Asa died and unable to return in time for the funeral. Buddie's son, John Howard Candler, sent this letter to him, dated March 15, 1929..

My Dear Father,

At a time like this it is very difficult for me to write you. I know what your feelings must be. There was nothing in the world you could have done had you been in Atlanta, but where such a bereavement strikes us we all have a strong desire to be with our own blood kin, and I know you must have wished that more than anything. How much you have lost no one but you can tell, but I know it is beyond measure. It is but necessary for me to substitute myself in your place to have a good yardstick by which to understand your grief. I can only say I wish you could have been here that I might have been near you when this happened.

I understood immediately that it was my duty to represent you, and I tried to do so as you would have wanted me to. I had seen Howard, Jr. Tuesday morning, and he said Grandpa wasn't very well, however, as he had

rallied from so many sinking spells, no great amount of
anxiety was attached to this particular one. However, at
sometime after three o'clock, Harry Carr came into the
office and said Aunt Lucy had just called Uncle Henry to
come. Since Mr. Carr had at that time been in conference
with Uncle Henry, he had come posthaste to tell me. I
hurried immediately to Wesley, and was the first to arrive;
(Aunt Lucy had been there all along) but, I was just too late.
Later Uncles Howard and Henry arrived, Uncle Howard
bringing a most remarkable document in Grandpa's
handwriting. The envelope was inscribed, "to be opened
immediately upon my death." Inside was another sealed
envelope, a formal announcement, and a short
autobiography that Grandpa willed to be all that the papers
would print of his life. We were, of course, unable to get
them to stick to it, in fact didn't try. It would have been
unjust to them, and would have undoubtedly brought forth
considerable criticism. I mention it simply as a further
evidence of Grandpa's modesty. Inside the second envelope
was this most remarkable document. It is beautiful, and you
will certainly want to read it upon your return. Couched in
beautiful English, without the waste of a single unnecessary
word, however in no sense ambiguous, Grandpa left this
short letter as directions as to how he wanted his funeral
conducted. I am happy to say we were able to carry through
his desires with only little interference from Mrs. Candler.
His forethought was remarkable. I recall this part of the
letter. Knowing his close friends would resent the attempt
to name any six as special friends, and therefore name them
as pallbearers, he requested that Patterson's [the funeral
parlor] men bear the casket from the home to the hearse,
and from the hearse to the grave. This gave the opportunity
of including all of his friends in his honorary escort, and
showed preference for none. A very thoughtful thing to do.
He had so many friends among the clergy, that he was again
faced with the possibility of offending if he chose any one,
as well as the possibility of having them precede him in
death; so, he nominated that the Dean of the Theological
School at Emory preside. He, therefore, chose an office
rather than a man, feeling assured that any one chosen to
hold that office by the University would make a suitable
clergyman for his funeral. Those two incidents from his
letter show you what painstaking care he went to not to

offend those in Death he had loved in Life, and give an insight into the man's character that is explanatory of his depth of feeling and his greatness of heart.

The flowers were beautiful, the library at his home being a profusion of hyacinths, lilies, and every flower now in season. The services were short. In accordance with his request there was no music, and only the short proscribed Methodist service followed by an even shorter prayer. It had rained steadily since the night before, and the grave being filled with water, we sent the body to Patterson. Interment will be this afternoon, and private, as he instructed.

Upon the advice of the family I had Martha & Helen, and Sam come down, and they will spend this weekend with us. This is the thought I have had constantly since Tuesday afternoon:

"Lives of great men, all remind us,
We may make our life sublime;
And departing, leave behind us
Footprints on the sands of time."

Know that everyone of our hearts have been with you at this time, and that we continue in our devotion.

Your devoted son, John.

Atlanta paid her respects to the man that perhaps had done more for the city's benefit than any other in her history. The day of his funeral was declared an official day of mourning. Offices closed and flags were flown at half-mast.

If Asa's funeral was modest and well-thought out, so was his will which had been written in January, 1925. The big surprise to all the nosy courtroom watchers was the discovery that Asa had given the balance of his fortune to Emory University as an annuity. It had been set up so that he received the income from it for the rest of his life and that at his death it would go to the university. May got her quarter of a million tax free; his loyal household staff received small bequests, and his beloved sister, Florence Candler Harris, who had died in 1926 received ten thousand dollars. His children, of course, had already received their inheritance at their mother's urging back in 1917.

Asa G. Candler was a naturally competitive man, a product of his times and his region. The Civil War and its aftermath gave him the background of poverty to spur him to achieve. It also freed him from an agrarian, circumscribed existence of the small, self-sufficient farms with which he was familiar. He was in every sense of the concept a New Southerner. He based his life on his faith which was in turn based on the literal acceptance of the Bible.

Asa was sentimental to the point of being maudlin, deeply affectionate, and possessed of an adventurous spirit and a strong sense of duty. He firmly believed in service to one's community according to one's ability and resources. Yet he was mischievous and liked pranks. He was not afraid to take a stand. He was ambitious, and probably came across as cocky in his youth. He was well organized, focused, and positive in his actions. He was also a bright, witty, funny, outgoing, friendly, and honest man.

As his granddaughter Laura describes him: "He lived his faith, he served his God. I believe, that loyalty to his church and to God was the reason he was successful. I believe that. But I would like to impress on my grandchildren that he was energetic and smart."

Asa Candler's legacy lives on in his many descendants, in Emory University, in good Methodists everywhere, in tall and strong buildings, and wherever people pause for a smile and to enjoy that drink that he made universal.

# Section Two:

# The Second Generation of Coca-Cola

# Coca-Cola in the Twenties and Thirties

With the sale of The Coca-Cola Company in 1919, *control* passed from the Candler family, but not their involvement. The Candlers were, and still are, as much a part of Coca-Cola as the coca leaf and kola bean. You would never find, say Pepsi, served in one of their homes. Such a sacrilege would send Asa and the others who have passed beyond spinning in their graves. The Real Ones drink The Real Thing. Admittedly, the focus here is on The Real Ones, but that does not mean that the eventual contributions of the new owners are not appreciated and applauded. The new regime, however, got off to a rocky start.

The first decade of the Woodruff control, the 1920s —the era of the flapper, the Charleston, the It girls, Al Capone and Elliot Ness, Prohibition and bathtub gin — started off with a bang. Nothing could go wrong, good times were ahead, real estate sales were booming, the stock market could only go up, and everybody was going to get rich, rich, rich. It was a heady time and no one had any hint that the stock market could ever fall. So they roared through the Roaring Twenties. It was full speed ahead for everyone, including The Coca-Cola Company.

December 6, 1920, brought great news for the company. It was on that day that the United States Supreme Court handed down its trademark infringement decision. The court ruled that the nickname "Coke" meant "Coca-Cola" and, even more importantly, forever established The Coca-Cola Company's right to its name as a trademark. This ended the fight begun by Dr. John Pemberton in 1888 to protect the name from imitators, a fight that Asa waged during his long stewardship. It had taken more than thirty-two years, but the name was now uncontested, and continues to be jealously guarded today.

In 1919, when Ernest Woodruff and his consortium took over the control of The Coca-Cola Company, they paid the Candlers $15 million in cash and $10 million worth of preferred stock. The preferred stock was eventually retired and converted in various ways into common stock, a goodly portion of which is still in the hands of various family members or in trusts in their names.

Interestingly, each of the five Candler children set up their estates differently. The descendants of one child, for example, have their stock in a ninety-nine-year trust. This means that they cannot sell the stock or even vote it, but do receive the income from it. Of course, there is nothing that prevents the Candlers from trading in Coca-Cola stock available on the open market without restrictions, and some do. Trying to calculate exactly how much Coca-Cola stock family members own or control, and its current value, is a daunting task. We estimate the total is perhaps in the hundreds of millions and without a doubt at least in the tens of millions of dollars. Put simply, it's a *lot*. That twenty-three hundred dollar investment of Asa Candler's in 1888 continues to grow rather nicely. There are now some four hundred descendants sharing in this legacy.

In the end, selling control of The Coca-Cola Company was a pretty good business decision for the family. Asa Candler was getting along in years and his children could not get along well enough to manage the company jointly. Asa had made Coca-Cola into a national drink that was sold all over the United States and had expanded into Mexico, the Philippines, Cuba, and Canada. However, it remained for new owners to launch an all-out invasion of foreign fields.

Still, the Candlers might have held onto the company if

they had known who was behind the deal.

Ernest Woodruff, like more modern takeover artists, bought profitable companies, dismantled them, and profited from the assets he stripped from those companies. He also bought small companies in financial troubles and built them up. He inflated their income and therefore their value and then sold them at high prices to sometimes unsuspecting buyers. The family objected to Woodruff because they believed he would "raid" and dismantle The Coca-Cola Company to make a quick profit for himself. Had Howard, Buddie, and the other Candler children been aware of his participation before it was finalized, chances are the deal would have been killed.

They didn't know because Ernest had stacked the deck. He had an inside man, Samuel Candler Dobbs, who helped orchestrate the sale and represented Candler family interests during the negotiations. As a reward, Dobbs replaced Howard Candler as president of The Coca-Cola Company, although at the end of his rocky twelve-month tenure, he might have wondered if it hadn't been a punishment.

Dobbs was faced immediately with a serious business problem. Economic conditions during World War I had created a severe sugar shortage. Dobbs needed sugar to make Coke. He purchased as much as he could at an elevated price during the height of the shortage. It was unfortunate timing since the sugar market collapsed shortly afterwards. When the price of sugar fell, Woodruff was furious with Dobbs, the company having lost several million dollars. Of course, had the price for sugar gone up, Woodruff would have considered him a near genius.

While Dobbs might have been able to survive the sugar debacle, he couldn't survive Ernest Woodruff's personality. Asa, if he had been consulted, could have told him he would have trouble with Woodruff. Dobbs found himself arguing with the meddling Woodruff on an almost daily basis. By October of 1920, it came to a head, and the sugar incident was used as an excuse for Dobbs' departure.

Ernest had made up his mind that he needed one of those Candlers back to run the company. Howard was the logical choice. He been with the company since his childhood when he did chores for his father and had already demonstrated he could be an effective president. Family members remember Ernest Woodruff coming over to Howard's home on more than one occasion to beg him to come back to The Coca-Cola Company.

Finally, Howard acquiesced and returned to The Coca-Cola Company. Waiting for him were declining sales, a pending lawsuit by the bottlers over the price of Coca-Cola syrup, and Ernest Woodruff's continuous interference and harassment. Howard later characterized this as "picayunish interference with the management."

The bottlers' suit was both complicated and important. They had gotten the right from Asa Candler to bottle Coca-Cola in perpetuity. The new owners wanted to rescind these rights so that they could resell them or license them out for limited periods of time. If they had succeeded, it would have meant *billions* of additional dollars of profit for the company over the course of the past seventy years. The bottlers, liking the deal they had made with Asa Candler, were not about to give up any of their rights and start paying license fees. The bottlers eventually won, and retained their perpetual rights, although they do have to meet certain conditions. In recent years, The Coca-Cola Company has bought into some bottlers, realizing this is the only way they will ever get a slice of the rights that Asa gave so freely. Although, at the time, it was really a masterful stroke on his part since it caused Coca-Cola sales to mushroom and brought additional millions of profit into the company's (and Asa's) coffers.

So, from the first, Howard's last stint as president of The Coca-Cola Company was not pleasant. In fact, as is obvious in his later writings, these few years were by far among the most trying of his life. Not only was Ernest Woodruff constantly meddling, but there were some questionable maneuverings going on behind the scenes. Howard seemed to have caught on pretty quickly and intimated in 1921 that Woodruff was attempting to manipulate the financial statements of The Coca-Cola Company, all in addition to being a general pain in the neck and regions even lower. Woodruff was continuously making demands in the form of minor suggestions and criticisms. These included sometimes ridiculous cost-cutting measures, such as hiring unskilled labor to do what only skilled labor could do.

By April of 1921, Howard had realized that what Ernest really wanted was a figurehead or a puppet who would take Ernest's orders as opposed to instituting sound management policies of his own. Howard set these grievances before the executive committee of the company in the form of a long and detailed letter (dated April 20). It was not a happy letter, and began: "I have been almost constantly harassed during the past three weeks by Mr. Woodruff's solicitude with respect to the possible passing of control..." The gloves had come off.

Ernest Woodruff, for his part, was running into the same problem with Howard that he had with Sam. The Candlers were hardheaded and had their own sense of what was right and wrong. As Howard suspected, Ernest was trying to manipulate the stock prices in 1921. He evidently planned to sell a large block of shares for an inflated price. When the company's audited statements did not support the line he had given to the potential investors, Ernest attempted to coerce the auditors and Howard as president to change the figures to reflect the values Ernest had given out.

In addition, "unsubstantiated rumors" were flying in New York regarding the increasing profits of the company. Woodruff requested that Howard deny these rumors of upcoming profits in a statement to the press. This denial would have pushed the price down. Howard refused. Also, Ernest was preparing a statement to be released later showing the increased profits, while at the same time doubling his inventory by counting it twice. This would have pushed the stock prices up. Howard and the auditors again refused to cooperate, and Howard went so far as to inform the preferred stockholders and the executive committee of Woodruff's attempted duplicity.

Howard was not exactly an innocent in these maneuverings. He was trying in his own way to discredit Ernest in the eyes of his peers. Although he does not say so in his papers, it is pretty obvious that Howard (perhaps with some backing from other family members) was attempting to regain control of the company from the Woodruff group, with whom he was already very disillusioned. However, the man that Howard was fighting, Ernest Woodruff, was a wily wolf in corporate boardrooms and had far more experience in such infighting than Howard who, after all, had spent most of his life just selling Coca-Cola.

In the end, Woodruff won the battle for control of the company, and Howard was out as president. It took nearly eighteen months for Ernest to replace him, however. Ernest's son, Robert Woodruff, took the office of president in April of 1923 as president of the company. Not wishing to alienate Howard completely, Woodruff gave him the chairmanship of a newly formed advisory committee. After all, Howard was one of the few men alive who not only knew the formula, but was perfectly capable of mixing up any size batch of it in his own basement as he had as a child. Thus, until his death in 1957, Howard continued as a director of the company and was treated with respect and not a little trepidation. The alliance was perhaps uneasy, but it did hold. There were no more attempts to wrestle back control of the company.

Howard Candler first learned of his ouster from newspaper accounts released while he was in New York on business. The situation had been coming to a head since 1921 when Howard first openly opposed Ernest. The newspaper accounts came out two full days before the board of directors voted on the transfer of power.

This was typical of the way Ernest Woodruff tried to manipulate people, companies, and the media. Perhaps he thought that by bringing in his own son, he would finally have the puppet he had been seeking, someone who would do exactly what he was told.

It has been legend for years in Coca-Cola circles that Ernest Woodruff was opposed to Robert's being offered the presidency. However, it is quite hard to believe, given the strong influence the man had within the company, that anyone would have been offered the job over Ernest's explicit objection. Ernest and Robert had butted heads for years. For one thing, Ernest had wanted his son to get a college education. But Robert wasn't interested and dropped out of Emory University as a freshman.

As former Coca-Cola archivist Franklin Garrett tells it,

"Robert Woodruff was in a hurry to go to work.... He paid a token visit to college. He attended elementary school in Inman Park. ... I think he did go through to high school. Anyway, Robert Woodruff was in a hurry to get going on working and a pox on all this time in school. His father didn't approve of that.

"He went to work as sort of a mechanic for the Grunnel Company. There are pictures of him in his grease stained coveralls. Bob was a born salesman. He soon gravitated into sales work. Mr. Ernest didn't think much of his son Robert quitting school so early. Then it wasn't so important to go to college as it is now—unless you were going to be a lawyer, or a doctor or a preacher, or some occupation where you had to have a college degree."

While they had had differences, they were certainly not estranged on April 28, 1923, when Robert was elected president of The Coca-Cola Company. Robert was thirty-three years old. He started right at the top at Coca-Cola and stayed there for next fifty years and more.

According to Franklin Garrett, Robert was also "president of the White Motor Company. He had a lot to do with the bottlers going from horse-drawn wagons to trucks. He retained that job for a little while and spent most of his nights on Pullman cars between Atlanta and Cleveland, rather than either there or here. Finally he gave up the presidency of the White Motor Company and was succeeded, rather ironically, by a man named Black. Mr. Black became president of White."

Robert soon found himself contending with the same interference from his father that Howard Candler and Sam Dobbs had endured before him. However, unlike his predecessors, Robert came up with a simple solution. He informed the company officers that anyone taking Ernest's orders over his would be fired.

The settlement with the bottlers in 1921 resulted in an agreement that allowed flexibility in the pricing of the syrup based on a complex formula tied to the market price of granulated sugar. This agreement may have saved The Coca-Cola Company in more ways than one. Gone was the opportunity for Ernest Woodruff to manipulate the company's books and inflate its value for quick sale and profit. Instead, Robert, who came in two years after the compromise settlement, was forced to take the long view and increase profitability of the company instead of priming it for a quick turnover. The money was in the long term and not the short. With the luxury of a seventy-year perspective, this certainly appears to have been the correct course.

As to someone else making a run at control of The Coca-Cola Company, the company has pursued a consistent strategy over the years of buying up its own stock to forestall such attempts. No new-age Ernest Woodruff, nor even a latter day Howard Candler, is going to have much chance of taking the company. Coca-Cola controls its own destiny. We just hope that the wild rumors that occasionally surface — such as selling out to the Japanese — stay just that, rumors. That, we fear, would still be a lynching offense in Georgia.

Even after Robert's edict to the executives, Ernest meddled. Robert would not be manipulated. He soon staged a successful *coup d'etat* and ousted his father.

Ernest Woodruff died in 1944 at the age of eighty-one. Not a man to throw money away, he made sure he was getting the cases of Coke delivered to his hospital room at the wholesale price.

Ernest Woodruff never came to be well-liked by the Candlers. In fact, some family members didn't like him at all. Buddie's wife, the family's "Aunt Florence," was a great Southern lady, but even she was driven to referring to Ernest as "that yellow dog." Bob Woodruff, she would say, had to spend his life paying for the sins of his father.

Robert Woodruff and the Candlers got along reasonably well — after all, they had known each other all their lives. He was even a groomsman in the wedding of Buddie's daughter, Lucy (whose husband worked for The Coca-Cola Company). He was also in the wedding party of Asa's grandson Henry Heinz.

One wonders, however, what the Candlers, ultra-patriotic Southerners that they were, thought when Robert Woodruff reincorporated the pride of Dixie in Delaware. For a time, the "official" headquarters of this most Southern of institutions was even moved to "Yankeeland."

Franklin Garrett tells the story.

"Robert Woodruff got very put out with the tax people in the state of Georgia in the early 1930s... Georgia wanted to tax Coca-Cola wherever it was sold and not just in Georgia. Bob Woodruff didn't want any part of that, so he moved the corporate headquarters to Wilmington, Delaware. I think it consisted maybe of just a boardroom. A good many of the annual meetings of Coca-Cola are held in Wilmington. Many of them are very brief. I remember one stockholder was going to attend the meeting [there], and before he could find just exactly what building it was in, the meeting was over."

The Candlers had to be happy with the way Robert Woodruff took the company to new heights, although he might not have been able to without the firm foundation built by Asa Candler. Woodruff made Coca-Cola the international organization it is today. (Robert Woodruff is held in such esteem at the company itself, that his office is preserved exactly the way the grand old man left it, even to putting a fresh flower in it every morning.)

Although Aunt Florence for one was never to get over the way the sale of the company was handled, Asa's great-grandson John H. Candler, Jr., gives Robert Woodruff his due. "I'm not sure Asa Jr. and Howard would ever have carried The Coca-Cola Company anywhere but into the ground."

The Woodruff era brought a new aura of success to Coca-Cola.

Ernest Woodruff had convinced all of the socially prominent people in town (in addition to many, many small investors) to buy Coca-Cola stock. This meant that the "in" people in town were a part of The Coca-Cola Company. It became quite fashionable. Suddenly, it wasn't family-owned anymore; everybody in Georgia had a piece of the action.

Coca-Cola was a vibrant, dynamic enterprise. It was where things were happening in the South and especially in Atlanta. The employees shared an *esprit de corps* about their work, belief in the business, and in the future growth of the company.

Young men employed by the company were seen as social equals to young bankers, attorneys, and doctors. They formed a new class of "white collar" professionals, young men on their way up. This got them included in many of the social events going on in town. They were introduced to socially prominent, nice young ladies.

Atlanta was excited about this new era of The Coca-Cola Company. Everybody wanted a piece of the company—after all, it had made millions for Asa Candler, why not them? This was the entree for many a bright young man with his eye on the future to not only establish a terrific career with a young, growing company, but to also be introduced into high society circles. This influx of eligible young men was certainly a boon to young ladies in Atlanta at that time. High society circles expanded to include these young Coca-Cola employees, franchisees, and their families.

Coca-Cola bottling franchises cost little to set up (about five thousand dollars in the early days) and produced great cash profits. Generally, once an operation was running, the owner would set up members of his family in similar operations. When you started up your Coca-Cola bottling franchise, your family automatically became a part of the family of Coca-Cola. For generations to come, these people and their families would produce and sell Coca-Cola and laugh all the way to the bank. The people who owned bottling franchises quickly became some of the wealthiest people in town and rapidly rose to positions of prominence in the civic and business circles.

Even during the Great Depression of the 1930s, The Coca-Cola Company continued to roll up profits. People were drinking lots of Coca-Cola at soda fountains and taking it home, too. In 1928, for the first time ever, in fact, sales of bottled Coca-Cola surpassed those of soda fountains. And, on July 27, 1929, an ad in the *Saturday Evening Post* featured the first use of the slogan "the pause that refreshes."

As America entered the dark days of the early thirties, the phrase "buddy, can you spare a dime" was a constant refrain. A dime, back then, would buy two Cokes and quite often did. People turned to Coca-Cola as an alternative to more expensive entertainments and refreshments. They got a little lift from the dire realities of Depression times by sipping an ice-cold Coke. Almost everyone could come up with the occasional nickel, so the company kept growing.

In 1930, as the Depression deepened, The Coca-Cola Company had record sales of $34,580,493, almost half of which (more than $13 million) was profit. In 1935, the first Coca-Cola coin-vending machines were set up, and in 1937 automatic fountain dispensers were introduced, finally insuring consistency in Cokes served over the counter. Also in this era, the six-pack of Coca-Cola was first offered, and proved to be a popular success.

Coolers were also designed and provided at very low cost to retailers by the company. Today everyone is familiar with soft drink coolers in stores with the prominent advertising logos on their sides. Then, however, it was a new and innovative idea that got Coca-Cola out from behind the counter and very visible.

And, of course, there were the constant advertising campaigns. The main thrust of advertising during the many Woodruff years was to equate Coca-Cola with American life. In that, the company's advertising has quite undeniably succeeded in the most emphatic way. Coca-Cola slowly shifted from a Southern to an American icon. We are Coke and Coke is us, and so the world perceives us.

The evolution of ad slogans is interesting. In the early twenties, there was "Enjoy Thirst," then came "Pause and Refresh Yourself," a theme that was to be repeated for years. Other slogans of the era were: "Refreshment Time," "Around the Corner from Anywhere," "Continuous Quality," "With a drink so good, 'tis folly to be thirsty," "Stop at the Red Sign," "A Hot Day Made Cool," "It Had to Be Good to Get Where It Is," and "7 Million a Day," the latter referring to the number of Cokes sold every day.

As more and more profits were pumped into the advertising campaigns of the 1920s, slogans included "The Shortest Distance Between Thirst and Refreshment," and "The Best-Served Drink in the World." Finally, in 1929, came the classic "The Pause that Refreshes."

By the time the Depression had ended and World War II began, The Coca-Cola Company was several times the size it had been under Asa Candler and was selling many millions of dollars of Coca-Cola, every year.

There is a perception by some that a company so large must pull the strings in the state's government.

We asked Georgia's famous governor and former senator, Herman Talmadge, if he ever felt much influence from The Coca-Cola Company or of the Woodruffs?

"No," Senator Talmadge said. "Bob Woodruff and I were friends. He always contributed to me. I think the only thing he asked me to do was shortly after I was elected governor. He called me and said, 'Herman, can you come out here and have lunch with me?' I said, 'sure.' So we agreed on a date. At the lunch, he said, 'there's something I want you to do for me.' I asked him what it was. He said, 'I want you not pave any roads through Ichauway.' I said, 'Bob, that ought to be pretty easy to handle.' Unfortunately, I had to pave one through Ichauway. So I didn't keep my pledge.

"That was the only thing he ever asked me to do in all my political career. However, lobbyists for The Coca-Cola Company came to me from time to time requesting things. I did them if I could."

Did Coca-Cola have a strong influence in Georgia politics? After all, the Candlers when Asa was alive had congressmen, the Judge, the Bishop, and at least one governor of Georgia (Allen Candler) in their court. Senator Talmadge was adamant about how little influence the company had during the Woodruff era.

"Oh, good God! Had no influence at all. I guess the word was passed around, 'Woodruff is supporting Herman' and probably his employees fell in line but, hell, that might have been fifteen hundred votes out of two million, so what difference did it make?

"People outside of Georgia think Coca-Cola and Georgia Power Company nominate the politicians. That's not true at all. They couldn't elect a coroner. Corporate influence has very little influence in Georgia on a state level, and even less on the Washington level, of course."

While The Coca-Cola Company was triumphing in the

twenties and thirties, so, too, were the Candlers. They now had a *lot* of money and, being no longer tied down by the company or, in Buddie's case, the restraining hand of their father, were ready to have a good time and — again, especially in Buddie's case — they enjoyed this era a great deal.

# Refresh yourself

*This lady appeared in a Coke ad in 1924. A glass of Coca-Cola was only a nickel then, at better drugstores and soda fountains everywhere.*

# Uncle
# Howard

Charles Howard Candler, Sr. — Uncle Howard — was the oldest son of Asa Candler. He was ten years old when his father took over the rights to Coca-Cola, did chores at the factory as a boy, then went to work for The Coca-Cola Company in 1899 — an association that lasted until his death in 1957. In all, counting his boyhood, Howard lived and breathed Coca-Cola for sixty-nine years. He was also president of the company under three different ownerships — his father's, during the time he and Asa's other four children owned the company, and under the meddlesome Ernest Woodruff. He was also on the board of such major enterprises as the Trust Company of Georgia, Atlantic Steel, Asa G. Candler, Inc., National Manufacturers and Stores Corporation, the Atlantic Company, The Davison-Paxon Company, and Druid Hills, Inc.

Howard was a hard-nosed, shrewd businessman, but was considered shy and withdrawn by family. He made money and invested it well — and used much of it for charity. These traditions were continued by his sons and grandsons. He married the woman his mother approved of, Flora Glenn. The Glenn family was prominent, sophisticated, and well educated. His marriage and family life were the most stable of Asa's children. He and his wife were well-matched.

Howard contributed many things over the years to the

145

success of The Coca-Cola Company, one of the greatest of which was technical. It was also one of the most significant changes in the history of manufacturing of the soft drink.

The year was 1918 and America was engaged in the First World War — that war to end all wars that didn't. Industry as well as individuals were required in those dark days to conserve every conceivable thing for war purposes. Most of the staple food commodities were being rationed. The Coca-Cola Company was not permitted to buy as much sugar as it needed.

As soon as the sugar rationing ruling went into effect, the Coca-Cola people went to Washington and found out definitely what the rationing board wanted them to do and did exactly as requested. Their attitude was so sincere that the food administration pointed to them as an ideally patriotic firm.

However, demand for Coca-Cola was increasing and could not be satisfied due to the restricted sugar supply. The company was forced to reduce proportionately the amount of Coca-Cola syrup sold to customers.

Making matters even worse, the use of heating agents, such as coal and electricity, was also rationed. Luckily, electricity was not restricted to as great an extent in the Atlanta area as elsewhere because of its water-powered generators. With these facts in mind, Howard Candler had a fortuitous brainstorm.

"It occurred to me," he later wrote, "that the critical situation might be relieved to some extent if a method could be devised to hasten without heat the solution of granulated sugar in the preparation of Coca-Cola syrup. I knew that sugar could be dissolved in cold water and without heat but reasoned that it would take a long time."

While sugar would still be in short supply, at least the rationing of coal would be bypassed if no heat was needed to make Coca-Cola syrup. That good old Southern staple summer drink, sweetened iced tea (which is always frustratingly impossible to find in Northern restaurants — ask for tea and they bring you *hot tea*, and not sweetened to boot) provided him with the answer.

"A couple of spoons full of sugar in a glass of very cold

tea," Howard said, "would simply settle at the bottom of the glass. But if vigorously agitated, despite the low temperature of the fluid, it would all go into solution and rather promptly. Of course, the amount of fluid in a glass of tea is vastly in excess, proportionately, of the amount of fluid we used in dissolving sugar in making Coca-Cola. The thought, occurred to me, therefore, that if I could sufficiently violently agitate the mixture of sugar and water, I could effect the complete solution of the sugar fairly quickly.

"Chance seems to have favored me in working out my ideas and in finally solving the problem which had been presented by our inability to buy and use coal for heating and power purposes. I happened upon an illustrated advertisement of the King Hardware Company (the same company which sold my father the first copper kettle in which he made Coca-Cola) offering for sale a Daisy glass churn. A square glass jar, this churn was fitted with a screw-top cover and a four-bladed revolving stirring apparatus with blades placed at an angle with the sides of the jar. To the shaft of this stirring apparatus was attached a pinion, meshed in a large driving gear which was propelled by a hand crank.

"The man who designed this little apparatus, holding about a gallon of fluid, intended it to churn buttermilk, but it was ideal for my purposes in that it produced extraordinarily vigorous agitation, throwing the liquid outward and upward against the sides and top of the churn. I bought one of these gallon-size churns, put into it the proper amount of sugar and water, based on our formula, and was really amazed to find how quickly the sugar went into complete solution.

"From this crude experiment, and after consulting with engineers and designers, we were able to devise a means of doing away with the necessity for heat in dissolving our sugar. Not only was the immediate problem solved, but savings were effected in fuel costs, upkeep on boilers and equipment, and in the saving of time over the old method. In the first place, it took less time to dissolve the sugar; in the second place, no time whatsoever was required for the syrup to cool, one of the bugbears of the early manufacturing days at the Peachtree store, the one on Decatur Street, and even after completion of the two successive plants on Edgewood Avenue and on Magnolia Street. At the latter factory, mechanical refrigeration was resorted to for hastening the cooling of the syrup. The installation and operating costs of this equipment were very high."

So Howard's process saved the company many millions over the years. When rationing of fuel was no longer required and again made heat possible for the manufacturing, the company no longer needed to make that expenditure.

Coke's arch rival, Pepsi, is making a big thing over their recent introduction of a "colorless" cola. However, Howard Candler beat them by a good many decades. In a letter dated May 1, 1953, and written on an Asa G..Candler, Inc., letterhead to Wilbur G. Kurtz, Jr. (archivist at The Coca-Cola Company), he details their invention of colorless cola.

> The facts about the question raised in our letter of April 30th are that during the spring of 1918, when the demand for Coca-Cola could not be supplied due to shortages of materials, the idea occurred to our Sales Department that we could successfully temporarily market an uncolored Coca-Cola. It was very difficult to obtain adequate supplies of caramel coloring due to War Time restrictions on the uses of corn.
>
> Dr. W. P. Heath and I made up one gallon of Coca-Cola containing all of the ingredients except the caramel coloring solely as an experiment. A few bottles, certainly not more than one case, from this sample were carbonated at Mr. Montgomery's plant. Suffice it to say that through blindfold tests there was no perceptible difference in the flavor and taste of this experimental product and that normally made with all of the ingredients; though when the testers tried it with open eyes, the assertion was made that the uncolored product tasted different. Aside from all this, Mr. Hirsch of our Legal Department would not tolerate the adoption of any such expediency; to have done so would have been suicidal. Obviously, none of this experimental product was ever sold and the presumption is that all of it was destroyed.

From the letters of Asa Candler, Sr., it is obvious that he planned on his eldest son taking over not only the business, but also to be the kind of brother that he himself had been to his own siblings — the one who provided the jobs, contacts, and help to the other family members.

Howard tried, if not always successfully, to fulfill this role. However, he was not always the loving brother that Asa was to the preceding generation of Candlers. Howard didn't get over being mad as fast and, of course, with a brother like Buddie, one's patience was often tried.

The oldest Candler son was subdued and restrained, very much the opposite of his brother Buddie. If personalities were colors, Buddie's would be fluorescent international orange and Howard's a more muted, tasteful and very proper shade of, say, beige. Howard, however, was a shrewd businessman and made many wise investments.

Catherine Candler Warren, Howard's daughter, naturally, remembers him well. She said that he was a very quiet person, not given to anything very flamboyant, however he did like to fish and hunt marsh hens. She said her father Howard was extremely close to his mother, Lucy, who was also shy and retiring.

One of Howard's idiosyncrasies was he didn't approve of earrings. When his daughters came home from dates on which they wore the brazen, forbidden ear baubles, they would always be sure to take them off before going inside. For some reason, Howard thought earrings were unladylike or cheap looking.

Caroline Candler Hunt, one of the Bishop's granddaughters, adds this about Howard's character: "He [the Bishop] liked Flora. Mama was crazy about Cousin Flora. Cousin Howard was so formal, so businesslike, not outgoing at all, and Flora was all outgoingness. And she and Mama had the same initials. So when my mother was getting her engraved stationery from J. P. Stephens, Cousin Flora just said, 'Frances, don't bother to get another stamp. Just use mine,' and she did! They used FGC all the time."

Howard was careful with his money but not parsimonious. He had simple tastes but still built a palatial home for his family.

"The one who was really tight with the money, in terms of spending it on himself and his whole family, was William," the Bishop's granddaughter said, "because he didn't spend on a great big house. But Cousin Howard had a beautiful home. I don't think he was maybe as conservative. He wasn't foolish with his money, but I don't think he was ungenerous. That house was just beautiful."

In his politics, Howard was very much like his father. Basically he did not take sides openly. He was quiet about his views and seemed somewhat apolitical. However, by the time that Franklin Delano Roosevelt came along, his family was well aware of his views regarding this particular politician. Howard was raised like most Southerners, a Democrat, but *this* president he could not support. He couldn't stand Roosevelt, nor did he support that Georgia kingpin and father of Herman Talmadge, Governor Eugene Talmadge (father and son were both governors of Georgia).

Howard got to be the kind of man he was because he was raised that way, and unlike Buddie or Walter, he was more adaptable and malleable to his father's wishes. As oldest child and son, Asa Candler expected him to be responsible for his brothers and sisters and to act as Asa would when Asa was not there.

Taught to be quiet, shy, but hard nosed about business, Howard's investment sense was conservative and practical. He was probably the child to whom Asa was closest.

Family letters and notes indicate that Howard was not always the healthiest of children. He seems to have suffered more from childhood illnesses than his next younger brother, Buddie, or Lucy and Walter. Asa's youngest child, William, seems to have also suffered from great bouts of illness. Health and the family's concern about health is a frequent subject of discussion in Asa's correspondence with his children. When Howard was away from home, his father used to send him medicine with which to treat his ailments and constantly reminded him to keep his chest covered to avoid "la grippe."

In a childhood accident when he was a year old, Howard had his four upper front teeth knocked out. This damaged the buds of his permanent teeth so that they never grew in. This increased his self-consciousness and, coupled with his natural shyness, made him a very reserved little boy. Asa decided that because of his shyness, Howard should go to the little military school known then as Moreland Park Military Academy, near their home. Howard would be graduated from this school and then enter Emory College at age sixteen.

The first is often the parents' experimental child. They try out their beliefs and parenting techniques on this one and keep those that work for the rest of the children. Asa would be so concerned with instilling in his children a sense of where they came from and giving them his experiences that sometimes he would go to the extreme.

Howard describes in his book how his father sent him to his first day of first grade with his lunch in a tin pail. The lunch consisted of biscuits left from breakfast with holes poked in them by Howard's finger (under Asa's instruction) and syrup pored over them. This mess was what Asa claimed he had to eat as a schoolboy. Of course, no other child at Moreland Park Military Academy had a lunch like that. Howard and his mother were soon able to persuade Asa that a more palatable meal was needed and acceptable.

Asa was trying, vainly, to give to his children the background he had had, the experiences he had suffered, so that they would benefit and be stronger for it. Unfortunately, no one can go back in time and re-create the past to give the next generation the benefits without the pain. Each generation must live in its own time. This would be particularly true for the Candler children because their lives would be so different in experience and opportunity from their father's, and the problems they encountered would be different.

It was difficult being the eldest, the son that was groomed to stand in the father's place, the one who was expected to be the example to the other children and to answer to the father for the other children's behavior. This is almost a form of primogeniture, and it could build resentment and frustration.

Howard's childhood was subject to setting the example. He couldn't quite be the child the others could. His siblings

might get away with occasional mischief making, not the
Good Son Howard. While this burden of responsibility can
develop qualities of leadership, it can instill a boy with a
sense of authority that makes him resent challenges, particularly from a younger brother.

By the time Howard entered Emory, he had been involved with The Coca-Cola Company for six years helping
his father at the factory. In a family that naturally promoted
itself and its business, it did not seem strange to Howard to
ask people to drink Coca-Cola, to tell people his father
produced it, or to try to get drugstores to stock his dad's
product. Thus, when he got to Emory it seemed natural for
him to try to get the local drugstore to carry and sell Coca-
Cola. However, Howard's natural tendency towards business and selling would earn him a small reprimand from Asa
if his studies suffered.

After Buddie joined him at Emory, Howard had the
additional burden of keeping his rambunctious, unpredict-
able brother in line. When Buddie got into trouble, which
was often, Howard was always expected to correct the
situation, not Asa, Sr., and not Buddie. This was an unfair
position to put Howard in given that he was only eighteen
months older than Buddie, and it put Buddie in the unfair
position of having to answer to a teenager, just eighteen
months older. Any kind of authority never sat well with
Buddie, but being under his brother's thumb was just asking
too much of him. It's little wonder that Howard's attempts at
being his brother's keeper didn't meet with much success, at
least not according to this letter from his father, dated
January 20, 1897.

> Dear Howard: I address this letter to you hoping that
> you can help me out of a great sorrow. Your Uncle Warren
> writes that Buddie has been acting badly.
>   How can my own child treat me so! He knows how I am
> already loaded down. For no fault of mine sued in court—
> annoyed by bad people who care nothing for me is very
> hard—but for my own son who bears my name & for whom
> I labor & work & pray to deliberately disgrace me is more
> than I can bear. My brother says he must be taken from

Oxford that he can't control him. Is it possible! Only last Sunday he wrote me how he was determined to do his duty — before a week has passed he breaks his word. I can't afford to write to him but want you to see to it that he reinstates himself with my brother. I cannot bear for him to be disgraced. I have for two weeks been going back & forth to attend to my poor old mother who is very sick at Cartersville. Having to leave your mother & the little children alone at night. My comfort has been in supposing that you boys were undisturbed at your books preparing yourselves with my aid to help & give me joy as honorable smart men in the near future. I cannot think that Buddie has deliberately made up his mind to kill me with remorse. He knows how to behave & ought not to treat me so. Write me plainly what wrong he has done & how he proposes to repair it. Let him write me that he will not again do so & let him say so to my brother. If I have to remove him I don't know what I will do with him. Now my son I put this case in your hand—to adjust. I will have to abide by the decision that is arrived at between you & my brother as to my future course with your brother. Let me hear.

Yr father Asa G. Candler, Sr.

Howard's exasperation with his younger brother at Emory eventually erupted with his getting even.

When the time came to pledge a fraternity, Buddie was interested in being a Kappa Alpha like Howard. This fraternity was the family fraternity. Buddie didn't make it; it seems Howard "blackballed" him. Buddie would be listed in the yearbook with the other nonfraternity men along with his cousin William Beall Candler of Villa Rica. Buddie's adventures in college were no more than a series of fairly lighthearted pranks; however, Howard didn't approve of any frivolity and resented his brother's activities and presence.

Overcoming the distractions, Howard was graduated, a Phi Beta Kappa, no less, from Emory in 1898.

If his career had gone according to his father's wishes, Howard would have gone into medicine. Asa was as determined for his son to be a doctor, a professional, as Sam

Candler had been for Asa. Both fathers had their hopes unrealized. Howard was very book smart and could have easily handled the schoolwork. In all likelihood, he would have been a very competent doctor, but his heart was never in it. He had a natural bent towards commerce, just as Asa had had. And like Asa, Howard would finally have to come to grips with the fact that he wanted to be in business, specifically in the Coca-Cola business, even if that meant disappointing his father.

After his graduation from Emory, Howard worked for the company and, while in New York City, attended medical school at night. Certainly, it was unreasonable for his father to assume that Howard could work all day (sunup to sundown) and then go to school at night, fully focused on his studies. While medical school instruction in 1898 was not as formalized as it is today and lots of the material covered was done by associating with a practicing doctor, still it was an arduous course of study, and Howard was not really given the time to pursue it fully. He was living his father's dream for himself, but not his own dream.

Fortunately for Howard, he had enough common sense, Candler stubbornness, and self-respect, to figure out that what he really wanted was to be involved with his father's rapidly growing enterprise. By 1901, he broached this subject of his dropping medical studies and was finally able to persuade Asa of the rightness of this choice; although from letters, it appears that Howard conned Asa into believing that New York City was not good for Howard's health. Of course, it may be that Asa didn't mind being finagled into letting Howard drop out, realizing that his son's academic background in chemistry, drugs, and medicine would prove valuable to the company.

Once Howard got back to Atlanta, the idea of medical school was allowed to die a natural death.

Howard was very conservative in business. In college he had to account for his money and send his father an expense report every week. He later used a similar tactic in training his own son, Howard, Jr. Howard and some of his descendants to this day are known for their meticulous records.

Howard's conservatism was so widely known within the family that it became a source of both kidding and pride. He was so careful with money and costs that he was able to parlay a small fortune into a very large one. Even today, in the other branches of the Candler family, the kudos given to a child that shows particular conservatism with money is to say that he or she "got it from Uncle Howard" or "shades of Uncle Howard." It's a compliment often said with a mixture of amusement and respect.

Mary Ripley Warren, who married one of Howard's grandsons, says there was a dichotomy to Howard's nature. "One of the main things that we remember were these things that he did that were so tightfisted but he was also very generous. He was really a great philanthropist and gave lots of money away. And he was generous with what he left his children and grandchildren and all that kind of stuff... But he was not generous to himself."

This cheapness with himself was the stuff of many family anecdotes. From Howard's niece Laura Candler Chambers (Buddie's daughter):

"Let me tell you, when I was working in my dad's office, Uncle Howard came in once, and he had on shoes that were getting old. They were cracked across the top. Papa looked at him and said, 'Howard, if you don't have enough money to get yourself a pair of shoes, here's a check. You go get yourself some.' Now I know Howard could buy Papa and forget it. They were just being brothers, you know."

Mary Ripley Warren has another story. "He used to go to the service station there on the corner. A guy named Jim Edwards and his brother Bill Edwards worked there. Grandfather used to go to Jim Edward's gas station to pay his bill, and he would park his car across the street, then walk across the street ... because he didn't want to block a pump while he was there. He wasn't going to block the man's pump so he couldn't sell some gas while he was paying his bill."

Howard was tight about his clothes, too. He would have Flora turn his collars when they frayed rather than buying a new shirt. His nieces who attended the same church he did (Glenn Memorial on the Emory campus) would delight in telling how they would see Uncle Howard in church taking a penknife and trimming the frayed places on his cuffs during the service. They would nudge each other and giggle, but they had to be careful, or their father would reprimand them for not paying attention to the sermon!

Howard was noted for driving his old car, a two-seater Packard, all over town. He refused to buy himself a new one. Flora decided that for Christmas one year, she would just give him a brand new vehicle. Howard was furious when he discovered she had traded the Packard. "I don't want that new car," he said. "I want my old car back!" And sure enough, he marched over to the dealer and retrieved his Packard, which he kept until the day he died.

Howard's pecuniary habits occasionally made him the butt of some good-natured teasing. Bradley Lancaster, a longtime friend of Howard, Jr., and something of a prankster, had some fun once with Howard, Sr., using the young Asa Candler V as an unwitting accomplice.

It happened when Asa V was perhaps four or five. The family was having a big barbecue at Buddie's house (Briarcliff). This is one of the few times that Howard visited his brother. People say, "Well, I never remember seeing Uncle Howard over at Uncle Buddie's with all the nieces and nephews" — but he was there this time. Bradley Lancaster grabbed little Asa and said, "Boy, do you know who that old man over there is?"

Asa V said, "No, suh."

Bradley looked at him, shook his head, and said, "Well, you ought to know that old man. That old man over there is your Great Uncle Howard. Did you know that?"

"No, suh."

Bradley continued, "I'll tell you something else about your Great Uncle Howard. He's got the first nickel his daddy ever gave him. You want to see it?"

Little Asa thought that was a fine idea. "Yeah, I wanna see it."

"Well, you just go over there and tell him who you are, and that you want to see the first nickel his daddy ever gave him."

Asa went scooting over and said, "Uncle Howard, can I see the first nickel your daddy ever gave you?"

Uncle Howard calmly reached into his pocket and kind of rumbled some change around in his hand. Then he pulled one out and rubbed it real good. And he said, "You look at it." He held it up and said, "There you are."

Howard knew that child had been put up to the stunt, so rather than gruffily putting him off, he went along with the gag. Asa says he still remembers seeing that nickel. Being Howard, of course, he did not *give* him the nickel.

Mary Ripley Warren adds, "He did things like that. He took his lunch to work every day in a brown paper sack. Every day he brought the sack back because he didn't want to waste it.

"When Billy [her husband] first went into business, he would get these notes from his grandfather, saying, 'Dear Billy' and signed 'Affectionately, Pops.' They'd be on short pieces of paper — a perfectly good piece of paper, the width of business stationery, except not as tall. Billy couldn't figure out why his grandfather was writing these notes on this funny little paper. Then Billy was in Howard's office one day, and his grandfather was opening his mail. What he was doing was, he'd get a letter from somebody, and it would only be written so far down the page. He'd cut the bottom off ... he was using that to write on to people!"

Howard married his childhood sweetheart, Flora Harper Glenn. She was a strong, positive influence on her husband. Unlike some of the wives of Asa's boys who lacked assertive personalities or as good health, Flora was strong. She could hold her own.

Flora was a sparkling, pert woman who approached life with humor and wit. She was as outgoing as Howard was shy and reserved. However, they shared mutual interests, background, intelligence, and education.

Flora was a hometown Atlanta girl with a wide circle of friends in town. Flora and Howard knew many people in common. She came to her marriage well-connected socially and financially. Like Howard she was smart, a college graduate (LaGrange) when most women were not. Her family lived in the same neighborhood as the Candlers; they all knew each other. She could politely stand her own ground with her Candler in-laws.

She was one of the first women in Atlanta to have a driver's license. Quite probably, Flora inspired Asa's wife, Lucy, to get a car and drive it herself.

Flora's parents were Wilbur Fiske Glenn and Florella Harper. He was a prominent Methodist preacher and a well-educated and socially polished man. Flora was one of the youngest of Reverend Glenn's large family of ten children.

One of Flora's older brothers, Thomas K. Glenn, knew Ernest Woodruff and may have sparked Woodruff's initial interest in The Coca-Cola Company with tales of Candler siblings' squabbles. In any case, Thomas Glenn was part of the consortium that purchased the company.

Tom Glenn was a brilliant man and similar in disposition to Howard. Because he was so much older and therefore more experienced, Glenn's counsel on selling The Coca-Cola Company would not have been taken lightly by the younger couple — even though, in 1919, Howard's age was forty-two to Tom Glenn's fifty-five. Tom Glenn's prominent position in the Trust Company of Georgia and close alliance with Howard would later prove a boon to Howard's knowledge of business affairs in Atlanta.

Flora and Howard shared a love of opera and were very supportive of the Atlanta opera week festivities. They entertained the immortal Enrico Caruso when he came to sing. Howard was a director and served for a time as the treasurer of the Atlanta Music Festival Association, which sponsored the performances of the Metropolitan Opera Company in Atlanta. He also helped to organize the Atlanta Municipal Opera Association which brought the light opera to the city.

Flora was very vivacious, a gracious hostess, warm and welcoming. She could overcome Howard's gruffness with his brothers and some of their children.

They had simple tastes in food and preferred Southern cooking as did all the Candler siblings. Even living in town, Flora had a large garden and grew her own vegetables at Callanwolde, as the huge house that Howard built was named. While they had an ample staff to take care of the house and grounds, Flora exerted control over every aspect of the management. She was involved in the day-to-day decisions. She always provided Howard with a warm haven from the stressful world of business and was quite domestic.

Lucy, Howard's mother, strongly supported this match. Howard had discovered Flora in the choir at Inman Park Church as a boy and taken a shine to her. But he was timid. Flora, on the other hand, was not. She was quite taken with Howard Candler and knowing a good catch when she saw one, and was not at all reserved about going after him. They really had been childhood sweethearts.

Of course, being a traveling salesman before his marriage — and we've all heard the stories about them — Howard was not as shy and retiring as one might expect.

During his years on the road for Coca-Cola, Howard lived mostly in New York City (with occasional time in Kansas City and a brief stint in California). He would write to his sister about his adventures, his dates, the sights of the big city, and his daily life.

He seems to have kept quite a number of young ladies on the string. He already had an eye on Flora, but while away from Georgia, dated several girls. One in particular became quite possessive, too possessive, in fact. Howard was relieved when this Miss Eubanks and her mother returned to North Carolina, although he did miss the mother's cooking.

By 1902, Howard had bought an automobile with the unlikely, if not prophetic, name of the Locomobile. His father had feared he would use the purchase for fun and games instead of work, which is exactly what Howard did. He wrote to his sister of taking various young ladies, including a Miss Inez Sledge "locomobiling..."

While squiring the ladies around, Howard kept up a warm correspondence with Flora. In 1903, this resulted in marriage, and Howard settled down after that to be a very faithful and loving family man for the rest of his life.

The wedding was held at the Glenns' home in Inman Park at 8:30 p.m. on December 3, 1903, one day after Howard's twenty-fifth birthday. Flora was twenty-two. The house was decorated with a profusion of cut flowers, palms, and wild smilax. Her dress was a unique design of pleated *palais de soie* smocked with pearls and trimmed with duchess lace.

Bishop Candler officiated as he had for Buddie and would for all of his nieces and nephews. Reverend Glenn gave away his daughter. The guest list numbered about three hundred and fifty people.

The wedding was elaborate. Howard's mother, Lucy, was later to remark to her sisters that, in her opinion, it was all a little overdone. This from a woman who had invited more than five hundred guests to her son Buddie's reception.

After a wedding trip to the North, they settled down at the Glenns' home not far from Asa and Lucy.

When they bought their first home, it was in Inman Park just down the street from Asa, Sr., and Lucy and just around the corner from the Glenns. They remained very close to both sets of parents. Asa's granddaughter remembered her grandfather Candler picking up the children in his horse and buggy and taking them to Sunday School. He loved to play with his grandchildren and frequently came down to Howard and Flora's house for breakfast when they were living in Inman Park.

As strict as Howard could be, and as conservative, he and Flora had a very loving and warm home. They presented, as a couple, a united front to their children and to the rest of the family. Their mutual love and affection for each other and for their children provided a stable base for their children. Howard, like his father, expected his children to work and contribute to the household.

In addition, Howard and Flora communicated well with each other. They were people who held a strong respect for their pasts and tradition, yet lived very much in the present. Flora wasn't about to go back in time to some nostalgic past that existed only in books and clouded memories. She knew that the present was great and enjoyed it. So did Howard, albeit more shyly. A subtle example of this was his children called him "Daddy," not "Papa" as was more the norm among Candlers. He and Flora arranged to have only three children, not a houseful as was more common in those days.

In 1917, Howard and Flora decided to build a larger, more elegant home out from town in the Druid Hills section being developed by Asa G. Candler, Inc. Howard's name for this elegant, Tudor-style estate reflected his love of history and his pride in his own heritage. The legends handed down generation to generation about Candlers in Kilkenny County, Ireland, certainly colored the family's history.

The Candlers were originally from England. In 1653 Cromwell gave Colonel William Candler Callan Castle in Ireland as payment for his services in the war against the Irish. William took his English wife and settled down to live in the Irish country.

In following generations, one of Colonel William's descendants, Daniel, was forced to emigrate to America as a result of his marriage to an Irish Catholic woman. By the second decade of the 1730s, the death penalty for marriage to an Irish person had been repealed. However, this marriage was still considered an outrage, bringing social and political ostracism to the Candler family. It might not have been so bad if Daniel hadn't been a third cousin to both Queen Mary of Orange and her sister, Queen Anne, the last of the Stuarts.

Daniel and his wife Hannah (Anna), after brief stops in Barbados and North Carolina, settled in the Virginia colony near distant relatives, the Moormans, and the Clarks, who would later marry into the Candler family. These three families formed the nucleus of a Quaker settlement known as the South River colony, located south of the James River. Daniel became a surveyor, served in the French and Indian War, and was a true frontiersman. The turmoil in Ireland certainly colored Daniel and his wife's approach to resolving differences. Like many of his descendants, he would prefer negotiated, bloodless settlements of differences and would fight only when it came down to a question of absolute survival.

Daniel died in 1765, naming as his heirs his son Zedekiah (the father of Zachariah, from whom the North Carolina Candlers are descended), his son John (progenitor of the Candlers of Virginia and Maryland), and William (from whom came Asa G. Candler and all the Georgia Candlers). In spite of their humble frontier background, these offspring would bequeath to their descendants a name, a coat of arms, and a tradition of striving to achieve great goals.

Asa and Lucy had named their beautiful home in Inman Park "Callan Castle" — so it was only natural that Howard and Flora would also find a use for the name "Callan."

Callanwolde was situated on twenty-seven acres in Druid Hills on Briarcliff Road. Begun in 1917, while Howard was president of The Coca-Cola Company. The house was completed in 1920. Delays resulting from war shortages caused the construction process to slow. Howard had the four-car garage with a six-room apartment above completed first so he could move his family there and be on site to personally supervise the construction. This was typical of both Howard and his father. They liked to be involved in the details of their projects.

This home, designed as an Elizabethan country house, was a reflection not only of Howard's interest in family and history but also Flora's elegant taste. They hired Henry Hornbostel to design the home. Mr. Hornbostel, of Pittsburgh, had designed the buildings on Emory University's nearby campus. In addition to the main house and garage, the grounds contained a swimming pool with clubhouse, tennis courts, greenhouse, conservatory, barns for horses and cows, plus buildings for the chickens and turkeys.

Informally landscaped with native trees and shrubs, the grounds had formal gardens, informal cutting gardens, and Flora's well-stocked and much loved vegetable garden. Essentially, Howard did for his family what his parents had done for their children. He moved his family to the country and set up a farm-like existence. It was a pattern repeated by all but one of Asa's children.

With all the money that came to him through the sale of The Coca-Cola Company in 1919, Howard could and did turn Callanwolde into a real showplace. His home was one area of his life in which Howard spared no expense.

Howard needed a haven, a place to get away from the problems of business — and siblings. It was all very nice that Asa, Sr., had envisioned his children working as a harmonious unit under the supervision of Howard in the lead. The reality was that as adults, the Candler children were divided by their views on how various family enterprises should be run and on life in general. Howard and Buddie had always been in competition and at odds from the day Buddie was born. Howard developed a similar, but perhaps not as volatile relationship with Walter. He worked well with William but saw him as his "little brother."

There were so many fundamental disagreements between the siblings. Just take the subject of second marriages. Howard had a complete mental block against people marrying again after a spouse's death — and divorce was not even to be considered. This attitude of the older brother would definitely affect his relationship with the others when they found themselves ready to remarry. Who's to say why Howard had such an adamant attitude? Was he reacting to his own mother's early death at fifty-nine and his father's remarriage? His Candler aunts, when widowed, did not remarry; but certainly there was nothing improper in taking another wife or husband if you were widowed.

Howard's uncle, the Judge, was married three times. The Judge, a charmer and a good-looking man with a twinkle in his eye, had a line to fit every occasion. He had lost his first two wives to early deaths, but "Judge Uncle John" could always find a nice lady to squire around and to marry (even if he did have wooden legs).

Howard was the only one of Asa's children not to have a spouse who got ill and died. He and Flora were both healthy and remained very compatible all their lives. When members of Buddie's family would make a reference to Howard's disapproval of second marriages, Buddie would reply, "Howard doesn't understand. His wife didn't die."

After Asa, Sr., became too ill to live at home and entered Emory Hospital, his children finally established their own individual family units and spheres of influence. Now instead of spending part of each Sunday with Asa, Sr., his grandchildren and their families spent the day with their respective parents.

Howard's children and grandchildren were very close to him, and he to them. He was loving and sweet, thoughtful with not only his descendants but also their spouses. And he was very generous. He gave Flora her own money and made no restrictions on the way she spent it.

Mary Ripley Warren has fond memories of Flora. "Oh, yes. Every year at Christmas, she'd buy a dress for every girl in the family, me included after I married into it. She'd buy suits for the boys. I was just overwhelmed with it all. I remember somebody saying, one of those salespeople in one of those places said, if they died, they wanted to come back as Queen Elizabeth or something. And one of them said, 'No, I want to come back as one of Mrs. Candler's grandchildren.' She did so much for them.

"He was not tight with Flora. Oh, no. He was not. He gave her a huge sum of money early on. I don't know when.

"At her death, she had quite a fortune of her own that she left. She got it from him. But of course enhanced it through the years. He used to grumble about it sometimes. I did hear him once or twice when she'd go out spending all this money on her grandchildren. He'd say, 'I know I shouldn't have given her that money.' He didn't really object to it, but he'd kind of grumble under his breath about it.

"He absolutely adored her. I don't think there's any question about that. He always adored her. She was an interesting person."

Other family memories of Howard come to us courtesy of Mary.

"Well, you know, Billy [Howard's grandson] told me two or three things he remembered. Of course, I don't know anything from the twenties, because Billy wasn't born until 1931, but he did grow up in the house [Callanwolde]. He would see his grandfather every day of his life. And Billy always said, 'I did so many things with my grandfather. We would go back and forth to Cumberland Island [an island Howard owned property on off the Georgia coast] together, just the two of us, riding down there and back. Because I lived in the house with him. I wanted to be just like him when I was a little boy. I went one day and I was looking at his bedroom shoes, and they had little specks of white all over them. I went and got some talcum powder and sprinkled it on my bedroom shoes, so they would look just like my grandfather's. But it all brushed off. I couldn't understand what I was doing wrong, why they wouldn't stay on there like his. I would go in his room and watch him. One time I went

in there and watched him brush his teeth, and I found out
how those specks were made — it was toothpaste!'

"Billy said, he and Sam [Sam O. Candler, Billy's cousin]
went to Cumberland Island one time with Popee — that's
what everyone called him was Popee... Anyway, they were
little boys. They stopped at a service station on the way
down... you know they were getting gas and going to the
bathroom, you know, the things you would do at a service
station. Coca-Cola had come out with a bigger bottle, a ten-
or twelve-ounce bottle. I don't know how big it was, it was a
bigger bottle. Sam saw this in the station's cooler, and his
eyes popped out. He wanted this bigger one. Well, Billy said
his grandfather had a fit. Howard was not familiar yet with
the new packaging and thought it was another brand. He
said, 'You go put that thing right back. You can't drink
anything but a Coca-Cola. That's belly-wash.'

"Howard smoked Camels. Many people did then. He
smoked it in a holder, which was kind of unusual for the day.
He smoked it all the way to the very end. I think that's why
he used a holder, because he was so tight, he wanted to
smoke the whole cigarette. And he smoked it all the way to
the bitter end, and then he had a little penknife that he used
to get out what was left and put it in the ashtray. It was a
regular little ritual he went through to do that.

"Billy told me about one time when he was a teenager,
and he had a car by then. He had this souped-up engine... it
was a Ford. A great Ford — 1947 Ford or something. He had
spent all this money. Of course, his family didn't know. This
was all done surreptitiously. He didn't want them to know he
had this motor because he would go out racing and all that.
He drove his grandfather down to Cumberland one time...
The car broke down. A belt broke or something minor that
they had to get fixed. They had to stop off the side of the road,
and Billy pulled up the hood.

"These guys stopped and [looked at] the engine, because
it had a big, big engine. And the car sat up high in the back
like that... And they said, 'Gol-ly. He must be a bootlegger.'

"Billy said, 'My grandfather heard them and he looked
at me, and I looked at him. I could see this stern look on his
face. I got the car fixed and jumped back in and closed the

hood down. And not another word was ever said about it. I kept wondering what my grandfather thought when he heard that he must be a bootlegger."

Howard had first become interested in Cumberland Island, one of the Georgia sea islands near Saint Simons, because of the great hunting there. It wasn't so much the deer, but the marsh hens. He helped form the Cumberland Island Hunting Club, which purchased and renovated an old hotel on the island. With the end of the Roaring Twenties, the club disbanded, and Howard bought the club's property. This became his family's retreat, which they would retain until the 1970's. At that time, the U.S. goverment bought the island from its several owners, including the Candlers and Carnegies. Today, Howard's descendants retain their vacation homes on the island through a lease. This decision to sell resulted in the preservation of the island as a natural habitat instead of being commercially developed.

Emory University is a common thread through five generations of Candlers and, as the sixth generation reaches college age, it is assumed that some of them will attend it as well.

Howard and Flora were strong supporters of Emory. Howard's years as a college student must have remained a pleasant memory for him in spite of the many additional duties and charges imposed upon him by his father. Over the span of his life, Howard would step in and fill the place that Asa, Sr., had filled and continue to support the college in its efforts to grow and establish its place in the state and the region. Howard contributed some seventeen million dollars to the university before his death. This would be in addition to gifts made to Emory with his brothers and sister.

The first gift to the college by the children as a group was the Lucy Elizabeth Pavilion, a maternity wing they donated to Emory Hospital and the college in memory of their mother. Howard also served as chairman of the college's board of trustees. In the late 1950s, shortly before his death, Howard and Flora gave the school the Candler Room, a memorial to Asa, Sr. and a repository for the Candler family papers and rare books that Howard had assembled and donated to the college. Flora supervised the decorating and furnishing of the room.

Over the years, Emory benefited from Flora's association with the college as well as Howard's. She and her brother, Tom Glenn gave the money to build Glenn Memorial Methodist Church on the campus in memory of their father, Wilbur Fiske Glenn. And, being a doting grandmother, when her grandsons pledged the Kappa Alpha fraternity, she paid to have the fraternity house done over.

Flora and Howard were strong supporters of Emory's Glee Club which fit in with their mutual love of music.

Charles Howard Candler, Sr., died on October 1, 1957, just two months shy of his seventy-ninth birthday. He died at Emory Hospital after a short illness. In his last few years, he had been plagued with a case of Parkinson's disease.

His funeral two days later was as understated as his father's had been.

Like Asa, Sr., Howard dedicated his life to both The Coca-Cola Company and Emory University. He worked hard to live up to the ideals of his father and to follow the example his father had set. He did not waver on issues that were important to him. He would see this strong stand cost him the presidency of the company his father had developed. It would set him against his brothers and sister on more than one business issue, but he would stand by his convictions.

*Every year, for many decades, Mr. S. Claus—in addition to his other duties—has always done a little moonlighting around Christmastime for The Coca-Cola Company.*

# Buddie!

The man kept elephants in his front yard. In Atlanta. For a quarter, anyone could walk up and touch them. And he had baboons, camels, leopards (not a good idea to touch the leopards), rare birds, and dozens of other animals in the largest privately owned menagerie in America.

Asa Candler, Jr., Buddie to the family, was creative and eccentric. He tried fitting into the mold society demanded but couldn't. So he laughingly went his own way.

Asa Candler, Sr., drove hard to create his cola empire. His eldest son Howard was studious, hard-working, and took his designation as heir apparent to his father's empire quite seriously, even after his family no longer ruled the vast Coca-Cola dominions. And Buddie? Buddie was just Buddie; but, in a way, he soared to heights that others in the family, more worried about responsibilities and appearances, dared not try. An inveterate showman, Buddie made a statement of style in everything he did.

Nancy Candler Nutter sums up Buddie this way: "For years I've mulled over the rather bizarre activities of my grandfather, Asa G. Candler, Jr., and thought an apt title for a book about his life might be *Elephants to Ride Upon*, a line for a song from the vaudeville days. In so far as he was able, I believe my Grandfather did as he pleased for most of his seventy-two years.

169

"According to him, he was the most attractive and liveliest of the four boys of Asa, Sr. He must have been a handful for he was sent to live and go to school for a time with Aunt Florence and Uncle Joe in Cartersville. While there, Uncle Joe taught him to smoke and chew tobacco. PaPa, as we grandchildren called our grandfather, must not have liked chewing tobacco because I don't recall his doing so, but he remained a cigarette and cigar smoker to the end, with cigars the smoke of preference. He was not a conversationalist as I think of the term with a back-and-forth verbal exchange. Rather, he was a storyteller or lecturer. Even an occasional poetry reciter, 'If Only You Could Be the Boy Your Mother Thinks You Are' being his usual choice.

"My grandfather was not given to much reminiscing but occasionally he would relate some tale from his youth. It was always humorous, nothing sad. He wasn't one to 'dwell in the valley of the Shadow.' This is much different from his father, I surmise [who in his letters, writes often of various illnesses suffered by family members and of his own coming death]. Perhaps Asa, Jr., had tired of this kind of conversation early. In any case, he wasn't one to look back and mourn what used to be or might have been. 'If only' wasn't in his vocabulary."

Exiled as a child to Cartersville because he was so hard to handle, young Buddie still had a good time. His uncle and aunt were perhaps not the best choice in reining in this free-spirited boy. They were older and tended to give him even more license than his parents. Although Asa, Sr., did try to market a Coca-Cola brand cigars (they flopped), tobacco was very much against his strict Methodist beliefs. Asa would have preferred to keep Buddie at home, in a cage if necessary, than let him pick up "that foul habit."

While growing up Buddie was drastically different from his three brothers and his sister, something of a holy terror.

Why did Buddie run wild as a youngster and go his own flamboyant way as an adult? There is conjecture in the family that his obstreperous, outrageous behavior may have been to compensate for dyslexia or some other similar learning disability. The rebellious behavior he exhibited as a child fits into this hypothesis. Children who are otherwise bright but see words as incomprehensible jumbles of letters are too often tagged "stupid" when they are anything but that. They become resentful and out of control when grown-ups push them without understanding the very real problems of the learning disabled.

In later life, Buddie still had problems with reading and writing. He usually prevailed upon either a secretary or his second wife, Florence, to write or type the letters he dictated. His early refractoriness and later flashy, dramatic behavior were all signs of the compensation a bright person with such disabilities makes.

Buddie, like the rental car company, Avis, was in second place, so he had to try harder. Only he wasn't trying hard to excel in academic or dutiful behavior. He was trying harder to be the center of attention. Lacking Howard's studious, more malleable personality, he engaged in all sorts of mischievous pranks, to gain attention if not approval. His busy parents had no knowledge of child psychology, and apparently it never occurred to them that this attractive, engaging child wanted his own place in the family limelight, at least occasionally. His sister, Lucy, often told her sons about their Uncle Buddie's boyhood escapades.

"Well now, there was the day Buddie sent little William down the well in the bucket and covered the well and left the little fellow hollering his head off. Fortunately Sister Lucy heard the commotion and called for help to rescue William. When asked, 'what are you doing in the well?,' back came his answer, 'Buddie put me down the well.' His mother would paddle Buddie as hard as she could and he would stand there like a monument never crying. Lucy would cry in exasperation, pleading with him to 'Cry Buddie, cry.' But he would not. When he threatened to join the circus, his sister and mother would beg him not to. By the time, Asa, Sr., arrived home from work, the entire household would be in an uproar."

One too many of these escapades made the Candlers decide that their second son would benefit by living with his aunt and uncle in Cartersville and attending her school.

Asa, Jr., was fidgety and hard to handle, much as his father, Asa, Sr. had been as a little boy. This child had his mother's darker features, brown eyes, and prominent nose. He was quick to finish his chores and then disappear looking for people to meet, fun things to do. He was not inclined to hang around the house as his older brother was. He liked to find some mischief and get his brothers to go with him.

Being sent off to his Aunt Florence's school would have an effect on him. Certainly Asa, Sr., saw this as a good solution to the discipline problem. After all, it had been Florence who had handled him. Eight-year-old Buddie must have seen it as being singled out for punishment just for being himself. None of the other Candler children would be sent away to school until they were teenagers. While he would return to Atlanta for holidays and summer vacation, Buddie was, in effect, exiled to the country.

In Cartersville, he would come under the influence not only of his devoted Aunt Florence and her husband, Colonel Joe Harris, but also his paternal grandmother, Martha Beall Candler. Florence may have mellowed somewhat since taking care of Asa, Sr., but she and her mother were still stern disciplinarians. They also had a very high opinion of the Candlers, and in Florence's opinion anything wrong with her nieces or nephews was a result of the "muddy streams" that had flowed into the Candler bloodline. This was her way of describing her in-laws. In particular, she was not overly pleased with Nettie Curtwright and Lucy Howard. Nettie was too flirtatious and high-strung, and Lucy had been spoiled as a girl and had a tendency to whine! So, Aunt "Sissie" (Asa's pet name for Florence) and Grandma Martha were more than glad to take young Buddie in hand and exert their "Candler" influence.

Florence's West End Institute was a girls' school, making Buddie's presence a novelty. He would laugh years later and claim that the reason he got along so well with the ladies was that he had gone to an all-girl school. Still, Buddie had to feel the pains of the banishment.

After Buddie finished his studies at Florence's school, he entered Emory College. His career there was marked by numerous pranks and escapades, and he was even expelled — twice.

Ever a prankster, one of Buddie's expulsions came from

an egregious offense — riding his bicycle on campus just as a faculty meeting was adjourning. His Uncle Warren, who was then president of Emory, promptly kicked him out. Buddie was readmitted only after Asa, Sr., interceded. This bicycle had been a topic of considerable discussion in letters between Buddie and his father. Asa, Sr., contended that Buddie and Howard needed to spend their time studying, not dreaming up frivolous things to buy. He would remind the boys that he had to work hard to provide them the privilege of an education. Nevertheless, Buddie got a bicycle. This is a pattern that repeats itself — both Howard and Buddie, but especially Buddie, had learned early how to manipulate their father and have their way about many things.

When he was older, Buddie loved to tell about the night some of the students filled the chapel with hay, thinking to avoid compulsory attendance the next day. Alas, no such luck. Uncle Warren stood on the chapel porch — out of the rain which had begun that morning — and conducted his service. Afterwards, he said he would not search for the culprits if all the boys would help remove the hay. He did indicate that he had a pretty good idea who was behind the incident.

In Oxford at that time there lived two elderly sisters who had never married. When new boys came to the campus, some upperclassmen would kindly offer to set them up with dates. Buddie would shake with laughter at the thought of a young, green country boy showing up at the sisters' house, expecting to find the young miss of his dreams, only to be greeted by the old spinster ladies. Buddie said the trick was done so often that the sisters were prepared with cookies and tea and would always invite the young man in for "tea and sympathy." The ladies appreciated the attention and took the joke good-naturedly.

Buddie must have had a thing about the chapel. Once he and some friends, including his cousin, William Beall Candler, decided it would be fun to take a goat up to the belfry. It turned out getting the goat up was the easy part. The critter refused to come down. It required much hay, apples, and coaxing to finally get that goat out of the chapel.

While Buddie's high jinks seem innocent by today's standards, it was upsetting for Warren as college president to have his nephew constantly in hot water. To make matters worse, Buddie did not act alone; he was great at getting a crowd involved. Once in awhile well-behaved Howard got roped in, as well.

Buddie finally went too far and got himself and Howard tossed out of Uncle Warren's house, where they had been living.

Despite all the controversy, Buddie was graduated from Emory in June 1899 when he was just eighteen years old. Asa, Sr., was anxious to get Buddie started in business. As usual, Asa turned to Howard for help with Buddie.

> June 8, 1899
>
> Buddie left this morning in the trap to attend Emory Commencement...Sister with a large party of girls goes down tomorrow. I want to be there when he graduates the 14th.
>
> If you have time to write him a letter on Sunday directing it to Oxford encouraging him, calling his attention to the fact that though he did not take first honor, that you believe he has taken a good education, and that he has every equipment necessary to being successful. &c. I have not decided yet what to do with him. Must decide positively next week.

Howard was in Kansas City, selling for The Coca-Cola Company and attending medical classes in the evenings. He had qualms about doing what his father had asked, but being Howard the Good, he complied.

Finished with his schooling, Buddie spent a week or so resting from his years of study. Then one morning at breakfast, his father told him to be at his office later that day. Young Asa dutifully appeared and was told by his father to prepare to leave for California to select sites for Coca-Cola plants. "But I don't know how," he protested.

Asa, Sr., slapped his desk with his hand, saying, "Never let me hear a son of mine say he can't do something he's asked to do. You'll go to California, and find sites for Coca-Cola plants!"

His protests not withstanding, Buddie was intrigued with the idea and was looking forward to this adventure. Although, once again, it is this child that is being sent as far away from home as possible. Even if Buddie didn't mind the distance, he wasn't above pointing out that he had not really lived with them for a long time when his parents wrote to say how much they would miss him.

July 10, 1899

> Dear Papa & Mama. I arrived here this morning after I had been delayed 36 hours in the desert in Nevada. I have just received your letter and I don't see why you are so lonesome without me for I have never been with you much in my life. I am not at all lonesome because I found such a hearty welcome for me from Sam. To tell the truth about it, I will tell you that I believe him to be the best cousin I have. I never was more charmed with any one than I am with him. I wish you could see our place it is simply fine. You could not improve on it if you were to try it is so convenient in every respect. We have been around to see some of the principle soda fountain men and I find them very friendly, so don't you think I will be lonely for I will not. Of course I will miss you but you know I cannot be with you always and I suppose I had just as well leave you now or never. You know I will always and at all times think of you and shall do just as I think you would like for me to if I were at home. I am just as much yours out here as I would be if I were at home and I expect to do and act as I would if you were by my side. Love to all and some one kiss my darling Mama and Papa for me. Your darling boy, Asa G. Candler, Jr.

California was a new frontier in 1899 when Buddie arrived, almost everyone there was new in town, so to speak. California was not "Yankee" nor was it steeped in old Confederacy lore; it was a breath of fresh air to this young Southerner. Most of the people who made the trek west were looking to make their fortune. The aristocratic Spanish families had been largely disfranchised and displaced by the westward-moving North Americans. It was a true melting pot.

Buddie had been sent to California not only to site Coca-Cola plants, but also to run the Los Angeles plant where his cousin, Samuel Charles Candler, a son of Congressman Milton Candler, had been in charge. Sam was older than Buddie and he originally had come to California because his young wife, the former Jane Porter of Savannah, had become ill with tuberculosis. They had been told that the weather in California would help her. His Uncle Asa had put Sam to work for the company and was hoping that Sam would show Buddie the ropes and get him fully introduced to life and work in California.

Sam certainly introduced young Buddie to life in sunny, Southern California. But, it wasn't quite what Uncle Asa had had in mind. Sam was charming, good-looking, and knew how to have a good time. He was a talented gambler. Young Sam would gamble on a variety of things like cards, dice, and most important of all, chess at which he excelled. He would became one of California's chess champions. Traditional work, such as his uncle provided, wasn't quite his cup of tea nor even Coca-Cola, for that matter.

Even Buddie quickly discovered that Sam wasn't the salesman that the other Coca-Cola men were, as evidenced by his letters to his brother Howard. This particular letter also confirms that Buddie already knew himself well enough to know that he would do what he pleased, that he was hardheaded — for example, if he loved a girl, no one could change his mind.

> 1899, Aug. 9: Buddie to Howard: "Your letter of the fourth was just received and I hasten to answer it. I would like to know how many times a week you write to The Coca Cola Company because I would like to find out how many times Sam should write to me. He has been out two weeks now and I have only received one telegram from him and in it he only said send me some money. Now don't that beat all, a traveling man out on the road and his nearest office does not know where he is. Between you and me I don't see how he can hold his place and continue in such a way because I see no reason why a company would keep a man

out on the road that was not doing any good. He must not be selling anything because if he did I would get the orders.

... You need not talk to me about Miss Nina for in the first place if I loved her so hard as you supposed no letters or advise from anyone would be of any good. I cannot do as you do about girls that is not my nature. I have to like a girl before I can have a good time and besides the girls out here are so much different than our girls back South that I don't care to have anything to do with them. You say to make all the girls think I love them. [This was written back in Howard's premarital, traveling salesman days.] I would never do that if I were to live always.

Your Loving Bro. A G Candler, Jr."

By spring 1900, Sam Candler had left The Coca-Cola Company, and Howard was on his way to California to help Buddie sell the family's product. The brothers seemed to get along together better now that they were far away from home and more dependent on each other. Assuredly they were anxious to have the California venture be a success. It would please their father. In all likelihood, this was the most carefree period in their lives. They were distanced from the scrutiny of their parents, earning their own money, which they could spend as they saw fit, and were engaged in a venture the success of which was measured in sales of syrup. This same spring, George E. "Pat" Patterson was hired to run the office. Business in California was growing, and the boys needed more help.

Both boys took trips out from Los Angeles to sell Coca-Cola. Howard was sent further afield while Buddie made short forays, returning to the plant to oversee the syrup production. It's obvious from Buddie's letters that Howard tended to want his orders filled quickly and could be rather high-handed in his requests. Howard had already been reprimanded by his father and Mr. Robinson back in Atlanta for similar requests the previous summer, but it would be up to Buddie to once again remind him that nothing happens instantly. It also appears that Howard would get depressed when business and sales weren't going as well as he wanted, and it was Buddie who cheered him on and encouraged him.

When one views The World of Coca-Cola Pavilion in

downtown Atlanta, or visits their corporate offices, or tours a modern bottling plant, it is nearly inconceivable that ninety-two years ago two brothers aged nineteen and twenty-one were stirring up batches of syrup, 150 to 300 gallons at a time, and peddling it from town to town in California. When not delivering the syrup, they handed out advertising fans, posters, and the like. They had youth and enthusiasm, an almost unbeatable combination. To anyone who knew them as older men, autocratic, aloof, and at times austere, it is hard to believe these eager fledglings ever existed. To those who were closest to them, from time to time, a glimmer of the boy that once was, would appear.

When not busy with Coca-Cola and its promotion, Buddie found time to investigate boats and the sea. Since early childhood he had been fascinated by water and the vessels that traveled on it. Perhaps this was a gene inherited from his long-ago ancestor, Mark Anthony, who signed on as a cabin boy at about age twelve and left his native Genoa, Italy, for life on the high seas. At any rate, Buddie earned his master's ticket (sea captain's license) while living in California. Even in old age, he could maneuver his boats to the dock with a sure and steady hand. His granddaughter, Nancy Candler Nutter, recalls, "He always told us that his grandmother, Martha Candler, had taken him to the seashore as a little lad. His first sight of the huge Atlantic Ocean so impressed him that he remained intrigued by it all his life long. After he came into his fortune, he had big boats and loved to ride up and down the Intracoastal Waterway or through the Panama Canal. He always took along a group of friends or relatives to share the trip with him."

Asa, Sr.'s, sons may have argued among themselves, but never with their father. His will, not theirs, prevailed. Howard and Buddie each developed his own style of dealing with decisions not to their liking. Howard usually pleaded ill health, which would panic his father into giving into his wishes. Buddie, on the other hand, told of some life-threatening experience, avoidable in the future if he were allowed to follow his own instincts, rather than his father's. It didn't always work. When Lucy Elizabeth Candler wanted her two older boys closer to home in Georgia, nothing could override their mother's pleas to her husband to bring them home. Asa, Sr., would have moved heaven and earth to please Lucy. Thus, the boys found themselves called home for what was ostensibly a vacation.

Once in Georgia, Buddie, who loved California and would have settled there, got the bad news. His father confessed, "Son, I've never lied to you before, but your mother missed you and wanted you home, so you can't return to California." Instead, Buddie soon found himself on his way to Hartwell, Georgia, to manage a cotton mill in which Asa, Sr. had invested some money.

The mill was a venture that Asa got into through his friendship with Mr. W.S. Witham. They had known each other through church and various Methodist organizations. Witham was a jovial, personable guy who was very popular in Atlanta. His wife was also a bubbly personality, and she and Lucy Candler got to be close friends. Mr. Witham was president of thirty small Georgia banks and also was the financial agent for eight small cotton mills, including his own Witham Cotton Mills located in Hartwell. Each of his financial organizations had separate charters and boards of directors.

In June of 1900, Witham talked Asa into investing in his cotton mills. Asa had agreed, thinking it would be a good business for Asa, Jr. It didn't bother Asa any more that Buddie had no training or knowledge of the cotton mill business than it had that he was unfamiliar with Coca-Cola plant sitings. All that mattered to Asa was to put his son in business in Georgia. Once again, Buddie was packed off to an out-of-the-way place, this time in the position of assistant secretary of Witham Cotton Mills.

Doing as he was told, Buddie gave up his dream of settling in California and headed to Hartwell. He arrived in style on September 4, 1900. Somewhere along the way, Buddie had acquired a Locomobile. He drove the machine to Hartwell on the red clay Georgia roads that ran north out of Atlanta. His arrival in a cloud of rust-colored dust, horn honking and brakes screeching, would be remembered for some years to come. (His grandson, Tommy Thompson, has been told that Buddie's was the first car ever seen in Hartwell.)

Buddie may have arrived in style, but this was a real change of lifestyle for him. Even Cartersville had been bigger than Hartwell, a small, rural, "one-train-a-day" town near the South Carolina line. Buddie didn't know anything about cotton, cotton mills, mill workers, or cotton futures. And, he didn't know anybody in town. It was a lonely situation, and he would be more than a little "homesick" for city life and friends.

Buddie set to work getting the mill organized. Witham Cotton Mills was in need of some hands-on management, since Mr. Witham was living in Atlanta and did not seem much interested in the actual management of the business. Buddie was responsible for rebuilding the factory and setting it back on its feet. To accomplish the needed construction, Buddie leased convicts from the state of Georgia. This was a typical arrangement for development projects and small factory-type operations in Georgia at the time. Asa, Sr., thought it dangerous, but at the same time felt that Buddie would set a good, Christian example to those under his influence. How much influence a twenty-year-old would have on a chain gang remains an interesting question. But, from this odd assortment of people, Buddie learned not only how to manage people of different backgrounds, he gained a lifelong friend, Landers Anderson.

As Buddie would tell it years later, if you leased convicts, it helped to have an informer among the men. The camp "spy" would report any trouble among the laborers and keep management apprised of possible uprisings or other problems. A tall black man, Landers Anderson, or "Brother Landrum," as he came to be called, was Buddie's camp spy. He'd report trouble so that Buddie could handle it before it blew up into a real problem. Brother Landrum was also the prisoners' cook and in a position to hear all the gossip.

Buddie and Brother Landrum developed a real rapport. They communicated well with one another and before long, Landrum was busy finding things he could handle for "Mr. Candler," other than cooking and spying. He was as much a character as Buddie.

Although Buddie was lonesome at first, Hartwell was a very small town and he soon found his way around. Like the rest of his family, he was a Methodist and quickly joined the local congregation.

It was in this church that Cupid let fly two of his magical arrows. For in the choir was a perfectly adorable, tiny (only four foot-ten), red-haired, blue-eyed soprano named Helen Arabella Magill. Young Buddie wasted no time in securing an introduction to this pretty miss, and with his usual flair for charming those he chose to charm, he was soon able to cut out his competition and have this little songbird all to himself. He would later tell his grandchildren about his "HMT" buggy. It was a two-seater and had a narrow front seat which put its occupants very close to each other; hence the name, HMT for "Hug-Me-Tight." This must have been the buggy he drove to court Miss Helen. No doubt Cupid's dart had hit her, too. Buddie was a "man-of-the-world" compared to other boys she knew, and he had "prospects." Why his salary at the mill was forty dollars a month, more than ample for two in those days.

Characteristically, once Buddie decided that he wanted to marry Helen, he told no one until they had set a date. They were young and headstrong, and no amount of counseling could persuade them to wait. After all, as Buddie had pointed out to Howard a year earlier, once his mind was made up, no one could change it.

By spring, determined to marry Helen, Buddie began to test his family's reaction to the idea. He started with his best ally, his sister Lucy.

May 3, 1901

My Dear Sister:
    Your sweet letter just received a few days ago and I thought I would write you to tell you I have been promoted and am now Secretary and Treasurer of the Mill. This is a very responsible place I am called upon to fill, handling other people's money and I must be very careful how I do it.
    I don't have as much time to think about going home as you do. I have too many other things that take my

attention elsewhere, besides I am here now to stay. There is no way to get me away except for the mill to go to pieces and if it were to do that my reputation would be lost, so I will have to make myself a little home up here and I intend to do it just as soon as I can. I am tired of boarding houses, having lived at them ever since I was eight years old. And besides you would like to have a sister. I cannot write much but you will take the will for the deed.

With much love, Yours, Asa Candler, Jr.

May 9, 1901

My Dear Sister:

Your sweet letter received a few days ago. Am sorry you take the position you do about me. There is no use in it. I will never be able to have a home with you all again and why not make me a home of my own. However, your advice will be of no use to me this time, for you are too late in giving it. Everything is now planned and I only wait for the day. It will be impossible for me to come home when you asked me to come. Now I am not saying this and mean to come, but I cannot come and that is all.

I wish I could be with you, but I cannot. I hope you will have a nice time at Emory.

With much love, I am your Devoted brother, Asa Candler, Jr.

May 14, 1901

My Dear Sister:

I received your sweet letter Monday and will write you now as I will not have any more time this week. I am going to tell you a secret. You must not tell it to anyone. Don't write it home for I am going down home on the 25th and I will tell it to Mama and Papa. And I want to be the one to tell it and not you...

But back to my original subject. You say you will stand by me. Now I am going to hold you to that. I may have to call on you to aid me. I hope not. We have been writing each other about marrying, well, I had long before I wrote you decided to do that thing and only wrote you to see what you would say before you knew I was going to be married. I am going to be married on June 12th and would like for you to come up here to see me and be with me when this happy time comes.

I will have to get me some clothes when I go to Atlanta. And you can now just consider yourself as having a sweet little sister that will love you real hard.

Write to your loving brother. Asa. Keep the above to yourself.

Helen's father, John Henry Magill, was the publisher of the local newspaper, the *Hartwell Sun*. Well-respected in his town and by his peers, J.H. Magill was a self-taught, self-made man. Born in South Carolina, the son of an Irish immigrant shoemaker, John had enlisted in the Confederate army at the ripe age of thirteen, quickly advancing from the rank of "drummer boy" to sergeant. Captured once and wounded twice, he found himself at the war's end with no home, no education, and no career. For next few years, he traveled through Georgia and Florida finding work with newspapers, doing a variety of odd jobs, and learning the business. His gift for gathering and writing the news was soon recognized. A group of men in Hartwell persuaded him to move there and start a newspaper for their town.

Magill managed not only to get a successful paper business going but also arranged to marry the local doctor's daughter, Laura Lepex Eberhardt. The Eberhardts were one of the more prominent families in town, and the connection was certainly useful to Magill's business. Laura's early death was a blow to John and all their children, but it was particularly hard on Helen, who had to take over running the household and caring for her brothers and sisters. Six years later, John married Miss Julia Dendy, an old friend of the family. The marriage came too late for Helen to re-enter school or catch up on those "carefree teen" years. She was no longer in charge at her father's home, and while she respected Miss Julia, she didn't want to live there any longer.

So you have two young people in the throes of youthful passion, neither one of whom felt they had a real home, old enough to marry, and both seeking someone with whom they could be number one.

From Buddie's letters to his sister, Lucy, it is apparent

that he had made up his mind to marry Helen and set up housekeeping. It is also apparent from other letters that his sister thought he was not ready to marry and shoulder the responsibilities it would bring. In addition, his father and mother weren't thrilled that he had picked out a girl they knew nothing about, a "country girl" as Asa, Sr., would refer to her in a letter to Howard. They were not able to get Asa, Jr., to change his mind, but they were able to persuade him to put the wedding off one month. That was long enough for his mother to make some arrangements for a party in the young couple's honor back home in Atlanta.

John Henry Magill must have had his own misgivings about his daughter's decision and preparedness for married life. He did not give the bride away, and it is not clear whether he and Julia were even at the ceremony. Buddie and Helen were married by Bishop Candler on July 16, 1901 at her uncle's home in Hartwell, Georgia. It was an elegant affair by any town's standards. The bride wore a simple dress of white *crepe de chine* over taffeta silk and carried a bouquet of white carnations and maidenhair ferns. Her only attendant was her young cousin, Helene Eberhardt, with her aunt standing as her matron of honor.

After a night spent at someone's home, the out-of-town guests plus the bride and groom took the train back to Atlanta where the newlyweds were subjected to a round of parties. Asa and Lucy entertained five hundred guests at their home complete with lanterns, festoons of flowers, vines, and ribbons, and topped off with a small orchestra— not your typical Southern reception of 1901. Judge and Mrs. John S. Candler held a small affair for one hundred guests at their home in Edgewood. In all, there were at least five large parties in Atlanta. Helen got her money's worth out of her wedding gown, but it wasn't a very romantic honeymoon.

The young couple returned to Hartwell to set up house-keeping. In his father's eyes, Buddie was now a "man." He was settled. He had real responsibilities, the mill, a wife, and (in no time at all it seemed) a baby on the way. He was doing it like Asa, Sr., had.

Buddie's mother, Lucy, was thrilled at the prospect of

being a grandmother. With her youngest, William, already eleven, a new baby would be such a delight. She began to make plans and was secretly pleased to learn in the fall that Helen's uncle, the only doctor in Hartwell, was moving to Texas. Well, of course, that meant that Helen would just have to come to Atlanta to have the baby. The baby wasn't due until June, but an accident intervened that would have a profound effect on the young couple and a ripple effect on the rest of the family.

The baby would be named Lucy and become the third Lucy in the family. Buddie — in one stroke — named his daughter after both his mother and his sister.

Mettelen Thompson Moore, the daughter of Lucy III, tells the story of the accident. "There was a cat that lived out in the barn. It was in February, so my grandmother, Helen Magill, brought the cat in by the fireplace because it had kittens, and she was sitting there watching the kittens play in front of the fireplace. They had just been born, so their eyes weren't open yet, and one of them got too close to the fire. She went to move it back but the kitten stepped on a hot coal, went mad with pain, and bit her on the hand.

"Later, the bite got very infected. That's what caused them to take the baby premature [almost three months premature]. They didn't think the baby was going to live. This was in March.

"Mother was born premature and very low weight. Danny [the grandchildren's nickname for Lucy, Asa's wife] just took her and laid her down in the other bedroom. Dr. Hurt was so busy working on Helen to make sure she would live and wouldn't bleed to death. They had to keep the baby warm. Danny had read that motion was good for a baby. She was caring for the baby all this time and cleaning it up and whatnot. She told Brother Landrum to go out to the chicken yard and get the egg incubator.

"It was an old-fashioned incubator on rockers that you kept heated with hot water. So Brother Landrum got that and cleaned it with alcohol. And then in went batting, which was like a cheesecloth,. He lined the oval-shaped inside with that. The outside circle, that's where they put the hot water.

"He did that and then took wet towels and put them

around that outside opening, and Danny said she would sit in front of the fire in a rocking chair and tend this incubator. It was on rockers, because you keep eggs moving also. She said she would sit there and rock this until her legs would be blistered from the heat. She would keep Landrum stoking the fireplace and keep rocking this incubator right in front of the fire.

"The fire on those hot towels would have the moisture you needed — as an incubator has moisture plus the heat. And he would pour hot water on these towels periodically. She sat there for days doing this. They fed the baby Coca-Cola with a dropper. That's the reason she was alive. There was no milk to speak of, women don't produce real milk the first day or so after birth, the baby just needed liquid. Helen never was able to nurse her, however. She had what is called childbed fever.

"After three or four days, PaPa went out and bought a goat. Landrum would milk that goat and then Danny would feed her. Helen was too deathly ill to nurse her.

"Somewhere in a New York journal, mother told me that Dr. Hurt wrote an article about this, and it became the first incubator for a baby in the South. It was a miracle that mother lived."

This cat bite incident left such an impression on the whole family that, years later, Buddie's brother Walter would not have cats on his place. Other Candlers developed an obsession on the subject of cats and would not have them around. Helen never really recovered from this difficult breech birth. She would go on to have twelve pregnancies, seven live births, and numerous health problems. But essentially, Buddie was going to find himself at a young age with a frail wife. This colored his behavior in the coming years. He was healthy, robust, and lively — and she wasn't.

Lucy Magill Candler, as the first grandchild, quickly became the apple of her grandparents' eyes. They doted on her, Lucy Elizabeth in particular. The little girl in learning to talk, couldn't say Granny, but instead struggled out a "Danny," and Lucy, once Lizzie, was forever afterward... Danny.

Meanwhile, Lucy III was raised on Coca-Cola literally.

She drank milk or Coca-Cola, but never coffee or tea. When she went away to school, she asked for and received special dispensation to bring Coca-Cola syrup with her to her posh finishing school, National Park Seminary in Washington, D.C.

It shouldn't be forgotten that at the time of Lucy III's birth in 1902, Coca-Cola still contained cocaine, but it also had more nutritional value than Coca-Cola does today. So, putting the narcotic aspects aside, it probably was not a bad choice in helping a premature baby survive. On the other hand, little Lucy's preference for Coca-Cola no doubt had more than a little component of addiction.

Things were not going well at the Witham Cotton Mills. Buddie had not been pleased with the situation he had found at the mill when he arrived in Hartwell in 1900. By early 1901, the situation was deteriorating. He was able to put the operation on the right track and gotten the daily management of the mill in good shape. However, Mr. Witham was handling the sale of the cotton. Witham by nature was a glad-hander. Affable and fun to be with, he was a gambler who was slick with his numbers. Witham much preferred the gambling side of the venture — the trips to New York to buy and sell cotton for the mill's account, which ultimately resulted in substantial losses. Asa, Sr., was blinded by the fact that he liked Witham and felt assured the business could be righted. In the end, it would fail.

The mill came to a disappointing finish when it was sold in December, 1910, to J.M. Geer of South Carolina for fifty thousand dollars. This was fifteen thousand less than Asa, Sr., had paid for it and was one of his few losing investments.

Buddie and Helen stayed in Hartwell until 1905. By then, he and his father had begun to invest in real estate, and it was in this field that Buddie found his niche.

Early on Buddie had shown a keen interest in real estate. Like his father, he enjoyed envisioning future uses of property and liked the give and take of the world of real estate development. He had a background in civil engineering thanks to his years at Emory, plus he had learned surveying in Cartersville. Asa was enthusiastic about his real estate ventures, and his naturally gregarious son was a good choice to send to meet potential lessors, lessees, buyers, and sellers. Buddie was tired of life in Hartwell anyway, so Asa brought him home to Atlanta to run the family's real estate division.

In the following years, Asa would acquire more and more real estate using the surplus funds of The Coca-Cola Company. When the income tax laws forced the company to divest itself of the holdings not related to Coca-Cola business, he formed Asa G. Candler, Inc., as a holding company to develop and manage real property investments. Asa established the corporation in 1917 with forty pieces of choice real estate as its initial assets. As with most of Asa Candler's companies, Howard was elected president even though he was also president of Coca-Cola. Buddie was elected vice-president and put in charge of actually running the new company for the family. This corporation would include not only all the real estate located in Atlanta, but also the Candler buildings scattered around the United States. Buddie would soon find himself traveling the country to oversee the financing, building, and management of these various ventures of his father. He began to hit his stride in a field that he enjoyed.

Asa had another real estate venture that fascinated him. In May, 1908, he bought out the holdings of the Kirkwood Land Company. Asa and his syndicate paid $500,000 for the property and the newspapers went wild with the report; this purchase was the largest real estate sale ever recorded for the southern states up until that time. In June, 1908, the Druid Hills Corporation was chartered. Asa, the principal stockholder, was named president. This elegant Atlanta neighborhood soon ceased to be a fantastic dream and became a reality. With Asa and Coca-Cola backing it, the master plan designed by the widely known landscape architects, Olmsted Brothers, of Massachusetts, was quickly developed. The beautiful rolling and wooded lots began to sell before the improvements could be completed. By 1910, important Atlantans were moving to Druid Hills.

Asa Candler, Sr. would remain president of the corporation until 1926 when Buddie was elected to take over the position. This was only one company of two where Howard wasn't automatically made the president.

There were many sides to Buddie. For one thing, he could be softhearted and quite capable of taking the "underdog's" side. It was whispered in the family that during the early part of the 1900's, Buddie spent a good bit of his money paying to rescue Jews from the pogroms in Russia. No one has ever said why this man, at this time, given his background, would choose to do this. But his descendants have said that it fit in with his character. He did not like seeing the "little guy" being picked on (unless he was the one doing the picking). To him, altruism would have had much less to do with helping the Jews than the sheer satisfaction of beating a government of thugs. For him it may have been as much a game or an experiment as a cause. He was always willing to try anything new or different, and his colorful exploits brought his family much enjoyment and embarrassment over the years.

An interesting footnote to the history of the Druid Hills development occurred in July, 1910. Atlanta had just a few short years before experienced the horror of the lynching of Leo Frank and had been brought face to face with anti-semitism. Asa, Sr., probably never met a Jew prior to his arrival in Atlanta. His letters indicate almost a curiosity with these "chosen people of God." He does not appear to shun or dislike them, but just expresses an innocent curiosity.

While Coca-Cola was involved in the federal case in Chattanooga, Asa was always reminding Howard and Johnnie to let Harold Hirsch, one of the company's lawyers who was Jewish, know how very pleased he was with Harold's work. It is almost as though he was worried that Harold might not feel completely included on the team by the gentiles with whom he was now associated.

Harold was also one of the incorporators of Druid Hills. In July 1910, the stockholders voted (with one individual opposed — this person was bought out by the Candlers shortly afterwards) that "no offer on any lot in Druid Hills

shall be refused solely on the ground that the prospective
purchaser is a Jew." Excluding Jews had been a practice of
residential developments for years throughout the United
States and was practiced with greater diligence in the North
than in the South. In making this decision, Asa and his
partners were departing from the norm; they were also
insuring increased sales to a very prosperous, cultured, and
educated segment of Atlanta's population.

Of course, Buddie was very much in favor of this action.
He had already begun his surreptitious moves on behalf of
Russian Jews. It is not known whether he was motivated
originally by his father's interest and concern for the Jews
that they knew personally, men like Harold Hirsch, or
whether Buddie's interest came from his association with
fellows in New York like Maurice Schotland and Charles
Goldsmith. Over the next forty years, both Mr. Schotland, a
furrier, and Mr. Goldsmith, a jeweler, would become Buddie's
close business and personal friends.

The other company that Asa formed and made Buddie
president of was created as an outlet for both Asa, Sr., and
Asa, Jr.'s, enthusiasm for their automobile hobbies. For all
of his "old fogyism" regarding Howard's purchase of a
Locomobile in 1902, Asa, like his sons, had really fallen in
love with the automobile.

Buddie shared with his father a love for gadgets and new
inventions. He enjoyed the speed and the possibilities that
the automobile represented. At Buddie's urging, Asa decided to develop a racetrack for automobiles. In August,
1909, they purchased three hundred acres in Hapeville,
Georgia, just ten miles out of Atlanta, which Buddie had
located and optioned. The tract cost $77,674.28.

Next, they formed a stock company called the Atlanta
Automobile Association (AAA) with Buddie as president and
Edward M. Durant, secretary. The investors of AAA were an
enthusiastic bunch of many of Atlanta's business and social
elite. They spent more than $400,000 to build a lavish
racetrack similar to the Indianapolis Speedway. A "rush" job
was undertaken by Nichols construction company, which
completed the development in time for the opening events

held in November 1909. It was called the Atlanta Speedway. Atlanta's mayor, Robert F. Maddox and Chamber of Commerce President, Asa G. Candler, Sr., made speeches welcoming the guests and the automobile show to Atlanta.

This was the first such show held in the South. The city was filled with automobile enthusiasts; the papers were full of articles about the show and the racetrack. Atlanta had automobile fever. The races went on daily for a week. Famous drivers were featured including Barney Oldfield, Louis Strang, Lee Lorimer, Charles Basle, and Louis Chevrolet (after whom the Chevrolet car was named).

To help promote the events, Buddie staged a race between his son, four-year-old John H. Candler, driving Buddie's Pope-Toledo and Barney Oldfield. John won. The adults tied the steering wheel down, placed a board against the gas pedal, and showed John how to stop it. It was a great week and everyone had fun, even Buddie, although his beautiful Pope-Toledo, nicknamed the "Merry Widow," did burn when its gas tank exploded while being driven by a racer. Fortunately, no one was hurt.

Unfortunately for the investors, the enthusiasm generated by the automobile show was not reflected in the receipts collected at the gate. In addition, Edward Durant had a falling out with Barney Oldfield and his agents as well as Buddie. The speedway closed after its first season and attempts to revive it failed. Consequently, Asa Candler did what he usually did when one of his incorporated ventures did not work out as expected. He foreclosed on the land. Quite a few prominent folks lost their investment in this highly speculative venture. This was seen by some as another example of Asa, Sr., and Asa, Jr.'s, shrewd operating methods. It was then, and is now, a typical method of raising capital for a risky venture. But some of Atlanta's high society types weren't too happy about their loss.

The property was leased the following year as a site for Atlanta's first aerial exhibitions, with Buddie the chief judge. This event would begin his fascination with airplanes and flying. It would also be Atlanta's first step towards becoming a regional air center. Ultimately the city would purchase Candler Field, as it came to be known. Today it is the site of Atlanta's very busy Hartsfield International Airport.

Buddie and Helen were thrilled and so was Asa, Sr., when in June, 1904, they greeted the healthy arrival of a son, named Asa Griggs Candler, III. The patriarch was truly delighted with the "boy" as he would refer to the little fellow. He was a good baby, full-term, mellow in disposition, bright-eyed, and much adored by his parents and grandparents. Then, tragedy struck.

In February, 1905, baby Asa developed what seemed to be a cold but quickly became what has been termed "galloping pneumonia." He was dead before anything could be done for him.

The first news Asa and Lucy had of this tragedy was when they saw Buddie coming up the walk of Callan Castle carrying the dead baby followed by Helen and little Lucy. The young parents had been unable to contact the family because an ice storm had cut off all lines of communication.

Joe Willard, one of Asa's nephews, in a letter to Howard in 1950 relates one of his most touching memories of how the old man reacted to the death of his grandson. "Your father told me of this one day and with tears on his cheeks said, 'I thought my heart would break when I saw my boy coming up the walk with his little baby in his arms.' In all these years, I have come upon no incident that touched me so deeply. The entire family was devastated."

Asa grieved over the death of his little namesake. In family photographs taken after the baby's death, he always included a portrait of the dead child.

Baby Asa III's, unexpected death was the first of a series of medical tragedies that would strike the Candler family over the next fourteen years. Until the discovery of the sulfa drugs and penicillin, there was little a physician could do with rampant infections but ease the pain and stand by waiting for nature to heal.

As he did with all tragedy, Buddie resolutely marched forward. He must have felt as King David did after the death of Bathsheba's son. He had grieved, but life moves on and so must he.

Nine months after Asa III's death, another son was born to Buddie and Helen. He filled a tremendous void for his grieving parents. This boy would become the child on whom both his parents depended, just as his Uncle Howard was for his grandfather. Buddie wanted to name this baby Asa III, also. Helen would not hear of it. She gently reminded him that their little Asa was dead, and this child should have his own name. And so he became John Howard Candler after his maternal grandfather, John Magill, and his Grandmother Candler's people.

Over the next few years, Buddie's business responsibilities increased as did his family. After the birth of John in December of 1905, Helen and Buddie continued to have children at rather frequent intervals with a few miscarriages in between. Laura arrived on Christmas Eve 1907. August 1911 brought a big surprise — twin girls, Martha and Helen II. Buddie was so taken aback by Dr. Hurt's announcement of twins, that according to the cook, he went to the basement and got drunk. Their last child, Samuel was born in November 1914. By this time, Helen's health was truly too frail to withstand any more births.

Helen's continuing sickness impinged greatly on her ability to shape the development of her later children in a positive way. They all had the exuberant Candler personalities and access to their father's money. Buddie's style of parenting included being generous with his money to the point of being excessive. He anticipated their desires before they had a chance to really express them. He gave them things before they even thought about wanting them. They had everything and little or no sense of responsibility for it.

John in his diaries describes a lifestyle not unlike the Great Gatsby — of having his own car, driving around with Howard, Jr., riding horseback through Druid Hills, flying to glee club concerts, and much more. He was multi-talented and yet inconsistent. He would do well at everything and yet not complete any one thing. Laura and Lucy, the two older girls, are the ones who got the benefit of their mother's training.

In contrast to Buddie's openhanded, mercurial, very inconsistent parenting, Helen was strict. Several of her

Candler nieces would later say that she came across as stern. Helen had to be stern; she was fighting an uphill battle. Her spouse encouraged her children to act like they were in a sideshow, and they had a genetic bent towards the theatrical, promotion, and a streak of showmanship. Not only was their Grandpa a master at promoting himself and his wares, but the Magills had a gift of the "blarney" as well.

Buddie encouraged his children to be eccentric or different. Their naturally creative and theatrical tendencies were encouraged, perhaps to their detriment, by him. All of the children had some musical ability. Laura, like her mother, would have a trained voice, Helen could play by ear, John was a trained tenor and played several instruments. They were all constantly "on stage."

Helen, on the other hand, was always trying to temper this. A gracious hostess and soft-spoken Southern lady, she tried to guide her children's development and instill in them a sense of quiet dignity and decorum. She was trying to ground her children with basic Southern values. She had grown up among small-town Southern society and would have liked for her children to have this same outlook. She found excessive publicity and ostentatious lifestyles offensive. She was so reserved and modest that it contributed to her early death. Helen adored Buddie but couldn't control him; perhaps she never understood him. Her daughters said that Helen admired Asa, Sr., but didn't understand him, either.

Helen Magill Candler would have her hands full with a houseful of little Candlers. With no living mother and living in her husband's peoples' hometown, she was without a strong base of her own. Unlike Howard's wife Flora, who had her own family and friends in Atlanta, Helen was dependent upon her in-laws and somewhat overpowered by them. They were kind yet, on occasion, overbearing. Asa and Lucy felt that Helen lacked maternal skills and that she was not the organized housekeeper that she should have been. This was quite an insult to a young mother who had essentially been keeping a house since she was twelve years old.

The feeling within the family was that Buddie had married someone not of their standing. Helen had been denied by fate a formal education and had to suffer comparisons with Flora who was a college graduate and Lucy Elizabeth who, while she had not finished her course of study, she had at least gone to college for awhile.

Helen's life in Atlanta was not easy. She was not close to her stepmother or her father. Besides, they had children who were contemporaries of Helen and Buddie's children. In 1913, Buddie moved J.H. and Julia Magill and their children to Atlanta. He purchased a home for them on Boulevard and helped support this family.

Helen suffered a great personal loss in 1923 when both her father and her sister, Lucille Magill Crawford, died the same week. Afterwards, her remaining siblings went in different directions, not all of them activities that fit Helen's sense of propriety.

Hartwell's small-town society had suited Helen. She had been active in her church's programs, particularly its choir where she had played a prominent part. She was also a charter member of Hartwell's chapter of the United Daughters of the Confederacy. Her family had some prominence there and she must have felt like an outsider in Atlanta's more sophisticated society. In time, Helen found her niche and adjusted to being one of Asa Candler's daughters-in-law.

Lucy Elizabeth Candler probably didn't consider herself a meddling mother-in-law, but Helen, for one, found Danny interfering. To Danny's way of thinking, however, she was concerned for her children's and grandchildren's welfare and could afford to indulge them if she so chose.

Her two oldest granddaughters, and namesakes, Lucy Magill Candler and Elizabeth Candler Owens, were her pets. They could get most anything by asking Danny, and in at least one case young Lucy III tried to override her mother's refusal by going to her grandmother.

According to Mettelen Thompson Moore, Lucy III's daughter, and corroborated by all the family members who have heard her tell this tale on herself, the saga of the plumed hat went like this:

"One day Mama and I were in town to do some shopping. As we passed an exclusive hat shop I noticed a particularly striking purple hat festooned with black plumes which were quite the fashion that year. So I told Mama I'd like to buy the hat. 'No indeed, you may not have that hat,' she said. 'It is entirely too ostentatious and showy for a girl your age.'

"Well, this wasn't the answer I wanted so later I told Danny about the hat, and the next thing I knew, she had sent the chauffeur to town to pick [it] up... Of course, Mama was furious. She caught me preening myself in front of the mirror and told me, 'Take that hat off your head. I said you could not have it.' 'But Danny gave it to me.' 'I told you no, and I meant no. You may have the hat, but you may not wear it.' 'But, Mama, it's from Danny...' She said, 'No, you will never put it on your head and go out of this house.' And I didn't. I kept that hat in a hat box on the top shelf of my closet for years. Do you know I never did wear that hat? I just couldn't."

Evidently when Helen wanted her way she could be very strong.

Danny was just delighted with her grandchildren and loved having them near her. She had a dollhouse out back especially for Lucy and Elizabeth and her other little granddaughters to play in. She could get quite put out with her daughters-in-law if she felt that she was not getting to spend enough time with her grandchildren. If Flora and Howard's children were over at the Glenns more than at the Candlers, Danny would be miffed. Danny ruled the roost.

On one occasion, she phoned Helen and asked in her deep voice, "Helen, do you know where Laura is?" and Helen said, "Oh, she's outdoors playing." Lucy Elizabeth replied, "She's up here in my yard." Laura had walked up to Callan Castle, several blocks away, and crossed the street to play in the dollhouse. What made this so scary to her grandmother and her mother was that she was just about two and a half years old and had wandered off without anyone noticing.

Buddie was enthusiastic about the Druid Hills purchase. He was also a little tired of life in town. In 1910, he purchased a fifty-acre acre tract of land from his father, located along what was then Williams Mill Road. That year he moved his family out to Briarcliff Farm. It was a working farm at the time of his purchase and he continued to keep it as such. One of his little sidelines was a chicken and egg delivery business. Buddie began assembling the largest and most unusual collection of chickens ever seen in the South. In addition to the chickens, he had pigs, cows, sheep, horses, and greenhouses. Buddie also kept the basement stocked with the everything he needed to mix up both ice cream and Coca-Cola for his big family.

Druid Hills was in the country when the young Candlers moved out there from their home in Inman Park. There were no public schools for the children to attend so they were sent into town to Washington Seminary, a fashionable girls' school on Peachtree Street. The school had been started after the War Between the States by two sisters and their niece had continued the school after her aunts died. Typical of Buddie, his son John, attended the school along with his sisters. As Buddie put it, "Miss Emma, you've got all these girls of mine, and you're just going to have to take John, too. I don't have anywhere else to send him." Miss Emma, a friend of Helen's, agreed.

The house Buddie and Helen moved into was a rambling farm-style home which suited a large, rural-based family, but wasn't exactly up to modern standards. Buddie found himself doing quite a bit of remodeling, not just because he had promised Helen, but because his "little Candlers" kept making it a necessity.

Nancy Candler Nutter explains, "This is one of Daddy's stories... He said, 'Lop [Buddie's daughter Laura Chambers] and I were playing doctor and nurse one time. So we started a fire in the vestibule to warm the water for the baby. In the front hall.'"

Laura Chambers adds, "Let me correct that. We did it in the back hall in the toilet. We would call it the ladies' room. Up under the steps, now mind you. This wasn't Briarcliff, but it was the other house there. It was not the one you know now. One of the servants smelled this smoke and wondered what it was."

They quickly put it out, but there was remodeling work for Buddie to do. Nor was that the only fire set by his children.

Mettelen Thompson Moore, Lucy III's daughter, has a

tale to tell about the second fire. "The twins were as mischievous as could be. One cold, rainy day, they had to play inside.
They decided to go into the storage room, which was just off
the hallway. Landrum kept firewood in there so it would be
dry when he used it to stoke the fire. There was no light in
this room when the door was closed. The girls got a lantern,
lit it, and were playing with dolls. Something got too close to
the lantern and caught fire. Frightened, the twins ran out of
the room and left the door open. Fortunately, Landrum
happened by, smelled the smoke, and called the fire department. Before they could get there, he had put out the fire.
This near-disaster scared Helen nearly to death. The twins
meant no harm; they were only playing and having a good
time."

While Buddie ran Briarcliff as a farm, he expanded it
into something a little more spectacular than your average
farm. In addition to the usual produce and animals, Buddie
did his farming on a big scale. He raised sheep. He kept pigs.
He had milk cows, and during World War I, he had a contract
to supply Fort Gordon with milk. Many times he loved to
relate stories of how he, Brother Landrum, and his son John,
would have to milk the cows and then deliver the milk when
the regular help didn't show up for work. In addition, he kept
those chickens. In fact, chickens quickly became a hobby
with Buddie.

A newspaper clipping from the early 1900s bears this
out, saying that Buddie's exhibit at the Alabama State Fair
in Birmingham was a good one.

> ...Candler's exhibit stood out prominently by reason of
> its size, completeness and uniform excellence. Where
> other contestants and exhibitors were content with showing
> a few pens, Mr. Candler entered a solid carload of fine
> chickens and the name of his mammoth poultry plant,
> Briarcliff Farm, was in evidence from the time one entered
> the hall until leaving. The Blue Orpingtons have never
> before been shown in the south, and the Diamond Jubilee
> Orpingtons are likewise a rarity. The foundation stock of
> these breeds was secured in England by Mr. Candler, who
> made a special trip to London for that purpose. The birds
> shown were immensely valuable and for some of the single

birds Mr. Candler has received and refused offers of more
than $2,000. Many other breeds were also shown by Mr.
Candler, including the White Buff and Black Orpingtons,
Leghorns, Lakenfelders, Anacona, Campines and
Ornamental Bantams of every conceivable variety.

By 1916, the house known as "Briarcliff Farm" had
become too small and no longer suited Buddie's tastes nor
reflected his much larger income. He rented a house across
the road for his family and proceeded to raze the farmhouse.
He hired architects, C.E. Frazier of Columbia, South Carolina, and Dan Bodin of Pittsburgh, Pennsylvania, to design
and build his new home. Briarcliff, completed in 1920, was
a twenty-two-room antebellum style-home complete with a
ballroom on the third floor. The elegant estate featured an
exterior of buff-colored brick with carved stone quoins at
each corner sitting on a rough granite base. The interior had
beautiful woodwork and carvings throughout, pegged wooden
floors, and massive fireplaces of carved Georgia marble.
Elaborate greenhouses were built to the rear of the building
where both Helen and Buddie could enjoy their gardening
hobbies. He raised prized orchids and she, unusual roses. It
was a grand home, the epitome of Southern elegance.

Buddie was a man of many hobbies, not only chickens
and orchids. He seemed always in search of things with
which to engage himself. According to granddaughter Nancy
Candler Nutter, "Asa, Jr., liked new inventions, gadgets,
magic, flowers, travel. He loved the ocean and kept a boat,
yacht that is, at some nearby body of water most of the time.
He developed the Savannah Marina [Thunderbolt Basin]
and had two boats which burned at the dock there; the
*Martha* and the *Helasa*. He had boats he kept at Panama
City, Florida. I accompanied him to Panama City to present
a trophy following a regatta in 1951.

"When anything new came out, he bought one. When the
first movie cameras were made available to the public, he
bought one and made movies of his many trips. He was
fascinated with the gadget and would film such things as the
wake his boat made as he sailed down the Intracoastal
Waterway. He and Landrum would set these home movies

up, and it was Landrum's job to run the movie projector and to help make the movies. When radio came along, PaPa bought a crystal set and spent hours in the attic listening to this radio; he was very dexterous and could take the radio apart and reassemble it."

This same dexterity led him to magic. Buddie arranged to meet and get to know Houdini, from whom he learned several tricks. He would do these tricks for the rest of his life. His grandson Tommy Thompson recalls that "PaPa was in the Society of Magicians or something like that. They'd put on a show and he'd participate. He had quite a few card tricks. A lot of people didn't realize how talented he was, but he had some card tricks that he would perform like a master. He entertained us. I'd always sit there, and he'd do a trick, and I would ask him how he did that, and he would say, 'Nope, nope, don't ever tell anybody how you do a trick. Nope.' And he'd do it again and he'd get through and I'd say, 'PaPa, I don't believe you did that.' He'd say, 'Yep, yep.' I'd say, 'Well, tell me how you did it.' 'Nope, nope, I won't tell.' And he'd be laughing and his stomach would be going."

Buddie had learned the tricks from Houdini with the promise to the master magician that he would never divulge them, and he never did. The other magician that Buddie knew well and admired was Howard Thurston, who was famous as a card manipulator and also for his large stage illusions such as the "floating lady." It was from Thurston that Buddie learned and purchased some of the illusion acts which he proceeded to perform — usually using his daughters, Helen and Martha, as his assistants. Buddie kept these elaborate magic boxes stored in the ballroom on the third floor of Briarcliff. He could cut a person in two or make them disappear and then return whole, plus many other tricks. Many of her cousins, still remember Martha being "cut in two" because she would play the part of being cut apart with real feeling.

"PaPa had an auto early, one of the first in Atlanta," Nancy Candler Nutter said. "He liked to drive in the middle of the road blowing his horn.

"In the 1920s, PaPa took Aunt Lucy and some of her school chums down to Miami on his boat. While they were sunning on the deck a plane flew over that offered rides to the public. PaPa said, 'That looks like fun.' Grandmother Helen replied, 'Oh, no. That would be dangerous.' A little while later, PaPa decided he needed to go to town on some errands and asked if the girls wanted to tag along; they mostly did. A little while after that, the plane comes buzzing overhead again with PaPa and the girls hanging out of the cockpit waving. This was before he owned his own plane.

"Of course, it was not long before Buddie purchased an airplane and hired Beeler Blevins to be his pilot. He and Beeler would then travel everywhere. Buddie quickly realized that being the quickest way to get from one point to another, flying was the wave of the future and he wanted to be involved in it. So he bought a plane for himself, one for his son, John, and later, another for his daughter, Martha. Buddie never learned to fly himself, however, Beeler Blevins taught both John and Martha to pilot their planes." Tragically, Beeler died in an automobile accident on May 24, 1934.

While Buddie was having a good time being Buddie, Helen was under a great deal of stress. She was not even–tempered and could fly off the handle at the slightest provocation. According to her daughter Lucy, Helen had a very mercurial personality. As the years progressed, she had more and more troubles to keep her anxious. Lucy would later say that her mother would get so blue that only one person could cheer her up and that was her son John. Like his father, he could sing, tell jokes or stories, and entertain her until she would laugh. But no amount of jokes and laughter could dispel the cloud that hung over the household at Briarcliff.

Buddie had married to have a home and to be number one with someone. Instead, he found himself saddled with a sick wife, a half-dozen children, and a position at work where he would always be second to either his father or his brother. He did have a great talent for real estate development and also for turning around small companies in trouble. He began to acquire properties for himself and to purchase undercapitalized companies that he could restructure and then resell. These businesses were his; he didn't have to discuss decisions made about them with anyone else. Before long, Buddie was traveling so much that he and Helen led different lives.

Never robust, Helen's health continued to fail. Taking care of her large family and overseeing Briarcliff took most of her energy and time. When she was able, she participated in activities at her church and with projects of the United Daughters of the Confederacy. She and Buddie travelled to New York City for vacations, as well as to Florida. He especially liked Florida, and thought it would be a good place for her. In the late teens and early twenties, they sailed to Cuba with the Charles Goldsmiths and other business friends of Buddie's. Helen preferred the mountains of Western North Carolina and vacationed there in the summers for several weeks at a time, often taking one or two of her daughters with her.

Buddie's behavior was becoming more difficult and eccentric than it had been in his childhood. He had always lived differently from the rest of the family, and now it was getting out of hand. In addition, he was drinking a lot. Asa G. Candler, Sr., was a staunch teetotaler. He disapproved of the use of liquor for anything other than medicinal purposes. He also disapproved of the use of tobacco, although even his dutiful son Howard would smoke cigarettes. But Buddie! Buddie smoked *and* drank.

Two things happened in 1919 that contributed to the onset of his heavy drinking.

First, the government decided to enact Prohibition, and that flew against everything Buddie Candler believed in. He did not feel that government should be involved in the personal lives of its citizens. He was heard to remark that he would do as he pleased; the government couldn't tell him what he could drink any more than it could tell him what he could eat.

The second and far more disturbing event in his life was the death of his mother, Lucy Elizabeth, that February. Buddie had loved his mother, but he had never really had her time or attention as he needed it. Now she was gone, and there was no chance to make amends, to create an understanding, nothing. He began to drink more.

Helen and Buddie would argue about the drinking. She was hurt and embarrassed by the displays he made of himself. She didn't want the children exposed to it, yet there he was at home, drunk. He didn't want to hear about it from her or anyone else. Buddie would get drunk and then, he'd sober up and be his same sweet self. Sober he was a lot of fun and a good businessman, drunk he could still be fun, but he was totally unreliable. They had their happy times, but the shadow of his drinking, coupled with her frail health, loomed over them. As the 1920s progressed, Buddie became more eccentric and drank more. He increasingly spent time on his boats and his private railroad car. And the parade of female companions began.

His older children were very much aware of the situation. Helen was bitterly hurt and unable to deal with it alone. She was beginning to waste away before their eyes. Their children decided to seek help and to try to make their father come to his senses. Buddie and Howard were already arguing vehemently about the drinking and the blatant affairs, in addition to their disagreements about the family businesses. They knew that Howard would not have any influence over Buddie, as the feelings there were too strong; instead, they called in the two people they felt he would listen to, his father, Asa, Sr., and their uncle, William Candler (Uncle Wittie).

John Howard Candler hinted at these growing problems his diary.

> Jan. 11, 1924: (from JHC's diary) Then we had a family discussion again about Liquor. There has to be a change soon we decided. "Man the Life-Boats there's reefs ahead."

> Feb. 18, 1926: Back in school after being out these two days. Mama, Lucy, and I talked to Uncle William tonight concerning Papa. Something must be done to relieve present situation.

> Feb. 19, 1926: Missed 8:00 o'clock class today. Went to Uncle William's office and nothing was accomplished. To show with Ed. I shall give them until tomorrow and then I get busy.

Feb. 26, 1926: Made 8:00 class today. Was called home by
Mama saying Papa had left us definitely. Went to basketball
tourney meet this afternoon. Dance tonight.

Feb. 28, 1926: Up about 10 o'clock. Grandpa came out and
discussed problem. Nothing accomplished. Over to Witties.
Took Mama to ride to Smyrna—home—started Eurights
novel.

Lucy and John worried about both their parents and
were furious with their father for his apparent neglect of
their mother's feelings. What had begun in the late teens as
a problem, was by the early 1920s a near-desperate situation in the minds of the eldest children. John was following
his father at night to find out where he went and with whom.
Buddie's drinking was bad enough but to couple it with
blatant womanizing so that Helen had to hear about it was
too much.

Buddie was seen all over town with women, but by late
1925, early 1926, it was one woman in particular. Buddie
began keeping company with his secretary of many years,
Miss Florence Stephenson. The rumors spread like wildfire.

Buddie's cousin, Caroline Candler Hunt, has unpleasant memories of this period. "He never thought anything
about being drunk. And I can remember being horrified. We
all had season tickets to the opera concerts in Atlanta. And
he would come to the concerts just as drunk as a hoot owl. He
was never embarrassed. Nothing embarrassed him.

"But Bud's drinking bothered me. It humiliated me in
public."

Buddie's family kept hanging together. And things were
not always totally dark. Buddie would do anything to amuse
or entertain. Despite his infidelities, he wanted to cheer
Helen, whose health continued to deteriorate, and sometimes went to great lengths.

He loved pranks as well as animals and, according to his
daughter Lucy, these two loves came together one Christmas. Buddie decided to give his youngest son, Sam, a goat
and a goat cart for Christmas. This was at a time when Helen

was not well at all. He wanted to show the goat to Helen, so he and some of the children led the animal upstairs to her bedroom. This was great fun until time came to take the goat back downstairs. Like the goat in the belfry from Buddie's college days, the little beastie refused to go down. They finally had to devise a sling to hoist it to the first floor. Lucy said there were hoof marks in the floor for years where that frightened goat had pawed.

Buddie's tragedy was to have a wife who was ill. His own mother had been in poor health for some of his childhood and most of his adult life. He was healthy and active and surrounded by invalid women. Helen loved Buddie deeply and he, in his way, cared for her. However, he had neither the knowledge nor the temperament to come to grips with his situation. Helen, likewise was hindered by her modesty, her cultural conditioning, and her temperament. His open infidelity while she was at her weakest tore her apart. She knew she was dying, and she knew he would soon find someone else. She could not be the wife that he needed, and he wasn't willing to be discreet about his arrangements.

Helen's health deteriorated rapidly in the early 1920s. She should never have had so many children, but was too modest to discuss this with her doctor. She probably believed any pain or illness she suffered was simply a woman's lot. Her health was ruined by her being pregnant most of her marriage. In addition to the blood poisoning from the cat scratch that caused little Lucy's premature birth, Helen developed a kidney problem, believed to have been "Bright's Disease."

Buddie sent her to specialists all over the country, but her own doctor finally had to tell him that she would never be cured. It was a long and painful illness. In 1926, after a reconciliation with Buddie, Helen went to Baltimore to Johns Hopkins to see if anything could be done to help her or, at least, ease her pain. Her son John and daughter Laura went with her for the five months she stayed there. On January 6, 1927, John would record in his diary that he had been out to see his mother and that she wanted to go home. He purchased the tickets to "go South" on January 7 and hastily packed to make the trip to Atlanta. Just three short weeks after her return home, Helen died on January 29, 1927. She was forty-six.

Her death certificate would say that Helen died of bronchial pneumonia brought on as a complication of a stroke. Her body had finally given out on her. But her children would always say that she really died of a broken heart.

# Buddie Again!

*This chapter is dedicated to the memory of
Florence Stephenson Candler.*

Buddie didn't mourn long after his wife Helen's death in January, 1927. By October 14 he was opening a new chapter in his life. It was on that day that he married Florence Adeline Stephenson, his secretary.

Miss Stephenson had been an employee of Asa G. Candler, Inc., since 1918 and Buddie's personal secretary since 1920. As much as anyone could, Florence kept Buddie from going too far off the deep end. She knew him well and was the perfect match for this wild man of Atlanta. Her common sense and nurturing were the counterbalance needed to his flamboyant enjoyment of life.

But, of course, nobody could stop Buddie from buying his elephants, gadgets, cars, boats, and planes. Buddie, under a good influence or not, was always Buddie.

The coauthor of this book knew Florence well during her later days and lived with her in summers and while in college.

Florence had an unusual background for a young woman of her generation. The middle child in a family of six girls and one boy, she and her sisters had to do work that in most families was done by boys. Florence's parents were William Jefferson Stephenson and Susan Rebecca Parks Stephenson of Lithonia, Georgia. Her father had a keen appreciation of his daughters' abilities and of the difficulties facing women with only domestic skills. Mr. Stephenson's own mother had been an aristocratic plantation-reared girl who never could adjust to the penury her family faced when the Civil War ended. He wanted a better life for his girls. Florence was a tomboy. She liked sports and could hold her own with the boys. She used her mind, not feminine wiles, to reach her goals.

Her father sold his farm and moved the family to Lithonia to pay tuition for the children's schooling (public education in Georgia was not free in those days). He always said he wanted his girls educated so they could earn a living and would never have to live with some sorry man.

Even so, he could only afford one year of college for Florence and her sister, LaRessa. They attended Bessie Tift College. Florence then taught school for two years but didn't like it. At the suggestion of her sister, Mercer, Florence took a business course. Mercer had taken one in lieu of attending college and already had a job in Atlanta. Florence was hired as a clerk-typist at Asa G. Candler, Inc.

With the World War raging, and most men off in uniform, the work force of American businesses had been depleted. Where men had once been the office workers, women would now have to do the job. Florence was in the forefront of the new movement that was bringing women into the world of business. The office manager quickly realized she was exceptionally efficient.

When Florence first started working in Atlanta, she and her sister, Mercer, rode the Accommodation Train, as it was called. These ambitious sisters awoke at daybreak for a quick game of tennis, weather permitting, then bathed, dressed, breakfasted, and caught the train at 6:15 a.m. so they could be at work at 8 o'clock. This long work day ended at 6 p.m. Later, the girls moved to Atlanta and shared an apartment. When Mercer married Alton Roberts, Florence rented an apartment at the Briarcliff Hotel, one of Buddie's many real estate holdings.

It is clear from stories told by many family members that Buddie had come to depend on his attractive, efficient, plain-talking secretary for more than just business. With Helen away in the hospital for long stays, he needed pleasant companionship and an understanding friend with whom he felt at ease. Who better than the young woman already well acquainted with his business, his extended family, and his wife's long illness, which they both knew was terminal.

Florence had often accompanied Asa, Sr., at Buddie's direction when the elder Asa would attend meetings at churches or at Emory. She admired and respected Asa, Sr., and he liked her.

Nancy Candler Nutter (Buddie's granddaughter) told us how Florence first came to Buddie's attention. "When she went to work for Asa G. Candler, Inc., I guess in the typing pool, she was good with figures and willing to work. She [was] a good employee, and they offered her a job in the payroll department as a bookkeeper. She said, 'I don't know bookkeeping.' And they paid for her to take a course in it.

"Well, one day, the regular person who prepared the payroll was out sick, and Florence was asked to make up the payroll. It took most of a day to prepare the envelope for the payroll. Each employee got an envelope with his name, hours worked, and wages earned written on it, with the cash enclosed in the envelope. At the end of the day, an office boy took the pay envelopes on a tray and handed them out to all the workers."

Charles Nutter added, "They were still doing it in 1938 when I went to work in New York City for the Home Insurance Company. They called it 'the eagle's going to fly today. Here comes the eagle' — money, you know."

"Anyway," Nancy continued, "when she got the payroll made up, it was a penny over. So she took it in to my grandfather and said, 'Mr. Candler, we have a penny over on the payroll, and it's your penny, and I've brought it back.' That's how she came to his attention. He admired her honesty.

"The opportunity to come to the attention of the boss wasn't lost on her, and since she really was honest, she wanted to underline that fact. Then he asked her to be his private secretary. She handled all of his correspondence and after a while, she just wrote the letters. He'd say, 'Here's this one from so-and-so, write him a letter.' He would read them and sign them, but she composed them, and I expect she was much better at that than he was. He didn't like to write and he didn't read often. He also sent her to board meetings in his place to take notes. He was paid to be a director of this company and that company, a fee, and he let her keep the fee. That's how she came to be making twenty-five thousand dollars a year as a secretary back in the twenties when, believe you me, very few secretaries made money like that. She was really more of an executive assistant...

"PaPa smoked cigars and cigarettes. And when his father would occasionally come by to discuss something with him and he was smoking, Asa, Sr., in that high pitched voice of his would say to Florence, 'I'll just wait out here until Buddie gets rid of that smoke. I'm not in that big a hurry.' PaPa would fly out of his chair, open the window, and blow his smoke out.

"They all stood in awe of their father, as well they should have."

Fifteen years Buddie's junior, Florence was a thoroughly modern girl of the 1920s. She was efficient, organized, businesslike, dependable, honest, and utterly loyal to Buddie and his father.

Although Florence was younger than Buddie, their backgrounds had many similarities. They were both essentially raised on a farm and respected and understood down-to-earth rural values. They shared their work, a love of good music, a strong sense of family, and a Southern heritage. Their marriage took place in Bishop Candler's parlor. Florence wore a brown velvet, two-piece ensemble. She had a lot of style and loved clothes. At the time she had a trim, if stocky, figure. Her father and sister Mercer were the only guests. She hadn't wanted her mother there because as she told it, "Mama's chin would have started to tremble, and I would know she was going to cry, and I don't think I could have gone through with it."

They cruised to Hawaii for their honeymoon, passing

through the Panama Canal, then staying at the new Royal Hawaiian Hotel. Buddie had enough orchids shipped from his greenhouses to the steamship for Florence to have a fresh one every day. He had a romantic streak, which was one of his endearing qualities.

Coming only eight and a half months after Helen's death, their marriage was considered a scandal in an era when one was expected to give a deceased spouse the honor of a year of mourning. Newspaper articles about their marriage implied that she was a scheming little gold digger. Since this occurred such a few years after the unfortunate publicity concerning Asa, Sr.'s, romances and second marriage, it is understandable that people drew this conclusion. To people who knew her well this was absurd. She just adored Mr. Candler, as she continued to call him for all the twenty-five years of their marriage. Occasionally, she'd call him "A.G." or "Darling."

The Atlanta newspapers wrote fairly polite articles on the wedding. The out-of-town papers played up her position as a former employee, resulting in snobbish pieces that hurt her feelings. The implication was that this millionaire had lowered himself. This first encounter with some newspaper reporters' anything-for-a-story attitude left her with a rancorous feeling toward journalists for the rest of her life.

In addition to the newspapers, polite society raised its eyebrows. Buddie's sister and brothers were not thrilled with the marriage or the publicity. Howard was cold. Lucy was upset with the impropriety of the early date. William, characteristically, was noncommittal and polite, while Walter, in his way, understood.

Buddie's children were bitter. The marriage was the ultimate insult to their mother and her memory. To have been seen all over with Florence before Helen died and then marry her before a year had passed was too much. Their mother deserved more respect than that, and they did not understand or forgive his decision. His eldest daughter was so furious that she gathered up all the silver and linens at Briarcliff while Buddie and Florence were on their honeymoon, and packed them away so they would not be available for Florence to use.

The staff became worried. What would happen when Mr. Candler came home? They enlisted the aid of young John, a newlywed himself, and he got all the items back into the house, barely in time for his father's return. John had to remind his siblings that, in fact, the house was their father's and so were most of the things in it. Therefore, they should not remove them. Unfortunately, everything didn't get back to the right spot, and Buddie noticed things were amiss. He was outraged when he discovered what had happened.

"No wife of mine has to live with secondhand finery!" he bellowed. He gathered up Florence and headed to New York where he went to Black, Frost, and Gorham and purchased complete sets of everyday, evening, and formal silver services all complete with Florence's monogram in heavy raised silver. "FSC" would adorn Briarcliff from that day forward.

After the brouhaha over the household accoutrements, Buddie decided to buy all new furniture for the master suite. While in New York, he talked with his friend, Charles Goldsmith, about some jewelry he wanted for Florence. Mr. Goldsmith worked diligently over the next few years assembling a rare and valuable collection of emeralds and diamonds. Buddie loved fine things and always had the best that money could buy. Buddie himself had designed Florence's spectacular emerald-and-diamond engagement ring and wedding band of baguette diamonds. Emeralds and diamonds were her favorites. This elegant and impressive collection that Mr. Goldsmith put together consisted of rings, bracelets, broaches, and watches. Buddie paid more than $250,000 for the collection. Sadly, none of these pieces were found after her death, nor was there any indication in her papers of their being sold, nor was there any codicil to her will about the disposition she wanted made of the collection. It was a little family mystery and remains so.

Buddie's insensitivity to his wife Helen's feelings during her last years and to the feelings of his children caused a rift that never really healed. Because he held the purse strings, his children accepted his second marriage, but they never liked Florence and seemed to feel that she had come between them and their rightful inheritance. Buddie was an uxorious man with a great fondness for women and had it not been

Florence, it would have been someone else. Furthermore, he was heard to say more than once, "If Florence dies, I'll be looking around at the cemetery for another one! There are too many women in the world for me to be without one." This was a kind of bravado. He surely felt she would outlive him. He did, however, love her very much. He was proud of his young, modern, career-girl wife. She was efficient and could work out the details after he dreamed up a project. Buddie had finally found someone with whom he would always be number one. They made a good team ... as long as he listened to her.

A big house like Briarcliff is sort of a combination private home and hotel. Life there was structured as it has to be when paid employees are doing all the work. One of the first tasks Florence faced when she and Buddie returned from their honeymoon was to bring some order to the chaos that reigned at Briarcliff. The servants and the teenage children still at home had been running it to suit themselves for sometime.

The servants had no authority over the children, and the children had no authority over the staff. Everyone just tried to keep things going like "Miss Helen" used to run it. In addition, Buddie's eldest daughter, Lucy Candler Thompson, her husband, and child, and her widowed mother-in-law, plus her young brother-in-law and young sister-in-law, all had been living there. Lucy had come home to help her mother, but her husband's people lived with them, so they all had to come. In the days before social security, the elderly lived with and were supported by their children.

Florence faced the job of bringing order to her husband's home with her characteristic forthright manner. She found that the staff was no more thrilled with the idea of the new mistress than the children were.

Soon after taking over, Florence told Buddie that she would need a steward to help her organize and run Briarcliff. They hired George Kampf. George had been their table steward on a trip to Europe in 1928, and he was hired to come back to Georgia and run Briarcliff, which he did most efficiently. For George, this was a great break. His native

Germany was still trying to recover from the first World War and moving to America must have seemed like a good idea. He would talk of his experiences after the war in his native land, and of being paid with a wheelbarrow full of marks which wasn't enough to buy one shoe.

America was on a great binge in the 1920s, and the Candlers enjoyed their wealth. Florence and Buddie spent months traveling around the world, and when in residence in Atlanta, they gave lavish parties. As his children and nieces and nephews came of age, Florence and Buddie did their share of entertaining. However, Buddie had a premonition that the excess of the 1920s could not last.

On a European cruise in the summer of 1929, Buddie wired his broker to sell everything in which he did not have a controlling interest. Knowing Buddie's propensity for heavy drinking, his broker wired back more than once for confirmation of the order until he received Buddie's last wire, "Do it or you're fired." As a result of this astute move, Buddie did not lose heavily on "Black Friday".

Most of Buddie's wealth was in his large real estate holdings. He had a marina, four hotels, commercial sites, and many apartments. He had a talent for taking a money loser and turning it into a money maker.

Sometime in the early 1930s, Buddie had the disappointment of discovering that a longtime, trusted employee had embezzled a large sum of money. Family problems had led the man to the embezzlement, and Buddie refused to prosecute. However, he now needed someone he could trust to oversee his business. Buddie asked Florence if she would be willing to come back in the business, which she was delighted to do.

In addition to his traditional businesses, Buddie could afford to indulge his whims and a number of them he turned into businesses. It was these unusual enterprises that he most enjoyed and that caused him the most trouble. One of these whimsical decisions came to him while traveling. Buddie — who supposedly was drunk when he did it — bought a bankrupt circus while in Eastern Europe. He wired home to his architects "Bought circus, build zoo." So a zoo was constructed in the front yard of Briarcliff.

The arrival in Atlanta of the circus animals was quite a spectacle. They came in by train and were unloaded at Emory University station located on the campus, about six blocks from Buddie's estate on Briarcliff Road. When the word of Mr. Candler's animals spread among the students, classes had to be canceled. Everyone went down to the train station to watch the animals being unloaded.

When Howard heard the news, he commented, "What has that fool brother of mine done now?" Walter headed over to see what was going on and told Buddie, "Bud, you've done some fool things in your life, but this is the damned foolest."

What a scene it was, with animals in cages, five elephants — Buddie named them "Delicious," "Refreshing," "Coca," "Cola," and "Rosa," Rosa being his cook — holding each others' tails and marching through Druid Hills to their new home in the front yard of Briarcliff.

This was just the beginning. Now that Buddie had the circus animals, he decided to create a large zoo and share it with the public.

Mettelen Thompson Moore adds this insight: "PaPa decided that the children of Atlanta didn't have a zoo, and that they needed one. So he commissioned a curator to go to Europe and Africa and get more animals to go with the ones he already had, and to tell him what kind of cages he would need. This man did all of the planning and buying for the zoo. He came back and drew up the plans for the zoo to fit in the front yard at Briarcliff.

"Some of the animals were shipped ahead. When the curator got it completed, he went back to make sure he got it all right and he wired PaPa, 'Have a stagecoach and six Shetland ponies trained in the circus to pull the stagecoach. It's a good buy...' It was a miniature stagecoach. Kaiser Wilhelm had commissioned the people that built things like that to go out north, south, east, and west to discover the best way to take his generals to see the front lines. They all came back saying that it would be best to go through the Black Forest in a black stagecoach, driven by four black horses.

"This stagecoach builder wasn't making any money, so he decided to make some money and sell it, maybe to a circus or something. PaPa wired back, 'no, it was too much money, don't buy it.'

"Well, the fellow wired back again, he'll take such and such amount for it, and he'd throw in the harness and everything else with it. So PaPa finally relented. PaPa knew nothing about trick horses. My father was a horseman and showed them, so PaPa got Daddy [Homer Thompson] to learn how to put the horses through the tricks. They would go around a little ring and they'd get up on their hind legs. They had a feather in the harness. And they would pull the stagecoach. My father was fascinated with it.

"Every Sunday, we would go to church, have lunch, then Daddy would lay down and take his nap. Afterwards, we would all go out to PaPa's. Daddy would hitch up the stagecoach and take the children for a ride around the zoo in [it]. Anybody's child could come. Of course, we didn't think about insurance then — what if one of the children got stepped on or kicked by a pony? You didn't think about those things. Nowadays you wouldn't dare do it."

Howard's family didn't react very favorably to Buddie's circus and zoo. Several of Howard's family members remembered that it was just horrible, because the lions would roar all night long and keep the neighbors awake, and they were always getting loose and getting into people's yards. They remembered the elephants and the monkeys. If his nieces and nephews could not imagine what in the world would possess him to want to have that many animals in his yard, they were not alone. Buddie's own children and in-laws were also dismayed by the spectacle.

Next, Buddie added another attraction to his Briarcliff Zoological Gardens, as it was called. He built a tremendous public swimming pool, complete with a beautiful neon-light fountain that came on at dusk. He put in a concession stand to sell hot dogs, hamburgers, chips, cookies, ice-cream sandwiches, Popsicles, and of course, Coca-Cola! In those hot, non-air-conditioned summer days in Georgia, this was a mecca for young and old. It only cost a quarter to get in. You were given a metal key to a locker in which you could stow your street clothes after changing into your bathing suit.

Florence's nephews, Alton Roberts of Lithonia, Georgia,

and Bobby Elliott of Conyers, Georgia, not only visited Briarcliff as children, but were able to land jobs working for their Uncle Buddie at the pool.

"Uncle Buddie was just a real good fellow. To me, what he did didn't seem eccentric at all," says Alton, "It was different [having the zoo and the pool] — and I assume that's why some would assume he was eccentric. But to me, as I say again, his business ability was greater than most of those other folks."

Bobby Elliott added, "He employed a lot of people during the depths of the Depression. He helped a lot of folks in a lot of ways. In those days, folks were glad to have an opportunity to work, and Uncle Buddie provided that opportunity."

Buddie had created a true fantasy playland for the child of the 1930s. This was the first of many enterprises Buddie would run from his estate on Briarcliff Road.

One such enterprise was a direct result of his zoo. Buddie became outraged at the price he was paying for city water he needed to run his zoo. So he drilled his own well on the property. The water from his artesian wells were enough not only for the zoo, but there was enough left over to add three more businesses: a laundry, a diaper service, and a bottled water service. After he had the water tested for purity by The Coca-Cola Company, it proved of such outstanding quality, he decided to share it with others. Not one to waste good business opportunities, Buddie quickly went into the business of bottled water sales from the "Crystal Pure Wells at Briarcliff."

But all was not rosy, as might be expected when one maintains a zoo in a residential area. There were lawsuits over such minor incidents as the baboon chasing a woman down the street. Slim, a member of Buddie's staff, told how the animals would occasionally get loose, and he and Mr. Dilbeck, who oversaw the zoo, would have to go catch them. Slim would make quite a story about how it was usually on a Sunday when people would be on their way to church or in the morning on their way to work. They would call Briarcliff and then Slim and Johnny Dilbeck would have to take the station wagon over and collect the lion or tiger — it was usually a cat. According to Slim, they'd coax it with food and soft talk, saying, "Here Simba, come here Simba," finally resorting to "Here kitty, kitty," which usually worked. The cat would get into the cage in the back of the wagon, and they would all go back home to Briarcliff.

Buddie had all these animals in his front yard before air-conditioning. Can you imagine the smells and the noise — lions roaring and elephants trumpeting all night and day? It must have been something, indeed.

Eventually, Buddie donated his menagerie to the City of Atlanta, and it became the basis for the city's public zoo.

Buddie loved to travel, and the fastest way to get anywhere was flying. According to Asa G. Candler V, "My grandfather immediately recognized that this was the best way to get from one spot to another. As soon as airplanes got to be commercial, he had one of them, and employed a full-time pilot, E.W. Hightower.

"Aunt Florence flew, too. She had her own custom-made flying suit. She'd take that map and follow everything. She was a good geography student, but sometimes they'd get lost and land in the cornfields and all kinds of stuff. Usually, they followed the railroads and had no trouble.

"PaPa loved to travel and always carried an entourage with him when he went somewhere. One summer he decided they should tour the West. So he gathered up Aunt Florence, his youngest son, Sam, and Florence's parents, Mr. and Mrs. Stephenson, a few servants, including Slim who was young at the time, a piano, a parrot, and Sam's pet goat. They stopped in St. Louis and had a suit tailored for Sam because he was at a stage where he seemed to be growing out of his clothes overnight. The ones he had packed were already too small. [They were traveling in private rail cars.] Anyway, not long out of St. Louis, the parrot, accompanied by Sam's pet monkey, opened the trunk, and somehow the suit ended up being eaten by the billy goat. Sam had to stop in Kansas City and get more new clothes."

Mettelen Thompson Moore added more about Buddie's propensity for travel. "He went up to somewhere on the Great Lakes ... and got a yacht. He had it customized to his liking, hired a crew, and he took mother and Tommy, Aunt

Laura, Aunt Helen, John, I think too, and maybe Uncle Sam. They flew up and got on the boat and came down through the Great Lakes, the Hudson River, and went to New York. Then they docked and went into the New York World's Fair [1939]. Then they came on down the coast."

When World War II broke out, the Coast Guard took over the yacht. Grandson Tommy Thompson isn't sure if Buddie gave it to the Coast Guard or whether it was just commandeered. "But the agreement was, he would get the boat back in the same condition that he turned it over to them. They pulled out some of the front decking and mounted a 50mm cannon out there. The rear decking, where they had some ample space, they mounted a couple of depth bomb racks. The master bedroom, they converted into a munitions room, and they converted other rooms to crews quarters. I think they had a crew of six or eight on board.

"It patrolled the coast of Georgia for several years during World War II. I think they also utilized part of the yacht basin for a Coast Guard base at the time. After the war was over, PaPa and I were talking one time, and I asked if he was going to get the boat back, and he said, 'No, son.'

"The thing was, there was no way they could take that boat and reconstruct it or put it back like it was without a lot more money than the boat was worth. The government says, 'Well we can only do so much.' That wasn't going to put it back like he wanted it to be, so I don't know whether they junked the boat or the government kept it, or what happened."

Tommy Thompson has yet more insights of Buddie.

"When PaPa was going to talk to me about something of pleasure or something when he's not reprimanding me, he'd start off saying, 'Son...' I knew then we were going to talk about something congenial. If he said, 'Tommy' or 'Thomas...' I knew right off the bat, I better stand at attention because I had done something wrong, or he had something on his mind that he wanted to get on my can about.

"One day he said, 'Son, me and the boys are going to go on out and do some hunting. Would you like to go?' And I asked when he would go, and he said it was going to be at the end of August or September. 'What are we going to go hunting for?' I asked, and he said, 'Moose and elk and deer and bear.'

"Daddy had told me that he and Uncle Tom Callaway ... had gone up to hunt bear and stuff at Jackson Hole, Wyoming. PaPa took me on the trip. I mean, it was a trip and a half. We packed back into the woods a good ways. Mr. Wirt who owned the Wirt Hotel, which I understand is still there, arranged everything. He must have arranged something pretty good for PaPa, because we all went out there. PaPa said he wanted to get a big moose. I think this was a forerunner of his wanting to go to Africa and hunt big game. I think this is where he really got the bug.

"They had a cook tent there, and we would wake up and they had food for us ... One morning, PaPa was through eating breakfast before we even got started good, and I thought this was kind of unusual. He went out and got on his horse and said, 'We're going to go and get a moose. We'll be back in a little bit.' Well, we're sitting down and I'm eating breakfast, and all of a sudden somebody yelled — and I thought to myself, 'Who's shooting in camp?'

"About ten minutes later, PaPa comes back and says, 'We got the moose.' I thought, 'Hell, they must have been hand feeding him there right in the pasture or had him tied down.' PaPa just had to ride from the camp to the bottom of the hill before he started shooting.

"We had a great time. I got an elk and so did Tom Callaway and Daddy and a fellow who worked for PaPa running the cemetery. The guy who later became president of Southern Airways, whose first name was Pete, Peterson or something like that.

Asa G. Candler V has some hunting remembrances as well. "The outgrowth of that Wyoming hunting trip was going to Africa. He wanted to go on a safari to Africa. At the time, I was living with him. I had moved in with him when I was sixteen. Being as I was there, he offered to take me. That suited me to a 'T.'

"He tried to line up one of the known outfitters over there, a safari operator, and he had been unable to. They were all booked up. He had pretty much given up on the idea of going, then through a friend he had written, Dr. Sangster, who was the head of the Methodist Church in England, to see if there was someone else he could recommend. He had come up with this guy Ikran Hassan, who was a young fellow starting his own thing, but a person of good repute. His father was an important veterinarian in Kenya. He was from an Indian family. Actually, they were Pakistanis, Moslems. I think I referred to him as Mr. Hassan. He was about thirty or thirty-one years old at the time. We couldn't have picked a better person. It was just fabulous. They waited on us hand and foot, met us at the airport when we came in. It was all a great adventure, going on that trip. My grandpa was very lucky in his hunting and fishing. You can't say he was good, but he was very lucky. We killed an elephant on that trip."

Buddie was reared in a Christian home where alcoholic beverages were never served and tobacco was never used. That didn't stop Buddie. He was a drinker. In time he became dependent on alcohol to console him when he was depressed and to add merriment and good cheer to happier times. In short, he was an alcoholic, one of those people who simply cannot take an occasional cocktail and leave it alone. He would drink until he would be in such a state that the family, fearing for his life, would ask his friend and physician, Dr. John Hurt, to give him something to help him recover from the alcohol poisoning.

After being called away from a dinner party one time too many, Dr. Hurt finally delivered his ultimatum. "Buddie, you're my friend, but you are killing yourself and I can't help you. So don't call me again. If you stop drinking, you might live to old age, if you don't you'll be dead within the year."

At this point, Buddie had reached the bottom of an abyss and realized he would have to crawl out of it or surely Dr. Hurt's prediction would come true. Once again, he called on Florence for help, and again she stood staunchly by his side. He asked her to get him a ribbon which he tied to the cork of his bottle of whiskey and then put it on the mantel. He told her, "I never expect to take another drink of liquor" — and he never did. That bottle, with the red ribbon around it, remained on the mantle for years as a reminder of his pledge.

As he turned away from his dependence on liquor, he returned to the church and to the steadfast Christian faith of his father and mother. He began giving testimonials about his battle with the bottle in which he would speak of hearing a voice telling him to renounce "self" and put his trust in the Lord.

With Florence's encouragement, he certainly tried.

Buddie gave up the drinking friends, dropped clubs where drinking alcohol was a part of the social scene, and ceased to serve it in his home. They became active in their churches. Florence was a member of the Baptist church and Buddie was a Methodist, so they went to both. On Sunday, the chauffeur took her to Druid Hills Baptist Church for Sunday School, then Buddie and the chauffeur picked her up and they drove to First Methodist to hear Dr. Pierce Harris. On Sunday evening, it was back to Druid Hills to hear Dr. Louie Newton preach. Bishop and Mrs. Arthur Moore were also close friends. Often the Candlers had these three couples for dinner and interesting conversation. These were worldly men in every good sense of the word, all engaged in trying to make the world better in any way possible.

Buddie worked behind the scenes to aid them when he could. He preferred to have the church get credit for his anonymous contributions, and he depended on these three Christian gentlemen to keep him informed about areas where his assistance would help.

In the last part of his life, he did exactly what he said he would do when he went around giving his talks about his battle with alcoholism, his renunciation of "self." He had come to believe that money did not bring happiness. He began to give more and more money away. "... capitalism," Buddie said, "teaches one great truth — to God we are always individuals and always individually responsible for our stewardship of his gifts. I plan to provide for my children; beyond this, it is my purpose to give everything to the service of my Master, and to give all I own away before I die. I want no part of it."

"After PaPa quit drinking," Nancy Candler Nutter said, "only two people that came to Briarcliff were served liquor — always on the front porch, that's where you sat. Lou Minear from Washington, D.C., a cemetery developer and Mr. and Mrs. Steven Scullen of Albany, New York. Steve Scullen and PaPa met in 1928 on a trip to Europe [by boat]; they liked each other instantly, discovered each had a wife named Florence, and were sure the girls would hit it off. They did, and the Florences became lifelong friends. The two couples, and later the two widows, took many trips together. After PaPa quit drinking, Aunt Florence kept liquor in her shoe closet. On Christmas, the men in the family would all go have a toast with her upstairs, while PaPa entertained the children.

If this were a work of fiction, we could stop right here with "and they all lived happily ever after." Real life rarely works that way. There were some very sad days ahead and disappointments enough for several lifetimes. As William Shakespeare said in *Julius Caesar*, "The good that we do is oft interred with our bones and the evil lives after us." Buddie had given up drink and taken up religion, but four of his six children could not or would not. Only his two older daughters, Lucy and Laura, managed to escape the clutches of demon rum and have what could be called a normal life.

In March 1937, his favorite son-in-law, Edgar Chambers, Jr., died unexpectedly of complications following a hernia operation. Edgar left Laura a widow at thirty with two young sons. Buddie's daughter, Martha, would be divorced from her husband, Jesse York, when divorce was considered a disgrace. When Martha moved back into Briarcliff, Florence told her, "Martha, when you lived here as a girl, this household revolved around you children. Now it revolves around two old people — your father and my mother — and you'll have to fit in as best you can." Florence's father had died and Mrs. Stephenson had a broken hip. She lived at Briarcliff with a companion, Mrs. Martin. Buddie was very fond of his mother-in-law and had been happy to make a place for her.

He loved to tease his mother-in-law, and he also tried to broaden her experiences. For example, he taught her to smoke cigarettes. She had always strongly disapproved of the habit, and her daughters never smoked in her presence.

Florence shared this anecdote: While visiting Florence and Buddie one time, her father came upon her smoking a cigarette. So she said to him, "Papa, I would just as soon you didn't mention this to Mama." Mr. Stephenson replied, "Don't worry, Florence, I'm not proud of it, either."

Bobby Elliott, one of the Stephensons' grandsons, adds this about smoking: "Once Granny started recovering, she never walked anymore except just to get out of the chair and go to the bathroom. Uncle Buddie told her, you're going to have to find something to do. She asked, 'And what is that?' And he said, 'Why don't you start smoking?' She replied, 'But I don't believe in women smoking.' Of course, Aunt Florence had smoked in front of her before, and she didn't like that. He said, 'Well, it won't hurt you.' So then, she did. She took up smoking, and every time we'd go up to see her, she'd say, 'Let's all have a cigarette.' She smoked Lucky Strikes. So we'd sit there, the three of us would sit up there and smoke a cigarette. She took up smoking after she broke her hip. She smoked until she died.

Martha soon married again, an old friend and kinsman of Florence's, Tom Callaway of Covington, Georgia. Her twin, Helen, eloped with Robert Hare III and moved to Tampa. Buddie's youngest son, Sam, married and moved. Briarcliff became a quieter place.

The automobiles that so fascinated Buddie were to cost him dearly. Not only did he lose his brother William, but his niece Elizabeth Owens died of complications following an accident.

Buddie had more than one accident himself. The worst one occurred in the summer of 1935. He, Florence, her maid, Rosa Logan, and Florence's two young nephews, Alton Roberts, Jr., and Bobby Elliott were returning from a visit to Panama City, Florida, where Florence and Buddie had a cottage. According to Alton and Bobby, it was the end of summer and the Candlers and their staff had closed up the summer house. They were returning in two cars. Buddie, Florence, Rosa, and the boys were in the lead car with Buddie driving. Slim and another servant, Lige, were following in the second car.

A mechanical error caused Buddie's car to flip end over

end and as it rolled, it threw everyone in the lead car out onto the pavement. Young Bobby Elliott was by far the most seriously injured. He spent months in a full body cast and missed a year of school, but as he philosophically says, "I'm still here." Both Bobby and Alton give Lige Brown, the chauffeur, credit for preventing an even greater tragedy. Lige expertly maneuvered his car to narrowly avoid running over young Bobby, thus saving his life.

In spite of the fact that his own kneecap was completely shattered, Buddie took charge, directing traffic, and getting help. Florence and Rosa had broken bones; everyone was badly hurt. When the ambulances came, Buddie insisted that everyone be taken to Emory Hospital. The significance of this is hard to understand today but Rosa went also. She was transported in the white ambulance to the white hospital, and as usual, no one dared cross Buddie.

Alton Roberts also remembers this accident vividly and Buddie's reaction. "He would not express his pain. He took control. We got in an ambulance. Came all the way from Griffin, which in those days you had to come up 19 through Jonesboro and Stewart Avenue, and you had the siren going the entire time."

"Uncle Buddie was sitting in the front seat with the driver and Bobbie, myself, and Aunt Florence were sitting in the back seat.

"When we got to the hospital at Emory, we walked in. Emory was small then... They brought us to the emergency room. I remember somebody said they didn't have a room or something, and Uncle Buddie said so-and-so you'd *better* have a room or something to that effect. Next thing I know, Bobby's wheeling by on the stretcher, and he went to a room.

"But he was a kind of person who could take control. And when I say, 'take control,' I don't mean he took it in an ungracious way. I mean that you knew that he was the leader. You accepted when a person is sitting there and you know he is a leader — he doesn't have to tell you. Uncle Buddie didn't have to tell you."

It was sometime after this accident that Florence said to Buddie, 'Mr. Candler, you are far too important a man to drive your own car. You should have a chauffeur.' She was ever the diplomat, and she knew her man. An appeal to his ego worked as nothing else could have. Thereafter, he rode in the back seat and let one of the capable and cautious chauffeurs do the driving.

There were happy times in the 1930s as well as tragedies. Nearly every year brought a new grandchild. On Sunday afternoons they gathered at Briarcliff to see their grandfather and play with their cousins while the grown folks sat around and talked or performed musically. Buddie and John liked to argue politics. Florence didn't like the arguments to get too heated, but the two men loved these debates. Buddie despised FDR and John thought FDR was great. They were both strong supporters of Governor Eugene Talmadge, but John could debate either side of an issue just for the sake of debate.

Christmas was the big celebration at Briarcliff. Buddie and Florence entertained his adult children with a black tie dinner on Christmas Eve. The next day they had a gift exchange and a sit-down dinner for the grandchildren. There was a tremendous decorated tree in the main dining room with huge mounds of gifts and a live Santa Claus [Buddie's son-in-law, Homer Thompson]. Even the Thompson grandchildren didn't miss their father or recognize his transformation into Santa — or if they did, they didn't spill the beans. It was a happy time. The other big event of every year was Buddie's birthday in August. This was usually a lavish event attended by family and friends, for which Florence went all out.

Buddie's sixtieth birthday present from Florence was his portrait painted by Emma Jennings, a well-known portrait artist of the day. Florence was out playing golf the day the picture was completed, so the artist gave the bill to Buddie, which he paid. Thereafter, Buddie loved to make a great story out of it by saying, "I know it's a nice gift, 'cause I had to pay for it and I know what it cost."

To celebrate the unveiling of the portrait, Florence held a big outdoor birthday party for Buddie at Briarcliff. They served Brunswick stew, which was almost a requirement for fancy picnics in Georgia during that era. The grandchildren all arrived in shorts, and some were very upset when they saw that all the grown-ups were dressed up.

Another famous party of Buddie and Florence's was the "Comic Strip Party," which they gave in honor of the twins, Martha and Helen, instead of a debut. Martha and Helen were costumed as the Katzenjammer Kids, a popular comic strip of the time featuring very appropriately mischievous twins. Buddie went as the Captain from the same strip and Florence as his wife. It was after this party when Florence and Bessie Little (the upstairs maid and main housekeeper) had so much trouble running the young guests out of the bedrooms and alcoves where they had repaired for some serious smooching that Florence decided no more parties in the ballroom! Thereafter, all bedrooms were kept locked when parties were going on because as Bessie said later, "Peoples just be curious to see what you has in yo' closets and drawers. They's snooping and it ain' nice."

With the onset of World War II, life became less lavish. Everyone had to cope with rationing and shortages. While Briarcliff continued as a self-sufficient farm, other durable goods were hard to come by. Buddie's sons-in-law, Tom Callaway and Robert Hare were in the service, his daughters and daughters-in-law found volunteer work to help the war effort, and before it ended Florence's nephews and Buddie's grandson, Tommy Thompson, would go into the service. These were anxious days for everyone with family members in uniform. However, Florence didn't quite see the army as other people did. Her nephew Alton Roberts, Jr. recalls:

"Well, this is typical of Aunt Florence. For Aunt Florence thought there wasn't anything too large. There wasn't any obstacle that you couldn't overcome. And I went out to Fort MacPherson and went ahead and enlisted in the army. When I went to Georgia Tech, I attempted to get in the naval ROTC. The basketball coach out there at the time and my daddy were good friends. I went Naval ROTC because that was an outstanding program back then. Didn't many schools have that. ... But I was color blind, so I couldn't get in.

"So anyhow, I went out and just enlisted in the Army. Way back in her earlier years, Aunt Florence had dated the fellow who was in charge of Fort MacPherson — the commanding general out there. And also this good friend of mine had dated him, Miss Bess Davis from out in Lithonia who grew up at Acworth. ... Both of them took it upon themselves to call him, just like you would do in those days if you had a friend in Macon. You would call and say 'My son's just moved to Macon...' or 'I have a niece that's moved to Macon...' Like they used to do. They wanted you to know they were there, and then naturally they would invite you by for lunch or so forth. Well, that's the way they were trying to do with the U.S. Army.

"Aunt Florence called and told him that she had a nephew coming out there and that she'd appreciate him looking me up. Miss Bess did, too. Well, I couldn't even get my leggings on straight — you know. Back in the early days of World War II, we wore leggings. I had them on the wrong side, and I was such a bad-looking GI. And there comes the Jeep with the star on it and picked me up, and all these jokers there in the barracks looking at me, wondering, 'Who in the world is he?'

"Off I went and got over there. He was obligated, I reckon, to both of them, to tell them at least that he saw me. All I remember now is that he said, 'Knowing the family you come from, son, I know you're a red-blooded young man.'

"I thought, 'Oh, what's this going to do to me now!' But anyhow, I think all it did at that time was keep me out of the infantry. I went to field artillery."

The end of the war brought similar special treatment for Buddie's grandson, Thomas Homer "Tommy" Thompson, Jr.

"I went into the service in '44," Tommy said. "When I came back to be discharged, PaPa had bought a Lockheed Lodestar, which at the inception of World War II, was really a twin-engine bomber. I don't know whether it was a used aircraft or not, but it had been converted and was very luxurious. It carried a pilot and copilot and eight other people. It was nice.

"The funny story about that was that Daddy, and of course PaPa, both knew several important Georgia politicians, including Governor Talmadge. Supposedly civilian aircraft were not allowed to land on the military bases except in cases of emergencies. So I called from New York and told everybody I had arrived, and I was safe and sound and that we were in New York. We would be there approximately two days, I said, and then I was going to Fort Bragg to be discharged. Well, Dad said, 'Son, when you get there, your grandfather wants to pick you up.' And I said, 'Where?' He told me, 'Well, there's an air base there on the military base.' I said, 'Daddy, they're not going to let you land there.' He said, 'Well, you call me from the base when you know the day you're going to be discharged.'

"The army made us go through a regular routine of getting all of our shots and everything before we were discharged, and they told us we'd be through approximately 1:30 or 2:00 on such and such a day. I called the family and told Dad I would be through tomorrow. He said, 'We'll pick you up in an airplane.' I asked, 'Where do you want me to be?' He said, 'You just be out there at the air base. We'll pick you up.' Then he added, 'Son, I think we might have a couple, three extra seats, if you've got any young men that want a ride to Atlanta, we could go ahead and fly them back.'

"There was this boy by the name of Fitzsimmons, we'd been in basic training together. He'd gone to Europe too, but he was being discharged at the same time I was. I ran into him and another boy who lived here in Atlanta. So I went up to them and said, 'Fitz, I can get you as far as Atlanta (I think he lived in Jacksonville or Orlando), the rest of it's up to you.' He said, 'Gosh, yeah. How you going to do it?' I said, 'They're going to pick me up in an airplane.' They said, 'WHAT?' and I said, 'Yeah, my grandpa is going to pick me up in an airplane.' They said, 'Come on, Thompson, don't give us all that bullstuff.' I said, 'That's what they told me, if you all want a ride, you can go with me.'

"Sure enough, we get out to the base, and I ask the major out there in charge if they were expecting an aircraft from Atlanta, because they asked me what I was doing and I said I was going to be picked up. The major asked, 'You Sergeant Thompson?' and I said, 'Yes, sir, I sure am,' and saluted him and. He said, 'The plane will be here in approximately another forty-five minutes. We've been talking to them and they've already left Atlanta.' These guys that were with me, you would have thought I was the vice president's son or something. They couldn't get over this fact. The plane did fly in and pick us up."

Before the war's end, another tragedy struck Buddie's family. In 1943, John's young wife, Lib, died after a long bout with cancer. This left John with four young children and Lib's widowed mother all dependent on him. Sadly, John had inherited his father's appetite for liquor and the inability to control his drinking. He did not have the faith nor the will to quit. Neither did he have a Florence waiting to take charge. John loved "Dearie" as everyone called Lib's mother, Mrs. Brandon, and she loved him, but she couldn't give him the strength and courage to bear the grief and go on with life.

John was a binge drinker. He would pass out for days and sometimes months on end, then finally sober up with promises of "never again," or "I've learned my lesson" — all the sad, sorry litany of remorse that addicts use. He tried it all — Alcoholics Anonymous, clinics specializing in such problems, psychiatry. He even fell in love again and remarried. Maybe, given more time, his second wife, Thesis Fowler of Union, South Carolina, could have helped him beat it, but he ran out of time on February 14, 1947. John had found a young fellow at one of the clinics who had been a doctor. He thought he could cure alcoholics by injecting them with insulin, which was supposed to shock them into sobriety. It shocked John — right into death.

Buddie was flying with a group of friends to a meeting out west when he got word that his son was dead. The men were in Westview Cemetery's Lockheed Lodestar, but he offered to catch a commercial plane and fly back to Atlanta. His friends would not hear of this and flew back with him. In one of those strange quirks of fate, Mrs. Stephenson, Florence's mother also died that day. Both were buried on February 17—John in the morning and Susan Stephenson in the afternoon.

With Florence's characteristic understanding of her husband's unspoken desires, she offered to make a home for John's orphaned children if he wanted her to, and he told her, "I would never have asked you to do it, but if you are willing to do it, fine. I am too old to try to rear young children." Florence told Thesis, "You are too young and have too much life ahead of you to be expected to make a home for these children when we already have a home."

John's two oldest children, Nancy and Asa V moved to Briarcliff, but their Grandmother Brandon fought for custody of the two younger children and she won. It was a bitter blow to both Florence and Buddie. Mrs. Brandon hired her daughter's cousin, Inman Brandon, to represent her in the battle.

Lib Brandon and John Candler had met as teenagers when she spent a year in Atlanta attending Washington Seminary and living with her father's uncle, Morris Brandon. The Brandons had been a wealthy and prominent family in middle Tennessee before the War Between the States, but Lib's father, George Clayton Brandon, had never quite found his niche. Morris Brandon was a successful and wealthy Atlanta attorney who had married into the very wealthy Inman family. He was in a position to help his more needy relatives. He and his wife had sons, but no daughters. Uncle Morris had provided for his niece and her brothers' education for years. He hoped to introduce Lib to an appropriate, marriageable young man in Atlanta. But John Candler messed up his plans. Morris was not at all happy with the match. The Brandons were dignified, educated, cultured people, and they were quiet and reserved. Uncle Morris didn't like the Candlers from Asa, Sr., to his grandson; he didn't like their self-promoting ways or the fact that he had lost money in their racetrack. When Lib opened her wedding present from her uncle, she found twelve full place settings of her silver, all embossed with the letter "B." Her uncle looked at her and said, "There is no finer name than Brandon."

Buddie's battle for his son's children took on a personal air; not only was it a case of the Brandons pulling together against the Candlers, but perhaps Buddie's reputation and escapades came back to haunt him. Florence said later that the judge didn't like Buddie and that helped decide against them; although the Judge said in court that because Mrs. Candler worked outside the home, it would be better for the children to live with their maternal grandmother, who was not employed! Little Helen III and John, Jr., would not move to Briarcliff until 1951, when Mrs. Brandon's health failed.

The loss of this suit had repercussions for two of Buddie's other grandchildren. When Helen II and Bob Hare divorced, she gained custody of the children. However, Helen was an alcoholic and, in her father Buddie's words, "an unfit mother." He told Florence, "We could try to get custody of those children, but what chance would we have if we can't get John's when the parents are dead and the Hare children have two living parents?" Their father finally got custody of the children and took them away to Florida.

Buddie could have avoided many headaches had he consulted an attorney before, instead of after, some of his actions. But that was not his nature.

Bad luck seemed to come all at once. Lib Candler died on April 20, 1943, and the Briarcliff Laundry burned to the ground two weeks later. Buddie had built a large commercial laundry on his estate back near the stables and Brother Landrum's house. There were small offices in different parts of town where customers could drop off their cleaning and laundry and pick it up. The work was done at the main plant on the estate.

The plant was insured for boiler explosion by an insurance agency in which Buddie's brothers had an interest. Unfortunately, the boiler didn't explode. The one saving grace was the fire occurred when the place was closed, so no one was hurt.

Buddie's sons, John and Sam were officers of the company and all three were sued for fraud because they advertised themselves as "insured." It was an embarrassing and expensive loss. Not only did they have to pay to defend the suit, but they had to find another business. Eventually they won. As John told his daughter, so many of the claims were unbelievable that the court decided for Buddie. "Would you believe," he said, "that no one in the entire city of Atlanta has anything but brand new Wamsutta percale sheets and no other kind of coat but mink?" The judge didn't either!

The laundry was not rebuilt. John went into commercial

real estate sales and development. Sam and a partner started Lullaby Diaper Service and Buddie turned his attention to Westview Cemetery. He had owned it for a long time and Florence had been running it. It isn't a complicated business as long as you sell lots, keep a record of where people are buried, get the grave dug in time for the funeral, and filled in after the services are concluded.

Buddie had built a large office and set up a sales office. People bought the lots on time so that when a loved one died, the lot was already selected. These grave sites were sold as "perpetual care" in a parklike setting. Perpetual care of raised graves with small hedges around each is very labor intensive. WW II brought a shortage of men to do this work. New cemeteries were being planned with lowered graves, no hedges, no trees, and headstones flush with the ground. Easy for a power mower to cut. It seemed like the way to go to Buddie, so he blithely started redoing the graveyard. There was one problem or there was at Westview Cemetery. Lots belong to the lot owner and changes needed to be cleared with the owner.

Buddie failed to get the necessary permission and lawsuits galore followed. Buddie's long-term attorney, Thomas Branch, had died just as these suits were filed. Buddie eventually won, thanks to his new attorney, John L. Westmoreland. But, Buddie was now tired of dealing with the public. He sold the cemetery on a long-term payout. He hoped this would provide an income for his wife and children when he was gone, and it did.

As his life wound down, Buddie still continued to be Buddie. For example, he bought a fishing boat. This was no rowboat — it cost about twenty-five thousand dollars, which in the 1950s would buy you a pretty nice cabin cruiser. It was, for Buddie, though, "a little boat." He and B.J. Jinks (his chauffeur) loved to go up to Lake Altoona and fish. Buddie always said, "I hope we don't catch any fish, I just want to fish." Nothing is quite as calming and peaceful as a large body of water. You can truly escape from your cares and concerns when you are quietly watching the water ebb and flow, and so Buddie did.

Buddie, even late in his life, rarely showed his distress, but the day his grandson, Asa V, went to join the Air Force during the Korean War, he sat and smoked one cigar after another and played solitaire. His anxiety was palpable because Asa was gone all day. When he finally came home, Buddie cheered up. His boy hadn't been sent off to war without a chance to come home. The war ended before Asa's flying course was completed.

In 1949, Buddie, as he had always done with his projects when he tired of them, sold Briarcliff estate. His health was beginning to fail some, and Florence had never felt any great love for the estate. He arranged to make a very favorable sale to the federal government. It benefited him tax-wise, and it allowed him to make other arrangements.

Originally they planned to put a Veterans Administration hospital there, but that never happened. The state of Georgia acquired the property. Ironically, Briarcliff Estate today is the home of the DeKalb Addiction Clinic, which specializes in the treatment of alcoholism.

Nancy Candler Nutter remembers Buddie's move after the sale. "Aunt Florence was an informal person and liked informal decorating. Fancy stuff was not really to her taste. He moved her to the hotel without ever telling her that he had that apartment all done. After Christmas dinner, he just said, 'C'mon, we're going for a ride.' ... We hopped in the car, and we rode up to the hotel, and we got in the elevator. It was her first clue that that's where they were going to go now that Briarcliff had been sold to the government. She knew they were going to move, but she thought they were going to buy a house or build a house.

"That was the first time she saw it and she was not happy about it. She didn't like living in an apartment. I'm sure she didn't like not being consulted; most women wouldn't. But she said, later, to me, 'Well, in every life, there are majors and minors. Your marriage is a major. Where you live is a minor.'

"She put some furniture there, and she got Mr. Argo, who really was an upholsterer, he wasn't really a decorator, to redo a few pieces. And she made do. Of course, a lot of people would say, 'How sad, to make due with the top floor of a hotel.' But it was not what she would have liked. And he could have afforded to have said, 'Well, honey, go get something you want. We can afford that. You find a house you like, you fix it up and that's fine.'

"But he wanted what he wanted. She said, 'The only thing your grandpa picked out in this whole place was where to set the TV. And he did. He had that fifty-two-foot-square living room, and he placed the TV and his chair, and she and Mr. Argo arranged the rest of the furniture. Of course, it was not a really convenient location. The living room was at one end, dining room and kitchens at the other. The bedrooms were strung up the way. But it was fine. We lived there for several years. After he died she said, 'Well, now I'm not going to rush out. I'm going to get a home, a house. I don't really like living in a hotel. But since we own it, it's better that we live here.' Which it was.

"Unfortunately, she had no interest in the hotel business. She liked the cemetery business, and they had sold that. She really disliked the hotel business. The very first chance she had to sell it, she did ..."

Florence and Buddie planned to return to Hawaii in October, 1952, with their friends, Ruth and Jim Thomas who had also spent their honeymoon in Hawaii. It was to be a silver anniversary celebration. Instead, Buddie was operated on for stomach trouble that proved to be cancer of the liver. It was already too advanced for a cure. He wasn't told, but, of course, he must have known. His doctor told Florence he would live about three months and he did. Buddie's turbulent and colorful life ended January 11, 1953. If he had been a singer, "I Did It My Way" would have been his theme song.

Buddie Candler had lived his life to the fullest.

*Actress Hilda Clarke was the model for this elegant 1900 Coca-Cola advertising poster. (Courtesy The Archives of the Coca-Cola Company)*

# Brother Landrum and Others

$S$ince the end of the Civil War, the Candler family has had black retainers, some of whom became as much members of the family as those born into it. A few, like Landers Anderson — the legendary Brother Landrum — were lifelong companions of their employer and more friend than servant.

Blacks working for wealthy families in the South sometimes had a better life than those who did not. Their employers served as a buffer from the excesses of oppression.

The stories about the servants are as much a part of Candler history as Buddie's elephants and Howard's penny-pinching. No offense should be taken at the use of dialect. *That is* the way people of deprived educational opportunity spoke. What racism there may have been, alas, was simply an accepted norm at the time — a part of history that none of us can rewrite. Like the classic "Amos 'n Andy" radio and television skits, such stories may no longer be accepted by all, but that doesn't make them any less humorous nor remove them from the fabric of history.

Brother Landrum was Buddie's boon companion for most of his adult life. Brother Landrum had first served as the chain gang camp spy, but quickly made himself indispensable. As Nancy Candler Nutter remembers him, "Landrum was a tall, very dark black man and in later life, he was palsied. In his youth, he must have cut quite a figure with the women. He was in prison for life for killing a man he caught with 'his woman.' PaPa wanted Landrum pardoned so he could work for him at his home because he was a very good cook and utterly loyal to PaPa. He also wanted to be sure that after he and Helen moved from Hartwell, Landrum's freedom would be guaranteed. So, Buddie went to see his cousin, Governor Allen Candler, whom he referred to as "Uncle Allen," a term of respect. He asked him this:

"'Uncle Allen, what would you do if you caught another man fooling around with your wife?'

"'Why, Buddie, I guess I'd kill the ornery S-O-B!'

"'Well, Uncle,' says Buddie, 'that's all poor, ole Landrum did, and they've got him in prison for life.'

"Landrum, called 'brother' as a term of respect by younger folk, black and white, was pardoned and worked for PaPa until he retired. Every Christmas, he made the rounds of PaPa's children to say 'Christmas gift' first, thereby getting the five dollars he'd come for. Being the first to call out 'Christmas gift' insured the caller the right to a gift. Every Christmas, Landrum would slowly make his way to the children's homes to catch them with the 'Christmas gift.'

"Landrum took care of the farm animals at Briarcliff. He prepared slop for the hogs, looked after the hunting dogs, managed the farm located on the back of the property, and lived in a nice groom house PaPa had built for him."

Nancy continues, "Landrum had worked inside while Helen was alive. One evening my grandmother had planned to have a Roquefort cheese dressing served with the salad. When the salad dressing came, it was another kind. After dinner, my grandmother asked Landrum what had happened to the dressing. 'Well, Miz Helen, after I'd picked all them spiled [spoiled] pieces out'n that cheese, there warn't nuff left to serve, so's I jest had to use sump'n else.'

"After PaPa was married the second time, his new bride took charge of the management of the household. She, being a good Baptist, took exception to Landrum's domestic arrangements. He had two girlfriends who alternatively lived with him on the place, as well as a regular parade of lady friends.

"One day, Aunt Florence, as Buddie's grandchildren called her, had Landrum come to the big house to talk with her. She asked him which woman he liked the best, and he replied, 'I believe I likes Jessie the best.' 'Well,' Aunt Florence said, 'if she'll have you, you are to marry her next Saturday because your present situation won't do.' Landrum pondered this decree and bowing to the inevitable put in a request of his own. He said he'd like a 'fresca' wedding like Miss Lucy had."

Nancy again: "Buddie's oldest daughter, Lucy Magill Candler, had been married to Homer Thompson in an elaborate alfresco affair in the sunken garden in 1924. Accounts of the festivities filled the Atlanta press. Of course, the staff had been present, and apparently Brother Landrum had been impressed. Florence arranged for Jessie and Landrum to have a reception in the summer house following their marriage. After the wedding, their thirteen-year-old daughter said to Jessie, 'Mama, I hope you and papa will be as happy as you has been.'

"Landrum also ran the movie projector. As a little girl I loved for him to run the movies backwards. He couldn't explain how it worked. I didn't understand it, either, and I was always trying to get him to run the elephants or ponies backwards while I was riding them."

Buddie's grandson, Asa G. Candler V, adds this: "After granddad, who was a young man at the time, got Landrum off the chain gang, he said, 'Well, you're free, you got your pardon.' And Landrum said, 'I want to stay and work for you.' PaPa said, 'Well, you can stay around here some, but soon I'm going to be done. I've got to go back down to Atlanta, and I won't have the need for you.' Landrum replied, 'Well, I want to work for you, though. I'll just be going down to the big house.' But granddad told him, 'Well, don't come on down there, because I won't have anything for you to do. You're free, man. You can go on your way. You can go home.'

"Granddad left and went back to Atlanta. The next day, there was Landrum on the back steps of Callan Castle. When Buddie asked Landrum what he was doing there, Landrum said very matter of factly, 'I'm come down here to work for Miss Helen,' and he lived around the place for the rest of his life. She put him to work.

"My dad was born in 1905. They say that Brother Landrum just kind of got to be a male nurse to my daddy from about the time he could walk. You can imagine this, a little two- or three-year-old kid, living on a big place like this. There wasn't a whole lot to do on a big place except follow a guy working around. Little kids like to be where the action is... Landrum was doing things, and that represented action so, in effect, he raised my daddy. There was a great deal of affection there.

"Apparently Brother Landrum also made moonshine whiskey on the back place there, and he was arrested several times. When my daddy was a teenager, as he told it, he came down to breakfast one day, and about halfway through breakfast, somebody mentioned, 'Oh, did you hear about Landrum?' And he said, 'What about Landrum?' They said, 'Well, they got him. The revenuers got him last night, and he's in jail.' Well, Daddy just quit right on the spot, put his napkin down, got out of his chair, went downtown, and bailed him out.

"As children, we would go over there and see Brother Landrum. He'd be in the back of the place. They kept a garden back there. They'd raise corn and, of course, pigs and chickens. He was old at the time and had an unstable voice; as some guys get real old, their voice will get to trembling a little bit. If I heard his voice today, I'd know that was Brother Landrum. He had a very distinctive voice. And he was a dark, rich color, and thin, not a big fat guy, but thin, with gray-white hair as I remember him. A very attractive kind of a guy. You could tell he looked at my dad with all kinds of love, and vice versa. And he liked us.

"I remember we were over there one time, and he had taken his wife, Jessie, over to the hospital. She had cancer. And he had come in to see my granddaddy. I guess I was a teenager. My granddaddy said, 'You know, Landrum, she's not coming home.' It was said with real empathy. Brother Landrum said, 'Yes, Boss, she's not coming home.' That's how they communicated."

Asa G. Candler V continues: "He was always there every Christmas. I don't know what all my daddy would give him.

I'm sure whiskey was part of it. He always lived on the back of the place and did the farming.

"There was an old Scot who lived back there named Mr. Stark who actually ran the grounds, which was a big job. There were forty acres with bushes and trimming those hedges and cutting the grass. It was a big job. Plus, at the back there, they were raising pigs and corn, and so forth. They had a regular village back there."

Mettelen Thompson Moore had this: "Mother always said, Brother Landrum would come up to Helen's room to see what was doing for the day. He would report. I'll tell you one of the stories about his coming to report, which I think is about as funny as can be. They had lived on Euclid Avenue and had this beautiful climbing rose. A couple weeks before they were to move out to Briarcliff Farm, Helen told Landrum that they wanted to get a cutting of that rose and go on and start it so that they would have it at the greenhouse out there at Briarcliff. He should get several started, and they could plant them later. So they moved to Briarcliff — I don't know if it was because of weather or what, but all of the landscaping wasn't finished when they moved in.

"So PaPa, of course, hired nurserymen to come and plant the landscape. Brother Landrum cooked biscuits in the morning and worked in the yard afternoons. He was just an all-around person. It was just a year later. Brother Landrum comes up to her room in the morning and Helen asked, 'Landrum, what is wrong with your rose bush? Everything else is just doing fine.'

"My mother could mimic him, and he said, 'Well, Miz Helen, I done everything I can to dat dere rosebush. The boss he done put so much shrubbery around dat, he done took all the subject outa de ground.'

"He'd transplanted it, and it just couldn't find enough nutrients. He was right — all the other plants took all that 'subject' out of the ground. [Helen] ran the household, but she ran it through Landrum more than anything else.

"He called mother 'Lucy' until she was about seven or eight years old. Then in one of those meetings, when Brother Landrum went up to Helen's room, Helen said, 'Landrum, I think we've got to start treating Lucy as a lady. I want you to call her Miss Lucy.' And he said, 'Yes, ma'am, I've changed her diapers and everything else, and now I've got to call her Miss Lucy.' But he did — and John, 'Mr. John.' I think by the time it got to Sam [nicknamed 'Pete'], it was just Pete."

Laura Candler Chambers recalls, "One of the cute stories about Brother Landrum was when he fired the nurse. There again, Mama had to go to town. She left me with a colored nurse. We always had a nurse when we were little, and Landrum was always there. He was a fixture. I went out in the yard and I was doing something. I was playing in the water, getting sopping wet, of course.

"Brother Landrum went outside, and he said to that girl, 'W'at is yo' doin' standin' dere like a donkey? W'at yo' doin' lettin' Laura play in all dat water foh? Don' yo' know she'll catch cole and die?' I mean to tell you, he gave it to her up and down. He said, 'You jes' get yo' hat and leave.'

"When mother came home, she noticed the girl wasn't there, and she said, 'Landrum, where's Odessa (or whatever her name was)?'

"He said, 'Miss Helen, I jes' plain fired her.'

"She said, 'You fired her?' He said, 'Yes'm. She was a lettin' Laura get wet, and I knowed Laura would have pneumonia and die. I jes' tole her to get her hat and go.' He would take charge, so Mama would never worry.

"She nearly knocked him out of commission, too, one time. With her rolling pin. Papa got cute and hired a white man as a chauffeur. I don't remember why. Anyway, the chauffeur and Mama and Landrum happened to come into the kitchen. Well, that white chauffeur turned around and sassed Mama, and that didn't suit Brother Landrum at all. He started to kill him... Brother Landrum had a knife in his hand and was going to stab him. Mama picked up the rolling pin — it was the closest thing to her — and she just hit Brother Landrum over the head and knocked him out.

"After he came to, he said, 'Miz Helen, I sho' do 'preciate yo' doin' dat, 'cause I was a going to kill dat man!'

"In those days, they had the marble top table, a little bitty thing, with the board and the rolling pin all set up for making biscuits. Mama didn't have anything else handy, so she just picked up the rolling pin and hit him. I don't think she meant to hit him as hard as she did. But she did it enough to make him fall out of the picture and certain he didn't commit a crime. From then on, *no more white chauffeurs!*"

All the grandchildren recalled the annual sausage making on the farm. One version of the great event comes from Asa Candler V. "[Buddie] always had some sheep there, up on the hill, eating some grass, sort of like a lawnmower deal. He just liked having animals. In the wintertime, it was pig-killing season. He and Brother Landrum and a couple of other guys would go back there, and Granddaddy would pick out the pig, and they'd bring him out.

"There was a bit of a ceremony about which one they thought should do the kill, then they'd bring that pig in and they'd kill it. Landrum would hit it in the head with an ax. He'd whap him on the brain, and down he'd go. First they'd put him in the hot water and scald him and get all that hair off of him. Then they would hang him up by his heels, and my granddaddy would butcher him. He just liked to do that.

"They had a big cauldron there. It was elevated, sort of a split-level building, completely open on one side, really more of a shed. In the upper level of this thing they had this cauldron. They'd keep a fire built under it and all of the scraps and garbage from the hotel restaurants they would bring out there and dump into this cauldron.

"They would boil all the food leftovers and turn it through a vat down into the troughs, and that's how they fed the pigs. There was a ramp that went by the door, down into the pigpens... That was sort of an early day recycling deal.

"On Mondays, he would kill that pig. On Tuesdays, they would have that big old marble table with all this meat ground up, and Slim would help. Slim was tall, about six-foot-four. They would have all that sausage spread out there on that table with a three-by-six-foot countertop. They'd start fixing up that sausage, and grandpa would supervise.

"They'd spread it over the entire top of the table, sort of even. Then they would shake salt out on it, and then they would mix it up. Then they would spread it out again, sort of even. Then they would shake pepper on it and mix it all up. Then grandpa would say, 'Needs a little sage on that, Slim.'

And then he would put the sage on it and mix it all up. Rosa would be in attendance baking biscuits so that we all tested the sausage until we thought it was just right. I don't know what all went into it. It was really the best sausage you ever had — hot. It had enough fat in it.

"I think people back then just grew up knowing how to do those things. He was born in 1880, and you can imagine he had seen some pigs killed between 1880 and 1900. Certainly by the time I was born — we're talking about the middle 30s when he was doing this pig killing I was watching — those were just some things that he liked to do, and he always did the things that he liked to do. If he wanted to go on a trip, he went on a trip. He was a guy that was out *doing* all the time. When he died, the editorial guy in the paper said that there are some men that are great, that are active. He was a doer. He did things."

Buddie had an extremely protective attitude toward his help. He had a chauffeur pick them up in the morning and drive them home in the evening. He said this was because he wanted his breakfast at a certain time — it was true, the streetcar system was not very efficient, and they would have had to walk a long way from the end of the line. But it was also a courtesy, an extra perk for employees at Briarcliff, plus a protection. During the race riots in Atlanta, Buddie locked the gates at his home and wouldn't let his help go out or anyone else come in. He kept them safe at his house during the entire period. They went home only after Buddie had determined it was safe.

Nancy Candler Nutter says that her grandfather, "Had good help ... they worked quietly and efficiently and they didn't ever quit. For that time, those jobs were as good as a black person in Atlanta was going to get, short of owning a life insurance company or a funeral home.

Charles Nutter guesses that the staff loyalty was partially due to Aunt Florence's policy of keeping them on even if she and Buddie were traveling for an extended period. "Other people in that era just laid them off when they went out of town."

Nancy Candler Nutter thinks that Florence's attitude

came out of having been a working woman herself. "Before she was a wealthy man's wife, she was a working girl, and she understood that you need that paycheck at the end of the week. You can't work at the pleasure of someone with plenty of money and then be out of work.

"I don't know exactly what they were paying, I just know it was more than the going rate. It wouldn't sound like much to you or me, but it was a secure job. They got to eat there. Their uniforms were done there. They had the laundry. They were provided transportation."

Mettelen Thompson Moore has another Landrum tale: "There was the time the Feds came up to PaPa and said, 'We've got to arrest you.' And he asked, 'Arrest me for what?' They said, 'Well, you're making whiskey on the back of the property.' PaPa said, 'You know I'm not making whiskey.' They said, 'You've got a still. You're making whiskey back there.'

"PaPa asked them to take a seat and called Brother Landrum. He told him to sit down. He said, 'Landrum, what are you doing in the back?' Landrum says, 'Boss, I ain't doing nothing in the back.' He said, 'Landrum, what are you doing in the back?' Landrum says, 'You know I've got this rheumatism and I need some help with it, so I'm just making me some medicine.'

"PaPa said, 'You know it's against the law.' And Landrum said, 'No it's not, not just for me, not just for me.'

"There wasn't much PaPa could do, so he turned Landrum over to the Feds, and said, 'There's your man.' It just broke Uncle John's heart. He just couldn't stand for him to be down there and be put on a chain gang and really have to do manual labor. Uncle John by this time was fourteen or fifteen years old. And, of course, Landrum did everything for him. All of them. Made the best biscuits and everything.

"So John gets himself up and goes on down to talk to the head jailer and talks to him. He says, 'Listen, if you want a good breakfast, put him in the kitchen, and make him the cook.' So they did. So Brother Landrum didn't have to spend any hard time. He just stayed in the kitchen. And John went down there every day to see him. He took him whatever he needed — soap, razor, clothes. It wasn't like he was really on a chain gang."

Mettelen Thompson Moore continues the story. "Anyway, about six months before mother was to get married. Helen went to PaPa and said, 'You've got to get Brother Landrum off that chain gang because I'm going to need him. The sunken garden needs attention, and I can't do all these things without him. ... PaPa said, 'Nope, he's learned his lesson for the last time now, I'm not going to get him out early. He doesn't have that much longer to serve.' So Uncle John went down there and told them how much he was needed and could he get out on good behavior? They said they would look into it. Anyway, about three days later, Helen called mother to come in there quick. She said, 'Come here. Is that Brother Landrum coming down the driveway?'

"Mother said, 'It sure does look like it.' And Helen said, 'Hmm. I wonder what he's doing.' So they talked a few minutes and then there was a knock on the door. There stood Brother Landrum in his white coat. He said, 'Well, Miz Helen, they done let me off 'cause I's so good. Here I is, so what yo' want me to do?'

"He was always into something, but they let him off 'cause he was so good. He was caught three or four times making whiskey back there."

Buddie stood up for Landrum and the other servants. He wasn't about to let other people's ideas about segregation dictate *his* actions. Asa G. Candler V remembers being told of what happened when with his parents were getting married. "When my daddy got married to my mama, Elizabeth Brandon, who lived in Richmond, Virginia, it was a big deal to go up to the wedding. And, of course, Brother Landrum had to go. Back in those days — we're talking about 1927 — we were a pretty segregated society with blacks living in their place and whites living in theirs. There wasn't any commingling while you were seated. Plenty of it while you were standing, but not while you were seated.

"They all got to the hotel in Richmond, and my grandfather says, 'Well, there's no place for Landrum to stay, he's just going to have to stay in that hotel.' Which was an unheard of thing, absolutely unheard of.

"They go to check in, and the clerk checking him in says, 'Who's that?' And granddad replied, 'Well, that's Landers Anderson. He's my valet. I want him to have the room next to mine.' The man at the hotel said, 'I'm sorry, but we don't rent rooms to Negroes. He'll have to stay somewhere else.'

"Granddad, he told me, 'I begged, I said I couldn't dress myself, he would have to dress me, he's my valet. I did everything I could think of, and the guy still stood his ground and finally they got the manager or the owner out and they just wouldn't let me check him into a room.'

"'Finally,' granddad said, 'they made me so mad, I just said to the man, 'How much do you want for this hotel?' And the man said to him, 'Does it mean that much to you, Mr. Candler?' And granddad told him, 'Absolutely, I can't dress myself without him.' So the clerk finally threw up his hands and gave in.

"And that's how they got Brother Landrum into a room in the Jefferson Hotel in Richmond, Virginia, in 1927. Brother Landrum stayed in the hotel and went to the wedding. He sat right down there next to my grandpa. He held him by the arm as they went down the aisle, like he couldn't get down there alone. It tickled my dad no end."

Mettelen Thompson Moore remembers the hotel incident, also. "When Uncle John got ready to get married, PaPa called Brother Landrum up there and said, 'Landrum, do you have a tuxedo?' Of course, Landrum said 'no.' So PaPa said, 'Well, go in my closet and find you one that will fit.'

"PaPa's weight then was still fluctuating, and Brother Landrum's weight stayed the same as long as I remember. He went in and found him a tuxedo, went in the drawer and found him a pair of socks, went in another drawer and got out a shirt and a tie. He went in the closet and got out a pair of shoes. He got the biggest pair he could find. Of course, patent leather shoes. Then PaPa told him, 'I want you to get a white suit.' Of course, that meant he had his own white shoes, and he had to get his own white things. He got a suitcase, and Brother Landrum packed his suitcase for the wedding. Then Brother Landrum packed PaPa's suitcase for the wedding.

"Then next afternoon, Brother Landrum was summoned

in and PaPa said to him, 'You're going to be my valet.'
Landrum said, 'I'm going to be your valet? I don't know what
valets do.' PaPa said, 'Well, you just do whatever I say to do.'

"Anyway, PaPa and Landrum went up on the train
together. They got a stateroom together with two lower
bunks and the upper bunks. So Brother Landrum dressed up
in his white suit, and with his tuxedo and his shirt and his
shoes all packed, they get on the train.

"Of course, with the black in a Pullman, the porter said,
'You can't stay in here.' Brother Landrum wasn't going to
argue with them. PaPa says, 'He is my valet and he stays
where I do.' Of course, they say, 'No black rides up here.' And
PaPa said, 'I bought his ticket, he rides up here. You can go
get the engineer or whoever you want, but I don't care.' PaPa
was a big shot back then.

"So Brother Landrum rode in the Pullman. They got
there and Brother Landrum got the suitcases, called the cab,
and they went to the hotel. They went through the rehearsal.
I don't know that there had ever been a wedding there that
a black man had attended the rehearsal. I don't think he
attended the dinner but was there to wait on PaPa. He
probably ate in the back with the others.

"The next afternoon came time to dress. They thought
they had everything, but it turned out that PaPa had
forgotten to put in a proper tuxedo shirt. So they sent
Brother Landrum to see if he could find one. It was about
4:30 on a Saturday afternoon and there was nowhere to go
for a tux shirt. Anyway, Brother Landrum lent PaPa his tux
shirt and put a dress shirt that he had on backwards. He put
the bow tie on it and wore that. He said, 'Boss, I didn't like
all them ruffles anyway.'

"And he rode back on the train that same way."

Brother Landrum and Buddie spent their lives together,
and they pretty much died together. Buddie passed away in
1952; Brother Landrum died only a few short months later.

The Candlers never could forget their rural background.
They had large mansions, but they ran them like farms.
They weren't quite comfortable having liveried white ser-
vants as did the Vanderbilts and the Rockefellers. In that

( Left ) Lucy II in 1900.
Courtesy of Mr. & Mrs. John Howard
Candler, Jr.

( Below ) The Real Ones in 1911
1st row: Lucy lll, Elizabeth
Owens, Howard Jr., John,
Catherine, Laura, Walter Jr., Asa
IV, and Eugenia II.
2nd row: Helen Candler, Lucy (II)
Candler Owens, and Eugenia
Candler.
3rd row: Florence Candler Harris
with portrait of the deceased Asa
III, Howard, Buddie, Asa Sr. and
Lucy holding twins, Helen and
Martha, William, Walter, and
William Owens holding William
Owens, Jr.
Courtesy of the family of Walter Turner
Candler, Sr.

( Above )  Charles Howard Candler.
Courtesy of Mr. & Mrs. Samuel Ozburn Candler.

( Left ) Howard as a senior at Emory, 1898.
Courtesy of the Special Collections Department, Robert W. Woodruff Library, Emory University.

( Below ) Asa Candler Sr., with his youngest grandchildren-- Emelie Heinz, Bootsie Candler, William Candler Jr., and Henry Heinz Jr.
Courtesy of Mr. & Mrs. Edward Harry Ruffner.

( Right ) The Candler
Building in Atlanta--Asa's
pride and joy.
From the collection of Elizabeth
Candler Graham.

( Below ) Howard Candler in
the company Locomobile at
the New York office of The
Coca-Cola Company in 1902.
Courtesy of Mr. & Mrs. Samuel
Ozburn Candler.

( Above ) The Real Ones in 1895. William, Asa Sr., Walter, Lucy II, Lucy I, Howard, Buddie.

Courtesy, Archives Department, The Coca-Cola Company.

( Below ) The house on Seaboard Avenue where Asa Sr. raised his children. Courtesy of Mrs. John Holtzendorff Wilson.

( Left ) Asa in 1888, the year he bought Coca-Cola. He is 36 this picture.

Courtesy of the Special Collections Department, Robert W. Woodruff Library, Emory University.

( Right ) Warren Aiken Candler, "the Bishop."

Courtesy of Mr. & Mrs. Charles Nisbett Nutter.

(Right ) Florence Candler
Harris ("Sissie") and her
brother, Asa Candler in
867.

(Below ) Martha Beall
Candler and her boys in
891. The Bishop
(Warren),
the Congressman (Milton),
Martha, the
Lawyer/Preacher (Ezekial),
the Judge (John),
the Banker (William),
the Coca-Cola King (Asa),
the Merchant (Samuel
Charles Jr.). Courtesy of Mr. &
Mrs. Samuel Ozburn Candler.

( Left ) Martha
Beall Candler
about 1833, Asa
Sr.'s mother.
Courtesy of Mr. & Mrs.
Charles Nisbett Nutter

( Right ) Samuel Charles
Candler about 1833, Asa
Sr.'s father.
Courtesy of Mr. & Mrs. Charles
Nisbett Nutter.

respect, Howard is interesting. He did have a white nanny.

In the North, the custom was that only the *nouveau riche* would hire blacks. No one who was "anyone" would have a black servant. They didn't want to be surrounded by people they perceived as ignorant. In the South, it was different. Black labor was cheap, and people were used to having blacks as servants and nannies for their children.

The Candlers, unlike some, treated their servants and employees well. Buddie and his brother Walter were really good friends with, or, at least, had a lifelong association with certain black people. Walter was very close to his Ernest and Buddie was very close to Brother Landrum.

Nancy Candler Nutter recounts, "PaPa loved his magic tricks and practiced them all the time. In later years, Aunt Florence loved to tell this story on him, or really on Rosa Logan, the downstairs maid. My grandfather was at home with a fever and in bed. Aunt Florence called from her office at Westview Cemetery to see how he was, and when Rosa answered the phone, the following conversation took place:

Mrs. C: "Rosa, how is Mr. C?"
Rosa: "He's all right."
Mrs. C: "Where is he?"
Rosa: "Oh, he's upstairs in his bedroom, playing with his little trick!"

PaPa and Aunt Florence found this response extremely funny and they had many a private laugh about it.

Rosa Logan had been a maid at the Briarcliff Hotel when Florence lived there before her marriage. Rosa had done personal laundry and other extra chores. The two women got along well together, so Florence hired her to work at Briarcliff, where she stayed for almost twenty-five years.

Nancy Candler Nutter says that "when Rosa married, PaPa invited her fiance to come by so he could meet him and see if he was 'good enough for one of my girls.' Rosa was not a young bride, and her groom was a man of some substance, but PaPa wanted to let him understand that Rosa was a special person and should be treated well. Tragically, theirs was not a long marriage. After a few years, Rosa became ill with cancer and died. Aunt Florence always said she had waited too late in life to marry, and the excitement was just too much for her.

Nancy Candler Nutter continues: "You may wonder just who was doing all the housework. Briarcliff had a staff of servants who moved silently and courteously through their daily routine. Most worked for my grandparents all their lives. As domestic jobs went, this one was probably choice. My grandmother, Helen, had as cook, Annie Little, called 'Nannie' because she also served as nurse for the children. My dad was her favorite, and she'd let him sit under the sink in the kitchen to play and eat cold biscuits or corn pone.

"When Daddy and Mama married, Nannie quit my grandfather so she would go work for 'Mr. John.' When she'd be miffed about something, he'd say to her, 'Nannie, the trouble with you is you're more Irish than anything else, and it makes you mean.'

"He was teasing and they got along very well.

"Nannie was very light-skinned and very proud. She'd never admit to being unable to read. She'd say to me, if Mama wanted something cooked that she had found in a cookbook, 'Nancy come here and call this recipe off to me. I don't have time to be reading recipes, and your mama wants this for supper.' I liked doing this, but was an adult before I understood the real reason for my reading to her.

"Because she had been Grandmother Helen's cook, Nannie was perhaps not thrilled at the prospect of working for Aunt Florence. After PaPa and Aunt Florence returned from their honeymoon, Nannie announced that she was going to work for Mr. John. Aunt Florence asked why she was leaving, and Nannie said, 'Cause he needs me to straighten him out and to fix his food, so I's going over there.' This was Nannie's way of leaving on good terms. (It was also news to my mother, because Annie just showed up and went to work at their house.)"

After Buddie's son John and his wife, Lib, began having a family, they needed a baby nurse. None of Buddie's staff was young enough to do that kind of work, so the word was put out that Mr. John and Miss Lib needed a baby nurse, which is how Buddie's grandchildren came to grow up under the guidance of Louise Benn, or "Nursie" as she was called.

Nancy Candler Nutter: "Nursie was a licensed practical nurse, which was one of the reasons that my mother hired her. Mother wanted to have reliable, responsible help. Nursie was nearly six feet tall and very dark. She was proud and rather standoffish with other help because she was better educated and could command better wages. Some of the people who worked in Druid Hills looked down on Nursie because she was so dark, and they were much lighter skinned. She used to tell me that she was 'mostly Indian.' Nursie liked to gamble or 'bet on the bug,' as she called it. When she'd put us to bed at night, she'd tell us to dream of a number, and she'd bet it for us. Sometimes she'd win. We loved being in the conspiracy.

"Nursie was a firm disciplinarian. She had her own way of getting her messages across; for example, she would say, 'Pretty is as pretty does, you being ugly.' It cut us to the quick for her to say that, and we would straighten up."

Nancy's sister, Helen Candler Griffith, adds, "The nurses would meet up and visit. Nursie would run us by the Bishop's house and by some of the other people that lived in that area. I guess it was a different route for her to stroll. Or maybe she just liked to hobnob with the swells. I don't know. But we used to stop by and speak with those people. I remember it. She always made sure we knew how we were related to various people, like the Bishop. It was very important to her.

"She was very proud of all that, of being a nursie, and getting to know the important people in town. She had a relationship with Eugene O'Neill's help at the beach where mother and daddy had their summer house. They had a house on Nineteenth Street; we had a house across the street. And she became friendly with the help — friendly enough to know that the O'Neills did not like children, which let us out. But *she* — they liked *her*.

"There was a sort of caste system that worked among the black help. They had their social order, and who you worked for had a lot to do with your standing. They hobnobbed back and forth and they knew everything about everybody."

What the little Candler grandchildren did not know at

the time, was that Nursie's thoughtful and constant attendance had more to it than just being a conscientious nurse.
John and Lib had received a kidnapping threat. And, they
took it very seriously. John's sister, Lucy Thompson, had
just been through a similar attack on her family in 1932.
Nursie understood the gravity of this situation and handled
it with a competence and dignity that was never forgotten.
Long after John and Lib were dead and the children were
grown, Nursie checked in on her little charges, sharing with
them her opinions and the important events in all their lives.

Bessie Little was the upstairs maid and carried the key
to the linen closet, which was always kept locked. She had
been Helen Candler's personal maid. Bessie and Lucy III
had washed and dressed Helen for burial because Helen did
not want strangers handling her body.

Nancy Candler Nutter said, "PaPa kept Bessie on long
after she was able to do much actual work because as he told
Aunt Florence, 'Bessie might as well be here where she can
sit down and rest and have someone to cook for her as to be
at home working herself to death looking after her nephews'
children.' Bessie also did all the flower arrangements at
Briarcliff, and there were always fresh flowers in the living
room, front hall, and side hall.

Tommy Thompson adds, "I remember the peacocks and
the parrot that they kept up there in the upstairs hallway.
I was little then. Bessie nicknamed me Puddleduck because
I liked water so much. She was more or less the upstairs
maid, and I guess Bessie was really the ramrod of all the
female colored help. She didn't have much to say about how
Rosa Logan and Slim behaved, because Aunt Florence hired
them, but Bessie was the princess.

"The story about the parrot was that Bessie would take
me from room to room as she was cleaning, and she let me
play in the bathtub while she was working. She carried me
around in a trash can. That kept me happy. She would put
me into these little bitty foot-tubs which were in a couple of
the bathrooms. She would put me in that foot-tub and run a
little water in there, and I was as happy as a dead hog in the
sunshine, and I would play and splash, and she could go in
and make up the beds. She would never put enough water in

there that I could drown, and she could hear me splashing.

"The parrot could imitate Bessie. I'd be out in by the garage and that parrot would get bored because there was nobody up there. I remember he'd hop to the window, because that was before air conditioning and they'd open the windows and he would let out with, 'Puddleduck, come here, come here!' Because he heard Bessie saying that when she was working upstairs, and I would go running down the halls. Mother always told me, 'Now you mind Bessie. Bessie tells you to do something, you do it.' And I was a little bit frightened if I didn't do it, I was going to get a spanking. That damn parrot would call me, and I would go running up all those stairs, and that parrot would be up there, walking back and forth across that thing. He was out, he wasn't in a cage. He was on one of those bar things, with a little loop around his ankle. He would just keep going. And there I would have run all the way thinking it was Bessie calling.

"I don't know what happened to that parrot. He died, I know, but I don't know whether somebody strangled him or shot him or choked him or what, but that parrot just all of a sudden disappeared."

The 'other Rosa' was Rosa Davis who was the cook and the person the fifth elephant was named for. She was in charge of the kitchen.

Nancy Candler Nutter tells this family story about her: "She had relatives that had gone up North to Chicago, and I think she had a few in New York. She didn't have any children of her own, but she would go on her vacations to see these people. She would always come home, and be agitated and unhappy for a few weeks after her vacation.

"Aunt Florence said, 'She goes up there, and these people put her down. They are always putting on airs like we live in Chicago, we don't have to be somebody's maid. I work on the train, or I work in a hotel, or whatever they were doing; they weren't somebody's maid.' They were always putting her down for that.

"She had finally just had enough of that. I guess she thought about it all year long. Aunt Florence would get these fur coats, and as they went out of style, she would give them to the servants. This particular year, she had given Rosa her fur coat. So Rosa decided she would go in the winter so she could wear her coat. Aunt Florence used to love to tell me this story. She used to tell me that Rosa finally learned something from her. 'You just can't let people walk all over you,' Aunt Florence said. 'I was always telling her that she just doesn't have to let people talk to her like that.'

"She got up to Chicago, and her relatives were going on and on about how they didn't have to be a maid in somebody else's house. They had this and they had that, and they had social security because Mr. Roosevelt had gotten them social security. They were going to be looked after forever and ever. The government's going to keep them up... Rosa said, 'Mrs. Candler, you know what I told them?' She'd come home and give Aunt Florence a blow-by-blow description of her trips. 'Well, I just looked at them and I said, 'Huh. Social security, what's that? A promise from some government is what that is. Who you going to trust in the government. Huh? You people ever heard of Coca-Cola up here?' Well, of course they'd all heard of Coca-Cola. She said, 'Well, Mr. Candler, his people gots Coca-Cola, and they's always got Coca-Cola. That's who my people are. That's who I work for. I ain't never going to need nothing, because I've got Coca-Cola backing me all the way to the grave.'

"And she did, she received stock in the company. She said, 'I put them in their place.' Of course, everybody had heard about the Coca-Cola millionaires in Georgia, and for some reason, it had not registered with her kin people.

"So she did that, and then Mrs. Steve Scullen, Aunt Florence's friend, told Rosa one time that when she went to New York to see her cousin, that Rosa should call her. They would have a party. When Rosa got there, she called Mrs. Scullen. She said, 'Mrs. Scullen, I'm here.' So her housekeeper arranged to have a big tea party, just like white folks had. Mrs. Scullen said, 'We've got to entertain her. She's just a wonderful person.' And her housekeeper entertained her, and she was entertained all around New York. Then she came back and told Aunt Florence all about it.

Nancy continues, "Rosa was a very good cook, and I remember with pleasure all the delicious food that came out of that kitchen. Rosa may have been the laundress, also. I rarely went to the basement where a large commercial-type laundry was set up complete with mangle for sheets and tablecloths, and so forth. I kind of think she was in charge there, too. Anyway, the servants went down there to rest between chores, smoke as some of them did, and just talk. The laundry looked out upon a pretty little grassy area across from the garage. It was here that Slim cut off the chickens heads for dinner. I guess the grown-ups thought we'd be entertained or informed by watching this ritual (or maybe they didn't know where we were). I was horrified that the poor chicken kept running after he'd lost his head. It was several weeks before I could eat chicken again. After Rosa retired, Florence's longtime cook was Louise Cornelius.

"Slim [Samuel Green] was the houseman, butler, and helped in the yard. He was the 'extra' chauffeur. Slim came to work at Briarcliff as a fourteen-year-old yard boy and worked for our family until his death at age sixty-two. He dropped dead in the barbershop on Saturday. I always thought this was God's way of rewarding a particularly faithful servant who had labored long in the vineyard — no nursing home, no long, painful illness."

John Howard Candler, Jr. recalls: "Briarcliff was a lot of fun. You talk about a fantasia. For a little kid? Like I was? I liked the opulence of it, and it was fun. There was always something to do. There were fifteen or sixteen of us that were first cousins. Think about it. Every Sunday afternoon you got together with your cousins and ran around one of the greatest mansions in the South and had a good time. That's a lot of fun.

"Sunday was wonderful! We liked to go over there. I know after we moved over there it was funny. I had always had such a super fun time, and yet when television came out, I remember that we weren't allowed to watch it on Sunday. No ma'am. PaPa didn't think that we should do that.

"Slim was always allowed to play pool with Asa and me.

"Aunt Florence was a good pool player. She could drive that ball so hard you couldn't believe it. But Slim taught me finesse. His favorite game was pool. That's the way he died, you know. Slim died at a barber shop downtown which also had pool tables. He died after he had opened a Coca-Cola. It's true. Slim was a great pool player.

"There's also a story," John Howard Candler, Jr. said, "about Slim polishing the black out of the silver. In the inside of the silver that Papa bought as a wedding gift for Florence, was this black enamel. PaPa went to Gorham's to buy that.

"The initials were a raised 'FSC' and inside of that was black enamel. So they go away to Europe. Slim and the staff were left at home. Aunt Florence said, 'Clean the silver.' Just, 'Clean the silver, clean the house, beat the rugs ... You know, all these things that you do when I'm gone for three or four months.' I'll never forget. She thought it was so funny. She laughed so hard ... She got back and she said Slim had the biggest smile on his face. She said, 'Now, Slim, you just look so happy about things. Why?' And he said, 'Oh, Miz Candler, I cleaned that silver. I finally got it clean. It had been worrying me. It had all that black in it. I cleaned it all.'

"He had gotten in there and cleaned all the enamel off. Can you imagine the patience it took? It took that whole three or four months!"

Once the coauthor of this book came home from Emory and Florence said, "Help me get some stuff out of the silver closet. We're going to wrap it up. Slim's anniversary is coming up. You know, he and Susie worked hard all their lives, and I'm going to give them some silver because I told Slim that anybody that's polished as much silver as he has as diligently as he has should have some silver." She was very amused about giving Slim silver, and it all harkened back to when Slim had polished off all that enamel.

"She just thought it was funny," John Candler said. "She just said that the hardest thing she had ever done was to keep a straight face. She said she sat there and she said, 'Oh, Slim. That's just beautiful. I really appreciate all of your help. You've done such a good job.' She said he just sat there and smiled. He said, 'Yas'm. I tried real hard. It took me all day, every day while you were gone.' And Aunt Florence told me, 'I thought, good God, it must have. He did it, but he never damaged the top of those monograms. He had gone in each little thing with the little instrument and he had polished up those things. Bless his heart, he got it all out, and it was wonderful. All thirty-six place settings.'"

Nancy Candler Nutter recounts these stories about other Briarcliff help: "There were several chauffeurs over the years, including Lige Brown and B.J. Jinks. B.J. drove for PaPa, helped wait on the table, helped my grandfather bathe and dress, and helped run the boat PaPa kept at Lake Altoona.

"Before George Kampf's arrival, there were two Filipinos, Jose and Felipe, brothers. They were housemen at Briarcliff. This didn't work out. PaPa hired them on a trip to the Orient and brought them to a very provincial Atlanta where they didn't have any fellow countrymen with whom they could socialize. They weren't really welcomed by either whites or blacks. One of them dated and wanted to marry a white girl, but her family objected. He committed suicide on the back of the place, and his brother went back to the islands. George Kampf's tenure came afterwards.

"Preacher was a short, tan-colored fellow who worked at Briarcliff doing a variety of odd chores. He really was a preacher. PaPa would ask him how many he had in attendance the past Sunday? 'Oh, Mr. Candler, maybe eleven or twelve,' he'd say. 'Well,' PaPa would answer, 'last week you had fourteen. Maybe you need a new sermon.' Preacher would say, 'No, Sir, I have a sermon. It's about selfishness. Trouble with those sinners is they ain't learned it yet. So's I'm going to preach it until they get it.'

"Another employee at Briarcliff was John Taylor. His wife was Appeline. John worked outside. Appeline would do laundry for members of the family but did not work for the big house per se." Nancy added, "She was a beautiful laundress and did the baby clothes for my first child. She said she loved to do baby things because they were just like doll clothes. She would also say about my baby, 'I bet Miz Graham wouldn't take a million dollars for her, but she wouldn't pay a penny for another one. That's the way I is.'

"The staff at Briarcliff, after the DeKalb County Alcohol Rehabilitation group moved in, say that the day they arrived, Appeline was standing on the front porch waiting on them. Someone asked if they could help her, and she said 'no,' she was there to help them. They were a little confused; Appeline allowed how she had come to work. They explained that they didn't have a job for her, and she just informed them that she had worked there always, and she planned to just keep on working. To make a long story short, she showed up every day and kept cleaning and working, so eventually she got hired. From day one, she was known to go around the place telling people to wipe their feet, use the door handle to open the door, and so on. She was always quick to say, 'Miz Candler don't allow folks to leave finger marks on de woodwork and to track in de house.'"

The relationship of black servants in the South to the families they worked for has always been greater than that of employer and employee. Such recent movies as *Driving Miss Daisy* and classics like *Gone with the Wind* show the deep affinities that can develop on both sides. It was far from a perfect system, but it gave a few blacks a chance for economic security that they otherwise could never have achieved.

Buddie's help did have a kind of pension plan. If they became disabled or retired, he would make up the difference between their social security and what he had been paying them. At his death, he left each one something in his will.

Brother Landrum, B.J., the two Rosas, Nannie, Preacher, Slim, and all the rest, they were all Candlers, even if their last names were not.

# Lucy, Walter, and William

W hen there is a Buddie and a Howard in a family, it's easy for the other siblings to get left by the wayside.

Asa had hoped and planned for his five children to follow his grand design. They would work in harmony, under the leadership of Howard, all for one and one for all. As today's children are apt to say — NOT.

Howard, Buddie, Lucy, Walter, and William didn't work well together as children, and they sure didn't improve with age. There were too many differences, too much diversity of attitudes, too much ego, and too little cooperation.

Howard and William were quiet and deliberate, Lucy and Buddie more flamboyant, and Walter was a mixture. In combination, there was often bickering. They simply couldn't have pulled together enough over the long run to have continued managing and building The Coca-Cola Company into the soft-drink colossus it now is. In view of that, their giving up of the company was the best decision.

After the sale of The Coca-Cola Company, Asa G. Candler, Inc. was the real estate holding company they owned together. Board meetings of this company were good illustrations of the contentiousness of the actors.

Howard was a stable, conservative force. He was interested in maintaining the family wealth invested in the real estate company. They had many valuable downtown office

259

buildings, apartments, and hotels in Atlanta, New York, Kansas City, Baltimore, and Chicago plus residential real estate.

Howard's was a good business strategy, but tell that to his younger brothers who viewed the property as collateral for borrowing money — or for making money by speculation. When Howard wouldn't let them expand, William and Walter simply went out and borrowed against their shares in the company. In the midst of the Depression, the company found itself borrowing money to cover William and Walter's individual debts. William would be heavily leveraged over the Biltmore Hotel in Atlanta. Walter would be in debt over his commercial real estate ventures.

Most meetings would end with all of the siblings going home mad and upset. Howard probably felt he was doing a good job conserving the family interests and needed to make his brothers toe a conservative fiscal line. Some of the others did not agree. Walter was heard on more than one occasion to complain that Howard might have money, but he never did anything for Atlanta. Walter would say, "I put up some buildings in Atlanta. My brother William built a big hotel, the finest in Atlanta. Bud put up buildings in Atlanta. But what did Howard ever do?"

The fight for control over company assets and direction of the joint real estate holdings was neverending. Brothers took sides over every company decision; their sister Lucy ended up mediating, just as she had in their childhood. Originally, her husband served as her proxy. But after a while, he threw up his hands in disgust over the brothers' bickering, and Lucy had to take over. Her children report Lucy II coming home physically exhausted after Asa G. Candler, Inc. board meetings. She didn't want to take sides, but was forced to when her brothers were arguing — thereby always alienating someone. Most of the time, Lucy voted with Howard to conserve the money, but not always.

Over the years, the factions would change. Originally, it was Buddie and Walter against Howard and William, with Lucy as the swing vote. However, in later years, they matured and changed. Their alliances shifted, and their needs were different.

By 1939, William, usually one of the conservative brothers, had died, leaving his estate heavily in debt. Walter was
expanding his commercial real estate and was also in debt.
The Depression had wreaked havoc with the banks' policies
on lending. By this time, Buddie had been sober for several
years, and in addition, his business-minded young wife,
Florence, was exerting a stronger influence over him and his
financial affairs. It all blew up when the siblings found
themselves having to borrow again in order to continue
covering William and Walter's notes. William and Walter
had pledged their Asa G. Candler, Inc., stock as collateral on
their loans. The bank was threatening to foreclose, and the
other siblings did not want the stock to pass into the hands
of strangers.

The board of Asa G. Candler, Inc., voted to take out
another loan and secure the return of the collateral. For
Buddie, this was the final straw. The commercial real estate
holdings had taken a beating during the Depression and
ceased producing their usual heavy cash flow, In some ways
the company was becoming a liability rather than an asset.
For once, Buddie wasn't in debt and didn't have his shares
pledged. He already owned less of the corporation than the
others and always had. Whether Buddie used this episode in
1939 as an excuse to get Howard to buy him out of the
company isn't clear. What is known is Buddie caused a scene
at the next board meeting, offered to buy Howard out, and
then, conveniently sold his part to Howard. Buddie was out,
but the battles continued with only Walter, Lucy, and
Howard in attendance.

By 1947 Lucy, too, had had enough. She forced her
brothers' hands by agreeing to sell her shares to an outside
real estate developer. Shortly thereafter, Howard, unhappy
at having strangers in the family business, bought out the
other shareholders. The end result had a surprising and
rather happy ending. Howard donated all his interest in the
corporation to Emory University. The entire real estate
transaction was considered to be about ten million dollars,
the largest in Atlanta's history at that time. It was another
first for the Candlers and another plum for Emory. Somehow it was fitting that the major love that Asa Candler had

after his family, Emory University, would end up with the
remaining assets of his life's labors.

Lucy, William, and Walter tended to lead quieter lives
than their more famous brothers, Howard and Buddie. But
the Candler name invariably pulled them into the public
glare. The five siblings could be such studies in contrast —
how different could brothers be than Buddie and Howard? —
that sometimes it was hard to believe they grew up together.

Lucy Beall Candler occupied a unique place in the
family. All of her brothers stood, if not in awe of her, at least,
they held her in high regard. She was exactly in the middle,
two brothers older and two younger. When Lucy spoke to her
brothers, it was with the authority of her mother, Lucy
Elizabeth. She was always her mother's right hand; so her
brothers listened to her. They also shared with their sister
their real feelings, secrets, hopes, and plans. She had a
special relationship with all four of the boys. In addition, her
parents absolutely adored her.

We know a lot about Asa's daughter Lucy from the
family letters she received. At fourteen she went off to
boarding school at West End Institute, Aunt Florence Candler Harris' girls' prep school, where she received frequent
letters from her parents and her brothers.

Buddie enclosed money to buy candy in the letters he
sent her "so she wouldn't have to take candy from boys"
(which gives you an idea of what Buddie thought of boys'
morals — no doubt basing his opinion on his own experiences with the ladies). Howard wrote her about his health,
homesickness in New York, and the social visits he made.
Walter and William were little and wrote notes about their
days at school, their pets, and their playmates.

Lucy shared everything with her mother. Her mother
would tell her all the news from home, keeping Lucy posted
on various family members, births, deaths, illnesses. They
were mother and daughter, but they were also best friends.
And, on occasion, when Lucy, Sr., had to be more mother
than friend, they would keep secrets from Asa, Sr. At least
once, their secret concerned a certain young man named
George Reed. George was a friend of Buddie and Howard,

and he worked for The Coca-Cola Company. Lucy was
bubbly, vivacious, blond, and a very pretty teenager. She
had lots of attention from the fellows, and her mother did not
want her to get carried away and marry too young.

> "My Darling Darling Girl. Your Aunt F. came Friday
> and I felt so badly that you could not come with her, she will
> be back here this morning, and I am going to fix you up
> something good and send by her. Papa and the little boys
> have gone to Sunday school and I will have a good time
> fixing up your box all alone. I carried your Aunt Paul to the
> matinee yesterday afternoon it was the Southern Romance
> it was splendid so pathetic and sweet. Your Aunt Annie is
> getting along very well but your Uncle Will is sick in bed
> again they do have a bad time I am so sorry for them. We
> liked to have had another fire last night from housing hot
> ashes near the fence. Mr. Mack came over and told us papa
> and Walter got the hose and soon put it out with out much
> damage. Ida is real good but she is easily offended. She
> keeps everything very clean and nice, she sends you lots of
> love and is always talking about you. Zeb talks about you
> too and seems to think so much of all of you. I let him go
> to the pony and dog show with the boys yesterday and they
> had a fine time. Lucy your Aunt F. said you got a box the
> day before she left and told me, if I didn't send it that Mr.
> Reed sent it, for it had Coca Cola and candy and treats in it.
> I just want to know, don't say any thing about it, but write
> me and tell me all about it, I don't want you to get any thing
> from any one but mama and papa she said you drink too
> much C.C. don't drink so much, papa says it is not good for
> you. Now hoping you are well and will enjoy what I send
> you, I am your devoted mama. (I just want to know
> something about it, they seem down on Mr. Reed.) PS
> William sends you three violets says they are all he could
> find. I would have had quantities if it had not been for our
> neighbors, they are contemptible."

Then later that same month, her mother writes, "I don't
blame you about the box, I recon Mr. Reed sent it I don't
know if he did he must not do it again, and about the Coca
Cola papa says you must not drink it too often for it isn't good
for you, he wont let me drink it often..."

The following week her mother wrote that she had talked with George Reed, and he agreed not to send Lucy, Jr., any more presents, because as she points out, it isn't proper for him to do so without Lucy's parents' permission. This is one little romance that they kept from Asa, Sr.

Lucy went on to attend both Wesleyan College and Agnes Scott College. Musically gifted, she studied piano and organ. As a young girl, she was the organist at the Inman Park Methodist Church, before her marriage to William Owens, a handsome young banker associated with Asa Candler's bank.

After their marriage in 1903, the newlyweds lived with Lucy's parents at Callan Castle. Her first daughter, Elizabeth, was born at her parents' home. Elizabeth was one of the oldest grandchildren, and one of Danny's favorites, along with Lucy Magill Candler (Lucy III). Although they told Lucy II she shouldn't have any more children because she had had too difficult a delivery with Elizabeth, she insisted. She refused her husband's request to move into a house of their own unless she was pregnant. She was very headstrong and could be very adamant about her desires. Suffice to say that William Davies Owens, Jr., was born in April 1911, at Lucy's new house.

Lucy and her little family had three happy years together before tragedy struck. She and her husband fell sick in the typhoid epidemic of 1914. The worried relatives kept a watch at their separate bedsides, expecting both of them to die very soon. Sadly, William did, without Lucy even aware of his passing. Her family decided she was too sick to handle the news. Convinced that she, too, would succumb to the fever, they put William's body in a vault at the cemetery so that they could bury them together. Lucy did not learn of her husband's death until she recovered several weeks later. It was a blow to the young wife and mother.

After her husband's death, Lucy and the children lived alone in their home on Little Ponce de Leon Avenue until she accidentally left a door open and a burglar paid them a visit. Lucy was playing the piano with Elizabeth and Bill, Jr., singing along when she saw the intruder. Fortunately, Lucy could talk fast. It's easy to imagine her with her rapid-fire delivery talking the surprised and quite possibly timid burglar right out of robbing her — which is exactly what happened. This incident did, however, scare her so much that she moved back in with her parents. By this time Lucy's mother was very sick, so Lucy ended up caring for her and managing the household.

Lucy Owens was remarried in 1917 to Henry Charles Heinz. She was later to joke that Henry only married her because Henry was at William Owens' bedside while he lay dying, and William had asked him to "take care of Lucy and the children." Henry had been a friend not only of William Owens but also of Buddie. He was graduated from Emory with Howard, and the truth was, Henry Heinz had had a terrific crush on Lucy Candler since the first day he laid eyes on her. One of her sons recalled that his mother loved to tell how Buddie, Henry Heinz, and John Hurt rode their bikes from Oxford to Decatur to see her when she was at Agnes Scott.

The Heinz' had two children: Henry Jr. and Emelie. Henry Heinz, Jr., was born at the Lemon Pie house on Ponce de Leon just six weeks before his Grandmother Candler died. Henry and Lucy with their four children remained there looking after Asa, Sr., until 1922. With the announcement of Asa's engagement to Mrs. De Bouchel, Lucy and her husband felt it behooved them to plan a home of their own. Their elegant estate was named Rainbow Terrace; it was just down the street from Asa, Sr., also on Ponce de Leon.

Her children report that Lucy ran her own house very much the way her mother had — she had a mini-farm behind the house, cured hams by hanging them in the ballroom, and bought her children ponies, dogs, and cats. Their Uncle Buddie gave them a monkey. Of course, as a part of the farm they had chickens, goats, and a milk cow.

Louise Owens (Lucy's daughter-in-law) adds more: "She was a very nice housekeeper, and she had the same three servants for years, up until the last few years that she lived in that house. She had lost her good cook — I think the woman moved with her husband to Detroit or something like that. When we first married and lived there, she had Parthenia the cook and Lila was the maid. John was the butler and the chauffeur, everything. Then they had a yard man that came every day. He came back twice on Sundays to milk the cow. They kept a cow down in the barn. Stokes came twice on Sundays to milk the cow.

"Can you imagine that nowadays having a cow in your backyard inside the city? They had twenty-three acres and the barn was way down in the back.

"I remember in the winter she would have a country ham. Stokes would bring the milk to the house, and John would take care of it, and he would pour up the milk and churn it. Parthenia would superintend the operation, but John actually did the churning. Bill and I were talking about it not long ago, that when they made homemade ice cream on Saturday or Sunday, John would crank the thing."

Lucy and Henry Heinz were well-suited to one another. He was a big, athletic, good-looking man. He was in banking as William Owens had been. But Henry's greatest talents were actually in the fields of civic and charity work. He made plenty of money, his wife was wealthy, and he could work hard on behalf of the organizations that he loved. Henry was elected president of the Kiwanis International, organized and helped fund the Atlanta Boys Club, and was an active Mason in the Yaarab Shrine. These activities required many parties and much traveling, which Lucy enjoyed as much as her husband. On the surface they had an idyllic existence.

At home, however, Lucy and Henry Heinz faced a personal sorrow. Their little girl, Lucy Emelie (called Mimi) was never well. By the age of two, it was obvious that something was seriously wrong. Lucy took her little girl to specialists everywhere in an effort to diagnose the problem and find a cure.

Emelie, like her great-uncle, Nobel, was encouraged to be the best that she could be. Her mother found two ladies who would give her the special schooling she needed. Every summer she went to camp near Sautee, Georgia, with her cousins. She attended all the Candler family events. There was never any question of Emelie being put away as was so common during that time. She was an enthusiastic and affectionate child, and her parents doted on her. Waiting in the wings, however, was more tragedy for Lucy Candler

Heinz's little family.

As Emelie's sister-in-law explains it, "They didn't diagnose, until the day she died, what was wrong with her. It was encephalitis, which is sleeping sickness. She had a chronic case, apparently. They had treated her for everything under the sun. They had said that she was retarded, but I guess that naturally affects the brain, because the illness was what caused the retardation. She used to go to sleep and sleep for two or three days, and then she'd wake up.

"They brought her home from the school camp — this was in September. We went over there to see her that night. I was sitting on the sofa next to her, and I noticed the pulse in her neck. I was holding her hand, so I just felt her pulse, and it was rapid. I realized she was hot. I told Miss Lucy, 'Mama, I believe Emelie's got a temperature. Her pulse is fast and she seems to be hot.' Sure enough, she was sick."

Very sick. After several days, the doctor called in a neurologist. They took her to Emory Hospital. They were preparing that night to do a spinal tap when she died.

Emelie's death in September 1934 caused Lucy to decide that she and the family might face the holidays a little better if they went away for Christmas. They chose Florida. Lucy's two older children , Elizabeth and William, Jr., were both married by then which meant they would be traveling separately and at different times.

"Bill and I went with them to Florida, but we wanted to be back in Atlanta for Christmas. So we fished for three or four days down there, and they put us on the train down at Inverness, Florida, to come home. Elizabeth and Dr. Vann were going to meet them in Miami. Mr. and Mrs. Heinz put us on the train at night, and they left early the next morning driving to Miami. Elizabeth and Dr. Vann had left for Miami by car sometime the day before.

"When we got off the train, the old chauffeur met us. He said, 'We's got a heap o' trouble. Dr. and Mrs. Vann done had a wreck.' They came in on the train. They finally put Elizabeth on the train down there. She wouldn't go to the hospital. The accident happened Friday afternoon, and we got on the train coming home Friday night. The next morning we got the message. We couldn't get in touch with Mr.

and Mrs. Heinz, they were traveling, too. When we got the message to them, they came home. They were going to Miami to spend Christmas because she didn't want to stay at home right after Emelie died and everybody was so upset about that. So she came back, and Elizabeth only lived a week. She died December 30... She was at home and wouldn't go to the hospital. They brought a portable x-ray out there to the house and took a picture of her chest. She had landed over in the back of the car, and Dr. Vann's golf clubs landed on top of her.

"Elizabeth had TB shortly after she and Dr. Vann were married. She had had a whirlwind debutante year or so, and then she got married... Back in those days you didn't talk about it, but her lungs were already practically gone. Her mother took her to Asheville when she first got sick. They took her to Asheville because the climate's supposed to be good for someone who has TB. The doctors up there said, 'Why did you bring her up here, you've got doctors that are just as good in Atlanta.' Well, she didn't get along with the doctors up there, so she brought her back to Atlanta and kept her in bed at 1610 Ponce de Leon Avenue with nurses. I don't remember how long it was, it could have been about two years. When she got up, she was real weak. Bill and I had just been married a year and a half when this happened. Elizabeth was my matron of honor. She was just twenty-eight years old when we married. She was thirty when she died. That's why they didn't have any children — she was too sick. She and Dr. Vann had been married eight years. So Mama [Lucy] lost one daughter the 17th of September and the other one the 30th of December. They were just three months apart."

Lucy, Henry, and the two boys picked up and went on with their lives. It was a sad time for her, but she had a faith that kept her going. She concentrated on being an encouragement to her sons. She, alone, of the Candler children encouraged her children to seek their own destinies, to pursue their own interests, and to be their own "men."

As long as he lived, John Howard Candler would take credit for his cousin, Bill Owens' career choice. As boys they each had their own hobbies, John flew airplanes, and Bill raced motorcycles. Each boy was secretly terrified of the other cousin's hobby. Of course, they continually egged each other to try the other sport. Finally, they made a deal. John would ride Bill's motorcycle, if Bill would go flying in John's plane (an open cockpit in 1928). As John would tell it, he could see from the expression on Bill's face that he loved flying; Bill Owens was hooked. John, on the other hand, admitted that being on a motorcycle that one time so frightened him that he never got on another one. However, he would say, "I was right, I won the bet and Bill became a pilot." Not only did Bill become a pilot, but his younger brother, Henry, Jr., did also. Bill flew for Delta Airlines from its early days, and Henry flew for Eastern. They got in on the ground floor and saw the industry grow to what it is today. Unlike Asa Candler's other grandsons, these got to choose their careers and to follow their hearts' desires.

But Fate was not yet through with Lucy. In 1943, her husband Henry Heinz was murdered.

The murder sent shock waves through the entire Candler family.

Mettelen Thompson Moore remembers it well.

"The fellow was a black man and came in through the window. Aunt Lucy had gone back to take a shower, and Uncle Henry was listening to the news. They think if he had never struggled with the man that he probably would never have been killed. But he was trying to protect his family and was struggling with the man and got shot. He died right there on the sofa instantly.

"She heard the shot but didn't have any clothes on, and ladies in those days wouldn't dare come out of the shower without their clothes. When she did manage to get on a robe or something and got there, he was dead. She called the police. She called her former son-in-law, Dr. Vann, she called Louise Owens, and my Uncle John. See all of them lived right there along Lullwater Road.

"Vann was coming up to the house when the police arrived. The police, thinking it was him who did it, said 'Stop. Stop.' They fired at him, thinking he was the intruder and hit him. They brought Vann into the house and she said, 'No, that's my son-in-law.'

"When they finally caught the burglar and had the trial, she went. They had his fingerprints from the windowsill and he confessed. This black fellow had eight or nine little children. When the trial was over, he was found guilty, and he was sentenced to however long it was. She sent the chauffeur up and got his home address, where he lived. Then she went to the grocery store and got forty or fifty dollars worth of groceries, which was a lot of money then. She took the groceries up to the man's house and said, 'You can't help your children, and you can't help what your husband did. I don't want you to go hungry.' That was the type of person my great aunt Lucy was."

Lucy was adored by her nieces and nephews in addition to being loved and respected by her brothers. What made her unique and special was, despite all the tragedy that she faced, she had an irrepressible sense of humor. Lucy had her father's personality; she was outgoing, a fast talker, and a fast thinker. Her thoughtfulness was legendary among her brothers' children.

When her niece, Laura Chambers, was widowed at thirty, other people did all the usual things, bringing food, flowers, and sympathy. But Aunt Lucy brought Laura a new, elegant, handbag wrapped up like a present. As Laura said, "It was her way of letting me know that she understood what I was going through and of telling me, that in spite of the sorrow, life goes on."

John Howard Candler, Jr., remembers his great aunt and the excitement that she created by just being in the room. "Oh, she was cheerful. She was a ball. PaPa loved her. If she walked in the front door, just everything changed. I mean, she was just a ball. She'd just get in there and start talking, debating, and soon they would all be almost screeching and shouting, and everybody loved it. It was just a ball.

"PaPa loved Aunt Lucy. Oh, he thought his sister Lucy starred in the book, wrote the book, could have been in the Bible. He just thought she was the sweetest, most wonderful thing in the world. Loved her. When he got sick, I remember when she went down in the kitchen in Briarcliff and cooked a cake for him. I stood there and just watched in amazement.

She cooked the cake and made the help crazy. She made all the staff mad and then they laughed, because she just took over. She got back in there [and declared] 'I'm goin' to fix this for Bud, fix this favorite cake for Bud.' And she stood back there and mixed it, I mean from the word go. She fixed it up there on that damned old wooden stove, baked it, and took it up to his bedroom. I don't know if the cake was any good, because we didn't eat any of it. He wouldn't share it, because 'Sister' made it. They just had a wonderful time, just like sisters and brothers. They had a great time."

June Rackley Candler added that she was surprised as a new mother to have her husband's great aunt arrive with presents for the new baby, Asa VI. "She took such an interest in all the family, even her brother's grandchildren and their children. Not everyone would do that."

Helen Candler Griffith remembers Lucy's bright blue eyes and beautiful pale skin and that "She always talked a mile a minute. With lots of gesturing with her hands. She would come to see my grandfather every Christmas and bring him some kind of cookies that she made that he loved. I remember that. Aunt Florence liked her... Aunt Lucy didn't seem to be a judgmental sort of person. She was easygoing. If you were happy, and that was your lifestyle, that was fine with her. Just allow her the same privilege."

After Henry's death, Lucy moved out of Rainbow Terrace. She could not bear to live there any longer. Usually able to bear the sorrows that life dealt her, she was in terrible pain, and the constant stories in the press did not help. Her spirit was at a low ebb; fortunately, she had Bennie Teabeaut Candler for a sister-in-law. Bennie understood Lucy's loss. Bennie arrived at Rainbow Terrace and told Lucy to just pack up and come live at the Biltmore with her — there was plenty of room. Lucy stayed at the Biltmore and then moved to New York for awhile.

In New York, Lucy renewed an old acquaintance with Enrico Leide who had been the conductor of the Atlanta Symphony for years. Mr. Leide and his late wife had been friends of the Heinz', and he had taught Henry, Jr., to play the violin. One thing led to another, and in February, 1946, Lucy and Enrico Leide were married. They would share a happy sixteen years together.

They enjoyed music, travel, and their families. Lucy learned Italian so she could converse with Enrico's mother and relatives when they were in Italy. She doted on his children and adored him. Enrico Leide was a romantic, affectionate man and made her last years very happy ones.

Louise Owens gave us this about her mother-in-law's character, hobbies and later years: "She did needlepoint. She played bridge. She did some rugs and chairs which I still have. Almost all of my needlepoint she did. She loved to go on a cruise better than anything else in the world. She would sit in a deck chair and do needlepoint. In the last few years of her life she had cataracts. She had two heart attacks, and that slowed up her needlepoint. After she had the second cataract operation and got her new eyeglasses, she was like a little girl with a new doll.

"She was so happy because she could see, and she was going on the *Coronia* on a cruise. She said many times that being on the *Coronia* was like being next to heaven. She liked that ship. She was going on a Mediterranean cruise.

"Two days out of New York — on September 3, 1962 — she had a massive heart attack and died... Mr. Leide had a real ordeal getting her body back. Fortunately Mr. Leide could speak seven languages ... two days out of New York and first port of call was Las Palmas in the Canary Islands. The plane service was bad. There were only two commercial flights a week out of there. So she died aboard ship, and he couldn't get clearance to leave in time to get on the first plane. He had to wait about three or four days. In all, it took eleven days to get her body home.

"They called The Coca-Cola Company for help, and the company worked on it. The Canary Islands are a Spanish territory, and the Coca-Cola people in Madrid and the State Department were involved. They had everybody working on it. Bill and Mr. Leide's son, Will Leide, they were both conferring back and forth, and they talked to Mr. Leide a couple of times, but the connection was so bad that they couldn't understand much. The plane, at that time, had to fly from Las Palmas to Madrid. Then from Madrid to ... it might have been Paris, and then maybe to Ireland. It was worse on

Mr. Leide because he was alone and trying to get home. It is hard to realize how hard it was to fly home from Europe then. Today, a few hours and you can go anywhere in the world."

Lucy's death brought to a close a life that was full of love, hope, and perseverance. She had been the glue that held her extended family together long after the deaths of her parents. Lucy set an example to all the family; she had faced repeated tragedy with a grace that few could equal.

Walter was a different story. He spent money on himself, his wives, and his horses, but he never reconciled his desires with other people's needs. He got himself into some trouble because of this. He was stingy with his children and grandchildren. As a result, his children all grew up disliking horses and stepmothers.

When he was younger, he was headstrong. His nickname was "Brick." His brothers used to beat him up, then they would pay him a nickel not to tell their mother. He wasn't averse to physical labor, and he would do his brothers' chores for money. Buddie would laugh in later years and say, "Well, Brick would always take the nickel." He showed an early love for horses and broke his arm more than once while training his pony to do tricks.

His youth was spent in Atlanta attending a series of elementary schools and finally the University School for boys. He has often been described as having a temperament similar to Buddie's; however, unlike Buddie, Walter was actually a good student when he chose to be.

In a letter to his sister, Lucy, in October, 1897, twelve-year-old Walter described his birthday present and his class standing:

> "The prettiest writing desk & 25 envelopes & one equire of paper & the prettiest pen which I am now writing you with & 3 pen points. William has a pencil box, but no sharpener and is after me to use mine. William really likes a pencil sharpener. I am tops in my class, the teacher said so!"

From his earliest days, Walter had a mind of his own. He

liked what he liked and he pursued it. What Walter really liked were horses. He would write his sister Lucy about his mishaps and successes with them, and he would save his nickels so he could buy the things he wanted. He learned early about horse trading. By the age of twelve he was already experienced at negotiating for a horse. His mother's letter to Lucy in the spring of 1901 shows how determined Walter could be about his hobby:

> "Walter broke his arm in the same place as before. He was playing with the pony trying to teach it circus tricks & the pony got tired & threw him against the fence. Now you know I have got my hands full don't you?"

By the time Walter had reached his teens, his father found it increasingly difficult to direct him. Asa, Sr., was often exasperated by the actions and the attitude of his fourth child. Writing to Howard in September, 1901, Asa, Sr., expressed his irritation with Walter's headstrong ways:

> "The boys entered Peacocks school on Monday. Walter complains already that it is a poorly disciplined establishment. ... I get a little annoyed with Walter's everlasting faultfinding with the schools, his attitudes — He is greatly interested in girls is hard to get waked up in the morning. He has always "done his lessons" & yet never seems to be deeply interested in them. I hope he will improve. He is smart & strong & should be a most useful man."

Walter was a healthy, athletic, sexy sixteen–year old boy. He liked the ladies, but they often distracted him from his studies.

Asa enrolled his hardheaded son on a "floating school" (a school on shipboard). The school went under, at least financially, so Walter wound up going to Emory like his brothers. He loved college. He seemed to do well, although not as well as Howard had done. His parents wrote him newsy letters as they had for their other children. And, like Howard, Buddie, and Lucy before him, Walter also received admonitions from Asa, Sr., not to spend so much money. Like the others,

Walter had a hard time sticking to the budget his father gave him.

The Emory yearbook described Walter as a flashy dresser and a ladies' man. He made friends at Emory and loved his years there. He was devoted to his class (1907) and eventually was elected its president for life. Walter would always be a big supporter of Emory.

Shortly after his graduation, Walter married Winnie Eugenia Bigham, a Methodist preacher's daughter and his childhood sweetheart. Eugenia was a classic Victorian beauty. Graceful, artistic, and musical, "Genie," as she was called, brought a joy to Walter's life. Her closest friend within the family was Buddie's wife, Helen. These young women had a lot in common. They both had trained voices, both were married to difficult, selfish men, and both had too many children.

Walter loved Eugenia passionately. They had four children — Walter, Jr., in 1908, Asa IV in 1909, Eugenia in 1910, and Mary in 1912. Like her sister-in-law, Helen Magill Candler, Eugenia was told she shouldn't have any more children. Perhaps she and Walter tried, but Eugenia would die in 1918, pregnant with their fifth child. Years later, Walter's sister Lucy would introduce her brother at parties as "This is my brother Walter. He killed his first wife. Got her pregnant too many times." As his grandchildren reported, Walter would just stand there and take it. After all, Aunt Lucy could and would say anything she pleased.

Shortly after Eugenia's death in September, 1918, Walter's mother, Lucy, died after her long battle with cancer. Walter sunk into a deep depression. He got so mentally distraught and withdrawn that his sister Lucy had to intervene to help his children. She went to Buddie and asked, "What can we do about Walter?"

Walter was completely neglecting his children. The youngest child was six. The boys didn't go to school, they went down to the barn every day and hung out with the colored help. Lucy saw that the situation was serious, and someone needed to take charge. She made a deal with Walter, she would take on the care and upbringing of the girls, if he would just look after the boys. Lucy had the aid of

Eugenia's widowed mother and her sisters. They bought the girls dresses and made sure they learned the things young ladies needed to learn. Walter eventually came out of his depression, but he never got over losing Eugenia.

With the money he received from The Coca-Cola Company sale, Walter purchased a 233-acre farm on Lullwater Creek. Lullwater Estate was to be not only his home but the site of his famous race track and trotting horse stables. His main focus became his racetrack and stables.

By August 1919, Walter found a young lady and remarried. Marion Penland was a very pretty, vivacious girl who worked at the bank where Walter was the cashier. The daughter of a successful Roswell, Georgia, businessman, Marion was headstrong and determined to pursue her own dreams. She insisted on being allowed to take a job in town, and her father relented. In addition to being a very modern girl interested in the world of business, Marion Penland had become a Christian Scientist, again against her parents' wishes. This would be a major source of conflict in her marriage to Walter. The other problem they would have would be her relationship with his children. Marion had no idea what she was getting herself into marrying a widower with four children. Lucy Heinz talked Walter into taking the children with the newlyweds on their honeymoon and it went downhill from there.

Their daughter, Marion Elizabeth, called Bootsie was born in May, 1921. By the following spring, the marriage was on the rocks. Marion left Walter and took Bootsie with her to California. The marriage might have ended with a simple divorce, but family pressure brought the two of them back together. Asa, Sr., wanted Bootsie back. Bootsie was his last grandchild, he adored her, and he wanted her in Atlanta; in addition, he was opposed to divorce. In an effort to persuade Marion to return, Asa, Sr., wrote to fourteen-month-old Bootsie.

> July 6, 1922
> My Precious angel child,
>      Grandpa thinks and prays for you every day. I want to see you so bad. Those chubby hands and arms I want to feel

round my neck. How I wish I had you here. I don't wonder that everybody loves you. They cant help it. I know you look like an angel in that bird-wash-hole (he had a picture of the baby sitting in a birdbath)... Eugenia & Mary left last night to across the Atlantic Ocean. Now I have no girls to go to see. Emelie has been sick but is well now and just as sweet as you are — that's as sweet as can be. Write me again my darling baby. God knows I love you and I know He cares for you. When you get ready to come home let me know and I'll go after you.

Your grandpa, Asa G. Candler.

Not only did Asa, Sr., want his grandchild back, he felt that Walter needed his wife Marion by his side to present a united front in what was soon to be called "the Byfield scandal." In Marion's absence, Walter had gotten involved with a young married woman, Sarah Byfield.

Walter was even more bullheaded than his brother Buddie — which is saying something. Buddie may have had affairs or "liaisons" with other women while Helen was ill, but at least they weren't with a married woman who might or might not have framed him to get his money. This incident flared into the public eye and was a great source of embarrassment and shame for the family.

Let's set the stage: It's the Roaring Twenties. Walter and his brothers had just sold a company, earning several millions each on the deal. Their real estate company, banking business, and other investments were prospering, and the good times didn't seem to have an end. Marion and Walter had separated in the late spring of 1922 when she left for California with their baby daughter. Not to be deterred, Walter continued his freewheeling existence in her absence. Shortly thereafter, he would freewheel his way into a load of trouble on a trip to Europe when he got caught in an illicit affair with a married man's wife.

In 1922, Walter left for Europe with his two girls, Eugenia and Mary. Accompanying him were Mr. and Mrs. Clyde Byfield, a couple he knew from business and racing circles. He encouraged the couple to go along for his companionship and "so the girls would have somebody to look after them." His sister Lucy could smell trouble, and she tried to get Walter not to take the Byfields, but to no avail. Helen Candler also saw the Byfield woman as trouble and begged Buddie to persuade his brother not to take the Byfields with him on the trip.

Nothing undue happened until July 16, 1922, the last night of the crossing, just before the ship's arrival in Cherbourg, France. While most of the ship's passengers feted the final night of the voyage with champagne in the lounges and public places of the ship, Mrs. Byfield suggested to Mr. Byfield that she would prefer to retire. He accompanied her to their stateroom, then he left her and returned to the festivities. Shortly afterward, Walter Candler excused himself from the party and left.

In his later testimony in court, Byfield claimed he was suspicious of Walter's absence after some twenty minutes had elapsed, and he returned to his stateroom to check up on his wife. When he opened the door, he found Walter Candler in the room with her. He claimed Walter fell to the floor, and he proceeded to soundly beat first Walter, then his wife in his fury. Walter said he was drunk and stumbled into Mrs. Byfield's stateroom by mistake. He denied attacking her in her stateroom or having any immoral or illicit intentions with her that night. When Byfield demanded money, Walter gave him a check for twenty-five thousand on the spot.

Later, upon sobering up, Walter demanded the check back. Before Byfield would comply, Walter had to issue a promissory note for $20,500, plus a smaller note for $2,500 and give Byfield $2,000 in cash. Later in court, Walter asserted that the whole affair was a frame-up perpetrated by the Byfields to extort money from him. It is difficult to believe that there were hard feelings at first, as other ship's passengers testified that the Candlers and the Byfields left the ship together, played cards together on the train to Paris, and lodged there at the same hotel.

The Byfields returned shortly to New York, and the next wrinkle of the scandal unfolded. They went public with their demands for "repairs" for their injuries, and Mrs. Byfield sued Walter in a widely publicized demand for one hundred thousand dollars in damages for assault. She claimed that his attack had led her to a nervous breakdown.

Walter's scandal hit the papers the same month as Asa's engagement to Onezima DeBouchel was announced and then retracted. The newspapers crowed over the Candler men's misfortunes.

Walter's family came to his aid —particularly Buddie— perhaps to excess in one case. Buddie, Walter, and two "friends" from the racetrack appeared to have been intending to enforce the return of the note from Byfield. This led to another lawsuit in which Byfield sued for damages, claiming to have been beaten by a Mr. McTyer, W. A. McCullough, Walter Candler, and Buddie Candler with a "large club." Buddie and Walter's attorneys later pointed out in court that this "large club" was Buddie's silver-handled walking stick, which would have broken in half had it in fact been used as a club.

There were lawsuits all around. Walter sued Mr. Byfield, claiming blackmail and demanding return of the note. Mrs. Byfield sued Walter for $100,000, charging assault. Clyde Byfield sued Buddie, McTyer, McCullough, and Walter for assault. It made the lawyers happy, not to mention the press.

Clyde Byfield got a judgment for $20,500 on September 1925. Mrs. Byfield's suit ended in a mistrial. When appealed to the Georgia Supreme Court, retrial was denied. Clyde Byfield vs. Buddie et al. was dismissed (for lack of evidence). It became apparent over the three years that it took for the suits to wind their way through the courts that the twenty-one-year-old Mrs. Byfield had been leading Walter on and had probably been involved with him before Marion left. Clyde and Sarah Byfield divorced, but Clyde did collect on his note for $20,500, because in that era a man's wife was still seen by many as little better than property. If a man ran around on his wife, she had to put up with it. But let a woman run around, and her husband was entitled to compensation. Clyde Byfield made a court believe that he had been cuckolded and it earned him twenty-five thousand dollars.

Walter pursued a more low-key profile after the debacle with Sarah Byfield. He devoted himself to his racetrack at Lullwater and to his increasing real estate ventures. He and Marion tried to work on their marriage, but they would violently disagree on the subject of religion and medical treatment for their daughter. Their daughter, Marion Candler Ruffner, recalls that difficult period in their marriage and her youth, "I was raised Methodist. I can remember as a child, Papa taking me to the hospital to have my tonsils out. And as he took me to the car, Mama standing there, wringing her hands in hysterics, saying, 'You are going to kill that child, you are going to kill that child!' And Papa saying, 'If we don't take her tonsils out, she is going to die.'

"It was not fair, and life isn't fair. And I found that out early on. This was part of my childhood, of having to deal with parents who were at odds about this weird religion. I remember Papa saying that Uncle Warren had even talked to Mama about it. They even called in the Bishop."

Walter divorced Marion in August 1934. The marriage had been troubled from the beginning and was never a great success.

Walter's third and final marriage was to Rebekah Skeen, the daughter of old family friends. She was a gracious Southern lady, who was well–liked by Walter's siblings. His children, however, were less than enthusiastic about the match, perhaps because she was their contemporary; or maybe step-mothers were just unacceptable to them.

Walter, like Buddie, took up drinking, although, unlike Buddie, he never seemed to have slipped over the edge. Unfortunately, his son, Walter, Jr., would. His son, Asa IV, went to work for The Coca-Cola Company in New Orleans. But Walter, Jr., couldn't hold a job, which isn't surprising considering he was a confirmed alcoholic before he turned seventeen. Walter took his son all over the country trying to find a cure; they tried everything from mud baths to weird diets. Nothing worked and Walter finally acknowledged that it was a problem that his son would have to want to solve before anything would change. Walter, Jr., just drifted. Newspaper articles in 1946 about "Soft Drink Heir Gets Job" hurt his family. He was working as a carpenter for ninety cents an hour in Florida. He was quoted as saying, "Don't get me wrong, I need the money. The Candler family owns only the minority stock of the company now. Dad owns a lot of it, but there'll be a lot of us to split it up among when he dies."

Tragically, this once handsome, blond, athletic man would never recover. In 1951, Walter, Jr., burned to death in Florida. He died at his cousin, William, Jr.'s, ranch where he was living. It was a painful sorrow that Walter, Sr., had to live with for the rest of his life.

Walter's life was not all sadness and scandal. He loved his children, but he never was able to really tell them so. He did however, find an outlet for his emotions with his hobbies. On his huge farm, he kept sixty purebred horses. He poured himself into his horses and developing his farm, seeming to prefer animals to people in his troubles. His favorite horse was the Duke of Lullwater, who was a champion in 1951. His neglected children never really understood his devotion and investment in his horses. He enjoyed breeding his trotter and tracing horses. In 1960, his Duke of Decatur won the Yonkers Futurity. His pacer, New Duke's Son, would pace the fastest mile in Maryland's harness-racing history at Laurel Raceway in 1966. He would also receive an award in 1966 for Duke's Son as the top pacer for the 1964-65 season at Pompano Park, Pompano Beach, Florida.

Walter's other strong interest centered on his love of Shakespeare. He had a group of friends that met regularly at his home on the weekends to read the plays and poems of Shakespeare aloud. This was something he shared with his third wife, Rebekah.

In addition to Shakespeare, Walter was interested in Spanish and Spanish culture. He left Atlanta after divorcing Marion and spent the next year traveling in South America. He learned Spanish and continued to be interested in South and Central America. This interest culminated in Walter donating the funds for several lecture series at Emory University, his other love after his horses and his family. In 1958, he arranged a favorable sale, that was half gift, half sale, of his estate to Emory University. Lullwater is today the home of Emory's president and, should the college ever wish to expand, it has Walter's acreage.

If Walter was openhanded when it came to his horses, he was tightfisted with his family. Where Howard was tight only with himself, Walter was frugal with everyone, except when it came to his clothes or his horses. It became a source of jokes within the family. When Marion left Lullwater, Walter's granddaughter, Mary Ann Bresee, remembered with wry amusement that her grandfather asked her parents to move to Lullwater so his daughter, Mary Edmondson, could keep house for him. Then he charged them rent!

Bob Edmondson (Walter's grandson) remembers Walter's tightness with a dollar. "Uncle Buss (Asa IV) was going to school, he was in the second or third grade. The school caught on fire. And he ran back into the burning school building because he had two new erasers he had just bought, and Papa would wear him out if he didn't come home with those erasers. He ran back into the burning school building to get those erasers.

"Walter was so patriarchal. By golly, he'd come over for Sunday dinner and drive up in that big Cadillac with the silver hood ornament of a trotting horse on it. One summer, I think it was between my senior year in high school and starting at Emory, I was very industrious. I worked construction during the day. I was out there digging ditches. And at night, I went to my father's drive-in theater and worked at the concession stand.

"[Having worked so hard], I decided that right before I had to start at Emory, some friends of mine and I would go down to Daytona Beach for a vacation. So the week before I was going to quit and go to the beach, my grandfather asked me what I had been doing. I said, 'Well, I had been on summer construction, and at night I'd work out at Daddy's drive-in theater.' He asked, 'What are you going to do when you start Emory?' I said, 'Well, before I start at Emory, some friends of mine are going to go down to the beach for a week and relax.' And he jumped on me and called me lazy and how shiftless I was and all this — and this was from an old man who never worked a day in his life. Never worked a day in his life, and I was going to take a week off between working two jobs during the summer and going to school. He just rode me unmercifully at the dinner table. So later on that day, I was back in my room, and my daddy came in and he said, 'Bob, I'm real sorry your grandfather jumped on you like that and I really don't think he should have done that, but you've got to understand, here's a man who started out with nothing but the shirt on his back and six million dollars.'"

Walter could also keep a secret. His children and grand-children loved to tease him about two things, a secret fraternity that he belonged to in college and the formula for Coca-Cola. As Bootsie Ruffner tells it, "We used to tease him all the time. We used to say, 'Papa, when are you going to tell us what the formula is?'

"Of course, he knew it. Papa knew it. And he said, 'I'm not going to tell you.'

"He was also a member of a club at Oxford. I forget what the club was. An exclusive club, that only had six members at a time, and if you were invited to belong to this club, you were really of the top echelon. But you were not allowed to say anything about the club.

"We used to tease Papa about it. He would get very stone-faced, and he wouldn't say a word. This was an old man. We would just tease him to death about it.

"He would tell us about making Coca-Cola in the back-yard... I remember him saying that his father, after the concoction was complete, he would drink it and taste it, and if it wasn't just exactly right, he knew what was wrong.

"It was Papa's job to cut up the vanilla. The vanilla came in beans, and it was his job to cut up the vanilla, and apparently he was allergic to it. He said he would break out. So they had to delegate that job to somebody else because it broke his arms out in a rash."

Walter Turner Candler died in April 1967 at Emory Hospital after a short illness. He survived all of his siblings and his death brought an era to a close.

William was Asa and Lucy Candler's youngest child. Born on January 24, 1890, he was the only one of their children not to have a middle name. He was named for Colonel William Candler, Asa's Revolutionary War ances-tor. Colonel Candler had led an interesting life on the Georgia frontier. Raised in a Quaker community in Virginia, he did not choose to follow all their teachings. William did find a wife at church, however. He married fourteen-year-old Elizabeth Anthony, daughter of Joseph Anthony and Elizabeth Clark Anthony. Once again, we have a Candler marrying a very young girl whose family has greater social and economic standing in the community. William and Elizabeth's marriage so enraged her father, that he left her only five shillings when he died, although by that time she was a widow with eleven children of her own.

William Candler moved his young wife to the Georgia Territory outside of Augusta in 1769. They settled in St. Paul's Parish. William began to expand his holdings and to continue in his field as a surveyor for the royal government. Like many Georgians, when trouble between England and the colonies began, William preferred to remain neutral and to encourage his fellow citizens to try to settle matters by peaceable means. However, when war became inevitable, William Candler became a patriot.

Along with Elijah Clarke, William Candler led four hundred refugees out of Georgia through the South Carolina Upcountry and the mountains of Western North Carolina in a desperate effort to hide from the Tories. Their destination was the Nolachucky settlement in the Cherokee lands (now Eastern Tennessee).

The Revolution in the northern colonies may have been a war against the mother country, but in Georgia and most of the Southern colonies, the Revolution was a bloody civil war with neighbor against neighbor and brother against brother. William and his son, Henry Candler, left their families along the trail and met up with those famous patriots, McDowell, Sevier, Campbell, and Shelby. The Candlers with their small party of Georgians joined the "Over Mountain Men" and fought the battle at Kings Mountain which proved to be a major turning point for the patriots. He would continue to fight until the war was won.

After the war, Colonel William Candler served in Georgia's first legislature. He died in 1784, but he left a legend and a long shadow that loomed over his descendants. All the Candlers revered Colonel William's memory, and Asa honored his memory by naming his last child for him.

In poor health most of his childhood, Asa and Lucy's baby, William was painfully shy and quiet. His nickname was Wittie. He was the one that Buddie's family went to when they were having problems with Buddie's drinking.

He was sensitive and perhaps the most approachable of their uncles.

William's health problems may have plagued his parents during his youth; however, he, like his brothers, had a stubborn streak. William loved to go fast. As a child he often raced his pony. On several occasions, he had serious accidents, one which nearly killed him.

William appears to have been a good student and opinionated about his schools. He insisted he wanted to attend Culver Military Academy in Culver, Indiana. This was a departure from the other boys. His mother was reluctant to let him go because he had been so ill the winter before; however, William won the debate. He returned to Georgia and entered Emory, but he did not graduate. By Christmas 1908, William was again too ill to be away from home. Once he recovered from this fever, he put his foot down. He had fallen behind his age group in school, and he wanted to go to work. Finally, his parents relented.

William's first job was working for Buddie, demolishing the old First Methodist Church and peddling the old material. By the fall of 1909, William got a job with The Coca-Cola Company starting in the mail room and learning all the various facets of the business as he worked his way up to the position of cashier. He would later be the secretary and treasurer for the company.

In February 1913, William married Miss Bennie Teabeaut, a daughter of Daniel Benjamin Teabeaut and Rena Sparks Teabeaut. Shy, modest William had discovered Miss Teabeaut in church. The romantic tale of their meeting as told by their granddaughter, Elizabeth Chambers, shows how love bloomed for William. "My grandmother was sitting in church and William came in and sat down next to her, and they didn't really notice each other at first. But she was fluttering her fan. This little blue bow fell off her fan, and he retrieved it. That's how they struck up a conversation and talked about the sermon. After that, they wrote letters or they talked. And he would sign the letters, 'From the Owner of the Little Blue Bow.' He had kept this bow. It was really sentimental and romantic. Apparently my grandfather kept the bow all those years and gave it to my mother for her 'something blue' in her wedding."

William made a good match. Bennie Teabeaut Candler was a cute, vivacious little woman. She was smart and well-educated. Bennie had been graduated from Randoph-Macon College at age sixteen and was trained to teach both piano and French. Where William was shy and retiring, Bennie was outgoing and friendly. Over the next few years, they would make a good team. Fortunately for William, he married a strong woman. He was easygoing and not as flamboyant as his older brothers and sister, but was considered a very solid citizen. He worked for The Coca-Cola Company under his father and under Howard.

William, unlike Buddie and Walter, was not given to stirring up arguments over the family businesses. He was heavily involved with The Coca-Cola Company, and even after its sale, he was on the board of directors of the Coca-Cola Bottling company of New York. But William chafed at being looked upon as the "baby" by Howard, and he grew restless with few real challenges presenting themselves. William was too smart to sit and count his money and too conservative to spend it.

This last child of Asa Candler's would do a great deal in his short life to uplift the city of Atlanta and to promote it as a regional center for business and tourism. This careful, conservative man was also a visionary. And, he had some of the Candler gambling genes in his makeup. While the rest of his siblings spent the early years of the 1920s building palatial estates, William and Bennie built an elegant, but modest home on a regular lot in Druid Hills. In this respect, William beat Howard for the title of "most conservative."

Instead of spending his money on himself or even on his family, William entered into a high-risk real estate venture. In 1923, he chartered the Atlanta Biltmore Hotel company. His plan included not only a hotel out from the heart of downtown Atlanta, but an apartment complex, as well. The Biltmore was not just the average hotel; William specifically designed it to become a convention hotel. He could foresee the increase in that type of travel and wanted Atlanta to become a convention center. Some folks in town thought he was nuts to do it. His sister and brothers were upset when he pledged his stock in Asa G. Candler, Inc., as collateral for the loans. But William had a vision and he was going to pursue it.

Bennie backed her man all the way. As soon as the Biltmore Hotel was completed, she began to entertain there frequently. This was her way of introducing all the people in Atlanta to her husband's new business venture. She worked hard at making the Biltmore the place to see and be seen, the place to go for tea, lunch, dinner, bridge parties, whatever. Bennie created a social whirl which resulted in business and profit for William's hotel.

In addition to the Atlanta real estate ventures, William saw potential in Florida. He loved the north central part of that state. After he received his share of the sale of The Coca-Cola Company, William began to invest heavily in ranchland in Florida. William had another vision. Today, what William planned for his property in Florida happens all the time in the world of real estate development. However, for the early 1920s it was very new and very farsighted. He called his dream Intercession City. Essentially what he envisioned was a planned community. He had the streets laid out, commercial sections planned, different densities of residential sections laid out, and even the locations for a variety of churches. It was a true planned urban development. William spent years dreaming about how he wanted this community to look. He drew plans and redrew plans. It was a special place, and he wanted it done right. This particular project would be slowed by the onslaught of the Great Depression, and it would fade into memory with William's tragic and early death.

When it came to describing his brother William, Buddie always said he was a saint. William was the reliable little brother, moderate in almost everything he did. If William had a vice, it was the same one that got him into trouble as a child. He just loved to go fast. When cars came along, it meant he could go faster than he could on a horse. His nieces laugh when they talk of Uncle Wittie, calling him a speed demon. It seems an odd appellation for such a quiet, sensitive man.

Speeding and driving too fast got William hurt badly in

several accidents. The worst one occurred in the early 1930s. On his way back from Florida, he hit a pig. He was nearly killed. It was three or four days before anyone even knew who he was. A black man coming along the road found the wrecked car and saw that the man was still alive inside. He got the injured man into his horse-drawn wagon and took him to the nearest hospital. William had no jewelry or any identification on him when he arrived. When he regained consciousness he was told that a colored man had been asking after him every day. Well, the colored man came in and handed him his wallet, his jewelry, everything else. He said something about not being able to read or write, but he had gotten his minister to look over the papers in William's wallet to see who he was. They then told someone at the hospital who was able to reach Bennie. The colored man explained to William that "I've kept dese things, 'cause we don't know dese people in dis hospital. They might take it. I figured if you lived, I'd bring them to you, and if you didn't, I'd give 'em to yo' peoples."

According to Mettelen Thompson Moore, "...Aunt Bennie hired a doctor and nurse and a Pullman car and outfitted it and took it down to Florida to get him. He was too sick to bring back home. He stayed down there on the railroad tracks for two or three weeks until they could get him stabilized. It was a very serious accident and they had to put a plate in his head."

William was not so lucky the next time. In October, 1936, on his way to meet some businessmen in an effort to restructure the Biltmore Hotel's debts and ride out the Depression, William hit a cow. He was traveling with his friend and attorney, George Spence when the accident happened outside Naylor, Georgia, a small community near Valdosta. William was killed instantly. Miraculously, George Spence survived with relatively few injuries.

William's death raised a hue and cry in papers across the South. Editorials demanded that the laws be changed to prevent animals from wandering at will and endangering the lives of innocent motorists. This controversy had been brewing for years, ever since automobiles became available to the average citizen. William's tragic death would be a catalyst for legislators in Georgia and Florida to revise their stockade laws. Prior to this, animals had the right-of-way.

William's tragic death at age forty-six left Bennie a young widow with an empire in debt. Not one to be defeated, she did what was necessary to save her children's inheritance. She sold the home in Druid Hills and moved to the Biltmore. She began taking a "hands-on" approach to management of the hotel. Although the Florida dream may have faded with William's blueprints, the Biltmore was up and running, and Bennie was determined to keep it that way.

Bennie quickly learned to put her charm and her feminine wiles to work. Bennie could be intimidating. She talked almost as fast as her sister-in-law, Lucy, and the two of them could both talk at once and understand perfectly what the other one was saying. This could be hard on a bank officer or developer trying to cut a deal in his own favor. She was famous within the Candler family for uproarious tales about her "poor sweet William" routine. Whenever some banker or businessman would try to take the advantage, Bennie was not above pretending she just didn't understand a thing about business. "... but my poor sweet William always said ..." In the end, she would get the deal she wanted by letting poor, sweet, dead William be the heavy.

Bennie did remarry some years after William's death, and it is a mark of her diplomacy and her character that she handled it the way she did. She had gone on a cruise to Europe and while on board, Bennie met Mr. Howell Ross Hansen of Pennsylvania. He was a prominent financier and banker from a long line of very wealthy "Yankee bankers." His grandfather and father had gotten in on the ground floor of many of the major U.S. corporations. Once they decided to marry, Bennie introduced Mr. Hansen to all of her family and her late husband's people. They were married in Atlanta, by Bishop Candler. All of the Candlers were in attendance and participated in the affair. Naturally, the reception was at the Biltmore. She and Mr. Hansen would have ten happy years together before his death.

Bennie strongly supported the Atlanta Chamber of Commerce, as William had. She continued to manage the Biltmore Hotel with a sharp eye towards service and southern hospitality. She was a super-organized, efficient little dynamo. Bennie Teabeaut Candler later became the Chamber of Commerce's Woman of the Year. She outlived all of her husband's siblings, dying in 1987.

# Section Three:

# Later Generations

# 12 The New Coke

Coca-Cola is one heck of a marketing triumph, maybe even the biggest in history. Asa Candler took Dr. John Pemberton's bitter-tasting patent medicine concoction, sweetened it and added fizz, then turned it from a headache remedy into The Real Thing.

After the Candlers gave up The Coca-Cola Company's helm, Robert Woodruff continued Asa Candler's marketing magic, building on and expanding the Candler tradition, taking Coca-Cola international. The present emperor of the vast Coca-Cola empire is Roberto C. Goizueta. He came originally from Cuba — that Cuba that so fascinated Asa and his brother, the Bishop — and is now the chairman and chief executive officer of The Coca-Cola Company. While benefiting from the Candler and Woodruff dynasties, Goizueta remains very much his own man and has brought his own considerable contributions to the company.

Of course, for all his accomplishments, Mr. Goizueta may end up being rememberd for making the biggest business boo-boo since ... well, since ever.

If Franklin Delano Roosevelt had still been alive, April 23, 1985, is another date he would have referred to as "a day of infamy." Certainly millions of Coca-Cola fans did, and still do, calling this day their "Black Tuesday."

April 23, 1985, the top executives of The Coca-Cola

293

Company called a news conference in New York City. The press being what it gloriously is, the purpose of the conference was no secret. Like the kings of old, Coca-Cola was dead, long live Coca-Cola! Or, in other words, The Coca-Cola Company was discontinuing the original formula and replacing it with "New" Coke, a sweeter drink similar to archrival Pepsi-Cola.

Hundreds of reporters attended the news conference, and many more participated via satellite hookup. It is hard to conceive of a relatively minor formula change in any other product creating that kind of interest among the otherwise hard-bitten folks of the working press. But this was different. Here was someone *daring* to change an American icon. Someone — the fact that it was The Coca-Cola Company itself was immaterial — was *tampering* with Coke!

The Coca-Cola Company had vastly underestimated the interest and reaction their announcement would generate. These ranged from Asa G. Candler V's rather laconic advice of "if it ain't broke, don't fix it," to various shades of outright fury by a legion of devoted Coke-aholics.

As far as Robert C. Goizueta was concerned "the best has been made even better." Little did he realize that if the president of the United States had gone on television and revealed that he was really a little green Martian, the shock could not have been greater. More, in fact, since a lot of people would accept that the president is from offplanet and simply encourage him to return home. But changing Coke? Now *that* was *personal.*

Ignoring the raised eyebrows of reporters present, Mr. Goizueta went on to say that The Coca-Cola Company's decision was based on more than two hundred thousand consumer taste tests, all of which resulted in preference for the new formula.

"To market research experts," Donald R. Keough, the president of Coca-Cola said, "to our bottlers, and to the retail trade, these numbers represent a staggering superiority."

Roberto Goizueta assured the reporters that this "bold change" was backed with "tremendous confidence and enthusiasm" by the company, and it was "the surest move the company ever made."

Thomas Oliver, in his excellent book *The Real Coke, the Real Story*, characterized the reaction of the American people to the new formula as "immediate and violent: three months of unrelenting protest against the loss of Coke."

Oliver, a native of Atlanta and reporter for the *Atlanta Journal* and *Atlanta Constitution*, was not just "a whistling Dixie." Stunned and humbled by an incredible outpouring of consumer outrage, Goizueta and Keough called another press conference on July 11, 1985. They bravely ate their huge helpings of humble pie, publicly apologizing to the American people, and literally begging for forgiveness. They announced that the company would bring back the original Coke under a new name, "Classic Coke.

The Black Tuesday announcement was such a public relations disaster that it was immediately immortalized in song by country music songwriter George Pickard. On that same day, after having heard the news, he rushed to Nashville, wrote, and recorded "Coke *Was* It." Pickard estimates that radio stations played his song between three and four hundred thousand times in the weeks that followed. There were also constant news stories giving people's negative reactions, such as "it's lousy!"

One must wonder, having lived through the those tumultuous three months in 1985, just who those two hundred thousand taste testers were? Perhaps fellow Martians of the president? Certainly, few real humans seemed to be admitting a preference for the New Coke versus the old. Instead, they were stockpiling old Coke by the caseloads and writing nasty letters to Atlanta, berating Coca-Cola's management for their "stupid, pigheaded" mistake. As Oliver reports in his book, these executives were no longer being invited to parties either. People in Atlanta take their Coca-Cola *seriously*.

The question that Asa G. Candler V asked "if it ain't broke why fix it?" is a good one. The answer is a simple one — *Pepsi*.

The Coca-Cola Company had become somewhat complacent during the late seventies and early eighties. Like many large corporations do, it had become stagnant and resistant to change, thus providing a standing target for its competitors, the largest and most aggressive of which is Pepsi. Coke's profits and market share began to decline while Pepsi's rose.

Pepsi, of course, was not helping at all. The famous "Pepsi Generation" ad campaign was proving highly successful during these years, and Pepsi was starting to catch on with the "thirtysomething" crowd — baby boomers and yuppies.

Like a brash young boxer sensing the champ weakening, Pepsi let fly a mighty roundhouse to Coke's jaw, not downing but certainly staggering the Cola giant. It was "the Pepsi Challenge."

The Challenge, as seen on countless televisions ads, was a simple but brilliant concept. People in the TV spots were presented with two cola drinks that had their brands covered over. The tester would taste both and make his or her choice as to which one tasted best. Pepsi won every time!

Coca-Cola did not respond well at first. They wanted Pepsi to stop its "misleading advertising" but, when they tried their own taste tests to prove this, they found that people *really did* prefer Pepsi. This caused some real panic at Coca-Cola headquarters in Atlanta. It was the first time a really *serious* challenge had been mounted against their product, and Pepsi's campaign was beginning to make inroads. Something, obviously, had to be done. Hence, the heretofore *unthinkable* move toward changing Coca-Cola's original formula.

At first, Coke tried fighting Pepsi by making fun of the Challenge commercials on the air. However, Pepsi countered every move with superior commercials of their own. Pepsi's market share jumped quickly from a lowly six percent to a respectable fourteen percent. The panic in Atlanta deepened. By 1983, the Challenge commercials were showing in 90 percent of U.S. markets.

The Challenge was boosting Pepsi's sales dramatically but taking far more from the market shares of other soft drinks than from Coke. Pepsi was not about to knock out Coke, but they were at least slowing down growth and planting seeds in the minds of consumers that could cause even more trouble in the future. And, although the Challenge was not truly hurting Coke that much financially, it was trampling all over the company's pride with big, hobnailed boots.

So, The Coca-Cola Company gritted its collective teeth and began doing the unthinkable, experimenting with ways of improving Coke's taste to the point where it could compete *and win* against Pepsi.

Alan Pottasch, the executive at Pepsi in charge of advertising for PepsiCo and the one who implemented "the Pepsi Challenge" campaign was delighted when New Coke was announced. He said (as Thomas Oliver reported) "it had to be pride, because we weren't hurting their numbers. They overreacted and if they hadn't, history would have been different."

Of course, there is one question — was it really overreaction or a canny stratagem on Coke's part to increase market share? Because the end result was that Coca-Cola (now New Coke) and Classic Coke came out of all the smoke and furor with *increased* sales.

In 1984, however, things were not looking rosy for Coke. Growth was down and Pepsi, which Coke had outsold better than two to one in the 1950s, was now only slightly less than 5 percent behind now. Worse, in the supermarkets, Coke was *losing* to Pepsi by almost two percent!

Since Coke was competitively priced and spent far more on advertising than Pepsi, the company could only conclude that the problem was with the product itself. So — over a long period and with much reluctance — the decision was finally made to change Coca-Cola's once sacrosanct formula and taste. Even Robert Woodruff, at ninety-five still alert, had agreed to changing it, although he died in March, 1985, before it was released. As far as we have been able to determine, none of the Candlers, and in fact, no other stockholders, were consulted on the change. The company played its cards close to its vest.

During World War II, the United States had its ultra top secret Manhattan Project, from which came the atomic bomb. The Coca-Cola Company's "Project Kansas" — the largest research project in the company's history — had just as much secrecy attached to it. Months of research, focus groups, and the other ways in which large corporations spread the blame before actually giving in to necessary change followed.

Pride, almost certainly it seems, ruled out simply introducing a second kind of Coke and keeping the old one as well. The company was obsessed with staying number one. Two Cokes would break up market share and perhaps allow Pepsi to become number one, a totally *unacceptable* result. So, the only way to go, or so it seemed then, was replacing the old Coke with a new, improved tasting Coke.

One unfortunate decision at this time was to go with a sweeter taste, just like Pepsi had. As this decision was being made, Coke was running a series of ads featuring popular comedian Bill Cosby, touting the fact that Coke was *less* sweet than Pepsi. These recent commercials would rise up to bite Coke when the new drink was released. The company was surprised that sweetness became the biggest negative the new Coke had. Worse, the new Coke also had more calories than the old one, something else that had not been considered and which became yet another negative.

Pepsi, happily, jumped on this latter difference in their ad campaigns. They pointed out that the new Coke had five more calories than the old Coke and that Pepsi, even though it was sweeter-tasting, had fewer.

Flatness was another point of contention for the new Coke. New Coke was "smoother" than the original and had less bite. It turned out that people missed the bite and wanted it back.

But all that was yet to come when Black Tuesday rolled around — the day of the press conference during which Roberto Goizueta was to announce the new Coke. Pepsi was not caught napping. They had learned of the change beforehand. Roger Enrico, the president and chief executive officer of Pepsi-Cola USA in 1985, was absolutely delighted about the new Coke and issued the following letter — which was sent to Pepsi bottlers *and* placed as an ad in the *New York Times* the day of the press conference:

It gives me great pleasure to offer each of you my heartiest congratulations. After 87 years of going at it eyeball to eyeball, the other guy just blinked. Coca-Cola is withdrawing their product from the marketplace, and is reformulating brand Coke to be more like Pepsi.... There is no question the long-term market success of Pepsi has forced this move... Maybe they finally realized what most of us have known for years. Pepsi tastes better than Coke.

Well, people in trouble tend to do desperate things... and we'll have to keep our eye on them. But for now, I say, victory is sweet, and we have earned a celebration. We're going to declare a holiday on Friday! Enjoy!

Best regards,

Roger Enrico
President, Chief Executive Officer
Pepsi-Cola USA

Declaring a holiday was a brilliant stroke on Pepsi's part. They sent out news releases to this effect the day of Coke's press conference. They suggested the press ask Coke executives about Bill Cosby's "less-sweet" ads and how they could reconcile this to the new Coke's sweetness. The uproar over Coke's change in formula would have happened anyway, but Pepsi didn't mind fanning the flames for all they were worth. It was a joyous and heady time for Pepsi people as shock and dismay came quickly to The Coca-Cola Company because of all this unexpected controversy and resistance to the new Coke.

The press, primed by Pepsi's news release, had a field day at the Coke news conference. Goizueta, visibly annoyed, tried to make the best of it, but this was just a forerunner of the growing storm.

Oliver, in his book, writes that within forty-eight hours of that press conference, according to a number of studies, more people knew about the new taste of Coke than knew who was president of the United States! The tollfree lines at Coca-Cola headquarters in Atlanta (unfortunately for Coke, the numbers were printed on several of their product packages) were deluged with irate calls. Still, the company was not overly alarmed. The consensus remained that, after some initial negative reaction, the new Coke would be accepted and things would go on as before.

That attitude was akin to George Armstrong Custer's if — during his little encounter with equally irate Native Americans — he had said something like, "Don't worry, boys. They'll shoot a couple of arrows, then ride on off."

Consumers and Coca-Cola fans, however, had a lot of arrows and were not about to go away. Within five days of the announcement, calls were in excess of a thousand a day. Plus, The Coca-Cola Company was being raked over the coals in the press and on the evening news.

People were just not taking it well.

Even in the South, once the unquestioned bastion of Coca-Cola, rumblings were being heard. Not so much in Atlanta — the city that has a love/hate relationship with the mighty Coke empire, of which Atlanta is the imperial city. People there were not so vocal at first (although, only at first). But next door in Birmingham, Alabama, Coke tried a fancy party to introduce the new Coke to consumers. Response was less than enthusiastic. The *Birmingham Post-Herald* quoted a number of these consumers — reactions were divided between dislike of the new taste and disgust at a perceived surrender to Pepsi. For, even though Pepsi was created in North Carolina, it had for decades been owned by and thought of as a "Yankee" drink and just not as good as the Southern-blessed Georgia nectar, Coca-Cola.

The Birmingham paper, for example, reported a Mrs. Maxwell's reaction. She had, she said, raised three generations on Coke and had been drinking it personally for over sixty years. "But to concede to competition," she concluded, "I think it cheapens them and makes them look yellow."

If, of course, this type of instant and violent reaction to new Coke had been restricted only to the South, the North might yet again have won a glorious victory (or at least the blue-clad forces of Pepsi)—after all, they had more bottling plants than the South and could have perhaps parlayed that numerical superiority into yet another victory, just as their railroads and factories had won the War Between the States. Well, yes, old U. S. Grant helped some but, luckily, he was not working for Pepsi.

However, the growing rebellion on Coke's hands was bursting into white-hot flames everywhere. Their heretofore true loyalists in the South were deserting them in droves. Across the North and East and West, and even overseas, the barricades were going up, and people were calling for the heads of those who had *dared* tamper with the taste of their sacred, their beloved Coca-Cola.

In Atlanta, Coca-Cola executives were virtually under siege — belabored by phone calls and letters of outrage. In those three months, they must have come to understand what people who suffered the great sieges of history must have felt — to Vicksburg, to the Russians in Leningrad, to Helen and Homer's Troy must be added Coca-Cola headquarters in Atlanta. In fact, speaking of Troy, there were those who felt that the new Coke was simply Pepsi in Coke bottles, an insidious infiltration like those of the soldiers hidden in the wooden horse that caused the fall that ancient city.

In other words, things were starting to get serious.

Meanwhile, the ad people at Pepsi were having a glorious time spoofing the change. There was one ad with some old men sitting on a bench. One old guy, "Wilbur," is bemoaning the fact that Coke had changed. "They've changed my Coke. I stuck with them through three wars and a couple of dust storms, but this is too much." He then says that it must have been something really big to make them change. One of the other oldsters replies, "Yep, big," and hands him a can of Pepsi. Wilbur tastes the Pepsi and likes it.

Even Roberto Goizueta's father, who lived in Mexico City at the time, was upset. He reported to his son that Mexico was in a state of uproar over the new Coke, even though it had not been introduced there yet.

Meanwhile, Coca-Cola was receiving a slew of irate letters. Here are three examples:

> Dear Sir: Changing Coke is like God making the grass purple or putting toes on our ears or teeth on our knees.

> It was nice knowing you. Your were a friend for most of my

> 35 years. Yesterday I had my first taste of the new Coke and to tell the truth, if I would have wanted a Pepsi, I would have ordered a Pepsi, not a Coke.
>
> The sorrow is knowing not only won't I ever enjoy the Real Coke again, but my children and grandchildren won't either. I guess my children will just have to take my word for it.

While a few letters actually did endorse the new taste, they were only a very, very small percentage. Most letters were absolutely against the change. Even famous radio commentator Paul Harvey said, on his nationally syndicated show, that the new Coke wasn't going to succeed and mused about the possibility of a revolt within the corporate halls of The Coca-Cola Company.

Nor was this ever-growing rebellion against the new Coke totally without organization. Two men in Seattle — Gay Mullins and Frank Olson, along with some of their friends — started (as it was later named) Old Coke Drinkers of America, Inc. They started out with an 800 number by selling a T-shirt showing a bottle of new Coke inside of a circle with a line through it, and the word "DON'T." Mullens became the celebrity leader of the anti-new-Coke rebellion, appearing on hundreds of radio shows and TV shows, and in national magazines and newspapers.

Coca-Cola executives, once stoutly in favor of the new Coke and constantly exclaiming "We will never go back," were weakening under the constant onslaught of protests. This trend was spurred on by the bottling companies, which were under similar pressures.

Finally the plunging morale at Coca-Cola and the continuing protests from people about how their Coke had been taken away succeeded. On July 10, ABC's Peter Jennings interrupted daytime television with a special bulletin to announce the joyous news. The official announcement, and The Coca-Cola Company's abject apology to the American people, came on July 11th, 1985.

But, of course, the company did not (and could not) suffer a total loss of face. The new Coke was retained and the old

Coke was renamed *Classic Coke.*

So Classic Coke came back, but is it the same Coca-Cola that Asa Candler made so popular? The Sugar Association didn't think so. They immediately launched an attack on Classic Coke, decrying the fact that it now contained high-fructose corn syrup instead of, alas, sugar. It was, they pointed out, no longer "The Real Thing." They took out ads in several major newspapers to let everyone know.

However, people generally were happy to have the new old Coke, and whether it was sweetened with sugar or high-fructose corn syrup or molasses didn't much matter. As The Coca-Cola Company maintained, "sweet is sweet."

So, finally, the Summer of No Coke which had begun on Black Tuesday was over. People once more had their Coca-Cola, even if it now had the word "Classic" attached. But what were the results of this second coming of The Real Thing?

By the end of 1985, exactly what the executives of Coke had feared would happen if they split the brand had occurred, Pepsi was now *the number one soft drink in the U.S.!* Once more, so it seemed, the South had lost, albeit this time by shooting themselves in the collective foot with a dull can of new Coke.

But, as a wise old mountain man once said, the winners "are them what are still on their feet when it's over." Classic Coke came back fast and soon actually surpassed Pepsi sales. Soft drink industry reports for the last two years — 1991 and 1992 — now show Coca-Cola Classic as the leading brand, with around a 20 percent market share. Pepsi runs second, at just over 18 percent for both years, Diet Coke and Diet Pepsi are third and fourth, followed by Dr. Pepper at fifth.

Where's new Coke, you ask? We have no idea, but it's definitely not in the top ten. With the return of the new old Coke, the new Coke has slid off the charts. We suspect it will eventually be allowed to die a quiet death.

Did The Coca-Cola Company commit a colossal blunder? One thing can be concluded for sure — judging by the industry sales figures quoted above — Coke could *not* make Pepsi as well as Pepsi does, hence the slide of new Coke sales. Certainly the Candler family thought little of the change to new Coke.

We also saw that it *did* need fixing. Coke sales were slipping, and the Pepsi Challenge was very effectively being used against them. Two more things are also certain, as well. First, Coca-Cola management had to make some sort of change, and they did. Secondly, when the public came down on them like a ton of lead bricks weighted with concrete, they were flexible enough to recover and bring back the old Coke. The change caused them to lose the number one place temporarily to Pepsi, but they came back stronger than ever, and now are once again firmly in first, although a hungry Pepsi continues nipping at their heels.

Maybe Roberto Goizueta planned it this way all along — he *is* a very sharp man, as is his number two and right-hand man, the president of Coke, Donald Keough. Actually, whether he planned it from the first or was simply fast enough on his feet to salvage the situation to Coca-Cola's advantage, the end result was the same. Coca-Cola, the once and future king, continues to rule its worldwide cola empire.

And *we* still have our beloved Classic Coke!

# Life in the Limelight: Later Generations

Asa Candler's grandchildren entered adulthood with a bang. In one case, it was a literal bang with near fatal results.

The millions that Asa's children — Howard, Buddie, Walter, William, and Lucy — had gotten upon reliquishing control of The Coca-Cola Company in 1920 has continued to grow throughout the years. The grandchildren were raised in wealth and, in the twenties and thirties, were beginning to make lives of their own, although these lives were often in the harsh glare of the limelight that great wealth attracts.

The first of the grandchildren to marry were Asa's two granddaughters, Lucy Magill Candler and Elizabeth Candler Owens. These girls had spent their childhoods together and were more like sisters than cousins. Their prenuptial parties and wedding plans made the social calendar for the spring of 1924. Their weddings were called the two "biggest social events of the season" by society editors. While they made the papers for their parties and their showers, it was the incidents after the vows were taken that gave the papers something to go on about, and quickly both girls found that the glare of publicity could be too much.

Both Elizabeth and Lucy were headstrong (a Candler

trait that has not been watered down over the generations). They had been their grandmother's pets; she adored them and indulged them. They were loved and doted on by their parents. They were not used to being told "no." And, they both married for love. Unfortunately, neither of the young men that they picked suited their parents.

Lucy had fallen for young Thomas Homer Thompson, one of those bright and upwardly mobile young Coca-Cola men that Atlanta had taken a fancy to. Homer Thompson was a likable, easygoing fellow whose main claim-to-fame prior to his employment with The Coca-Cola Company had been his position as a star of the All-Southern baseball team at the University of Georgia.

Thompson was from East Tennessee; he had no famous kin folks anybody in Georgia had heard of, few prospects, and his only connections were through his job. Buddie, Lucy's father, wasn't impressed. He told Lucy, "No, he hasn't any money. He can't support you. We don't know anything about him." Buddie and Helen snatched Lucy up, along with young John and Sam, and headed for an extended tour of the Orient in 1923. They hoped this little cultural expedition would distract Lucy III and make her forget her charming suitor, who found himself transferred to Charlotte, N.C. No such luck. Homer was waiting on the platform at the train station in Atlanta when they returned. Soon after, Lucy announced she was marrying Homer and planning the most perfect and unusual wedding Atlanta had ever seen.

Meanwhile, Elizabeth (Lucy II's daughter) had fallen for a young, struggling dentist from Alabama. Dr. Bryant King Vann had not endeared himself to his future in-laws, either. The year that the cousins made their debut, the society editors had written a sappy article about the most eligible and richest girls in Atlanta. Kat Haverty, Lucy Candler, Elizabeth Owens, and Louise Inman were among the young ladies mentioned. Vann, who was staying at the Bell House (a boardinghouse in Atlanta for young single men), announced to his friends, "fellows, look here. I'm going to marry one of those girls, just watch me." And, he did.

The weddings were both planned for June, 1924. Their Grandfather Candler even suggested that if they were going to marry in the same month, why not have a double wedding at his house? No, they each wanted their own elaborate affair and, in typical Candler fashion, even prevailed over their own grandfather (who was not unknown for his own strong will). And, no doubt, their mothers each wanted to plan that most special of events.

Elizabeth's wedding was held on June 11, 1924, at Rainbow Terrace. The altar was in front of a wide Dutch fireplace banked with massive palms, baskets of lilies, and hundreds of white burning tapers. The house was decorated with pink roses and sweet peas throughout. Family friend and orchestra leader Enrico Leide directed the music while Miss Vivian Fender of Valdosta, Georgia sang. The brides-maids and groomsmen met at the top of the spacious front stairs and descended in pairs. The bridesmaids' gowns were shades of the rainbow reflecting the name of Elizabeth's home. Little Rena Candler and her brother, William Candler, Jr., were the junior bridesmaid and groomsman.

After the elaborate wedding, the young couple was driven to the station to catch the evening train for Asheville, N.C., where they were to spend their honeymoon. The first of the "Candler Jinxes" occurred. On the way to the station, their car crashed into another automobile. Both vehicles were demolished — not an auspicious beginning to their marriage. Fortunately, no one was killed, but it was a serious accident. The newlyweds were injured slightly, enough to delay the honeymoon for a week.

And that following week — on June 18, 1924 — Homer Thompson and Lucy Candler were married in a sumptuous *al fresco* affair in the sunken gardens at Briarcliff. Orchids from Buddie's greenhouses adorned her altar; Buddie had a collection of more than two thousand species of orchids. The newspapers the week before described Elizabeth's wedding as being marked by "brilliance and beauty."

By the following week, they were running out of adjectives. Lucy's wedding was described as "unsurpassed brilliance." The Bishop united Lucy and Homer in matrimony as he had Elizabeth and Bry. Their attendants were dressed for an outdoor pageant.

As the party wound on, the newlyweds made a surreptitious escape, in order to avoid the rice and the teasing of their friends. Fleeing down a hidden garden path to the back of the estate, they jumped into Homer's car. They quickly drove to an alley, parked the car, and started to walk to the back of Mrs. Thompson's house so Homer could pick up his suitcases. Suddenly they heard what sounded like shots. Someone was shooting at them! Another shot was fired, this time brushing through Lucy's hair and actually cutting off some. Homer grabbed Lucy, pitched her into the car, and they sped away. Their honeymoon, also planned for Asheville, was postponed for a day so they could collect their wits. One of the neighbors, it seems, had mistaken them for burglars, deciding to shoot first and ask questions later. Lucy had said she wanted her wedding to be different. It was.

The next week brought the report to the public that Asa Candler, Sr., had filed for divorce from his second wife. The papers came to refer to him as the "lovelorn monarch of the Southern Soft Drink Dynasty." For his grandchildren, the hoopla and press coverage was a real bath in unwanted and undesirable publicity. After all, who really wants everyone in town to know that your parents were not happy about your choice in a mate? The papers made fun of the Candlers and the Candlers, with their usual wit, made fun of the papers among themselves. Before long, the "Candler Jinx" was a family joke.

By 1929, Lucy III and Homer were headed to Texas to live. He and Buddie had purchased a bottling plant in Galveston. Buddie's idea was to set his son-in-law up in business. Buddie had reconciled to Lucy's choice of a husband; after all, Homer was a lot of fun even if he wasn't an Atlanta boy by birth. Galveston was a beachfront town with good potential for Coca-Cola. Homer's first priority was to get out and establish outlets for sales. And, he was surprised to find that he had trouble. Even the pool halls didn't want to stock and sell Coca-Cola.

It was getting serious. He couldn't understand it; after all, this was Texas. It's even hotter in Texas than it is in Georgia. Homer quizzed his salesmen. What were they running into? Why were they having difficulty? After much

hemming and hawing and shuffling of feet, someone explained to Homer that the Maceo brothers didn't want Coca-
Cola in Galveston. They especially did not want Coca-Cola
in their pool halls, because it just might cut into their liquor
business. They also found Coca-Cola's "super-clean" image
offensive. The Maceo brothers were Galveston's version of
the Mafia, the local organized crime family.

Like every fully indoctrinated Coca-Cola man, and married to the chief's granddaughter, at that, Homer Thompson
would not accept "no" as an answer. He decided he would just
go see this Mr. Sam Maceo that everyone said was so opposed
to Coca-Cola. It took him a week or more to get the guy
tracked down.

Homer wasn't accustomed to dealing with mobsters, and
he wasn't what you'd call "street smart," but he was sold on
his product and determined to sell it in Galveston. He finally
got an audience with Sam Maceo. Maceo told him point
blank, Coca-Cola hurt the bootleg business, and it wasn't
going to be sold in Galveston. Homer tried all his usual,
company-approved arguments. It didn't work. Homer kept
going back to see Mr. Maceo, however, and the guy decided
he liked Homer's persistence. Finally, Homer broke through.
He asked Sam Maceo just to let him try to sell some Coca-
Cola in one of the nicer pool halls and let his patrons know
that it was available because down in Cuba it was getting
real popular to mix rum with Coca-Cola. Maceo agreed; rum
sales picked up. Next thing, Coca-Cola was suddenly wanted
all over town by all the retail outlets, and Homer had made
a business alliance, of sorts.

Things went well in Galveston for the young Thompsons.
Homer was active in clubs: the Rotary, the Boosters, a
member of the advisory board of the Chamber of Commerce,
the board of directors of the Beach Association, and vice
president of the Men's Club of the First Presbyterian Church.
Lucy III was busy with her two young children, Tommy and
Mettelen. They made the news as little as possible; although
it didn't help to have an eccentric father like Buddie. Every
now and then, the papers would write a page about Buddie
and Florence flying all over the country in either Buddie's
Lockheed-Vega or his open cockpit Waco biplane. Stories

would feature Florence flying to Galveston for a "tea" honoring Lucy, in less time that it would have taken to drive from Atlanta to Savannah.

By midsummer of 1932, Homer noticed something was amiss. The collections and expenses weren't right. Something was either wrong with the books or wrong in the plant. He started working hard to find the problem. It didn't take long; he found that one of the company's administrators, Bill Hall, was doctoring the books. In short, he was embezzling. Homer set a trap to catch the man, and Bill Hall was fired. A few evenings later, Hall came to the Thompson home, drunk and mad. He threatened Homer, he threatened the family, and he threatened the company. Quiet, affable Homer got the man out of the house, but not before young Tommy had seen and heard the angry exchange — fortunately so, as it turned out.

August, 1932, was a happy month for the Thompson family, they greeted the birth of another little girl. On the evening of the twenty-second, while Homer was down at the hospital visiting Lucy and baby Suzanne, Bill Hall came back to the Thompson house. Homer's mother, Mrs. Metta Thompson, was back in the kitchen when Hall entered the house (no one locked their doors back then). She thought it was Homer and called to him. When there was no answer, she came towards the front to see what was going on. Hall pushed her aside, "yelling I've come for his kids."

Hearing the shouts downstairs, five-year-old Tommy sneaked to the top of the stairwell and saw the scene below. Instinct told him to hide. As he has told it later, "All I knew was that that man had upset my daddy and that he was a bad man. I was too little to really understand anything else." Tommy ran to his little sister's room. Only three years old, Mettelen figured this was a great new game. Tommy grabbed her, ran to a guest room at the end of the hall and scooted the two of them under the old four poster bed. He shushed Mettelen; this was a game where you had to stay quiet. Bill Hall pushed past Metta Thompson and went through the house room by room. He opened closets, slammed doors and tramped through the entire house. But he didn't check under the old bed. In a rage, he ran out the door, just as sirens were heard headed towards the Thompson home.

The police arrived because they had not been able to get an answer by phone, and they really needed to get in touch with Homer Thompson. The Coca-Cola plant was on fire! They calmed Mrs. Thompson, Tommy finally coming out of hiding when he heard his grandmother calling, and the police tracked Homer down at the hospital.

The fire was definitely set, and it didn't take long for anyone to come up with a suspect. Just one problem, no one could find Mr. Hall. Days went by, Lucy, Homer, and Mrs. Thompson lived in fear that another kidnapping attempt would be made. Should they ask PaPa to send the plane? What should they do? Homer didn't want to back down from a threat; it wouldn't look good for business. It would set a bad example. But the police were not having any luck finding their arsonist. Finally, Homer went to see Sam Maceo.

Sam Maceo listened to Homer's story. He said he understood how worried Lucy must be about her children, and he understood that certainly, no one would want to appear to not have implicit faith in the law enforcement personnel; that wouldn't be a good image for a young businessman. However, a real threat was something to worry about, and, yes, he did understand that if the man was actually in jail, everyone would rest easier. Maceo agreed to keep his ears and eyes open.

Very shortly after Homer's little visit, maybe just a day or so, a large car pulled up outside of police headquarters and deposited one Bill Hall, suspect. The Maceo brothers had delivered. Hall was sentenced and served his time. That fall, Buddie and Homer sold the bottling plant to a holding company for The Coca-Cola Bottling Company that included Homer Thompson on the board of directors. The holding company would sell out in 1934 to another group. The Thompsons headed back east.

Homer and Lucy III would lead a happy, all-American, all-Coca-Cola kind of life. They would raise their family, participate in community activities and be happy. Lucy III had her friends, her clubs, and her home. Like her grandmother, Lucy, she was very domestic and focused her time and energy on her home and her family. Lucy III would typify most of the Candler granddaughters; clubs, causes, and social activities would take a back seat to their husbands, children, and homes. In this respect they would reflect their grandparents lifestyles and values, and for the most part, these would be the most content of Asa and Lucy's grandchildren.

Homer would continue his life's work as a Coca-Cola man. After his death, *The Coca-Cola Bottler* published a warm tribute to Homer's dedication to the company and reminded all the bottlers that it was Homer Thompson who first convinced the coaches of the nation to allow their players to drink Coca-Cola during games. As the writer pointed out, prior to that time, a player had to eat or suck on oranges and lemons or just suck on a sponge for liquid during games and at half time. Homer Thompson with his quiet persistence changed that practice. He was the man who finally convinced the coaches to allow coolers and Cokes in the locker rooms. He convinced them that the carbonated water would ease the acid in the players' stomachs and that the sugar would give them quick energy. This was a big achievement on behalf of The Coca-Cola Company in the late 1940s.

The publicity and the notoriety that accompany great wealth were a nuisance in the lives of Asa Candler's grandchildren. It was an intrusion they would learn to deal with; certainly, the novelty of being in the news wore off quickly.

After the tragic kidnapping and death of the Lindbergh baby, that kind of threat became more popular with the extortionists of America. Wealthy people everywhere lived in fear of an attempt being made against their children. Lucy III's experience and that of her brother John and his wife were not really that unusual, only more frightening because it was really tried. Even Buddie was threatened. After he established the zoo at Briarcliff, a young man attempted to extort money from him by threatening to kill his animals. Following the example set by Asa, Sr., Buddie like Homer and John, turned it over to the police. They solved the crime and saved the animals.

Of Asa and Lucy Candler's twenty-two grandchildren,

two would die as children — Asa III and Emelie. Of the remaining twenty, fully half would become alcoholics. Of those ten, six would die as a direct result of their addiction. The remaining four would win their battle with the bottle. What makes this sad tragedy more noteworthy is their grandfather's strong Methodist-fueled stand against alcohol. If it had been only Buddie's children who had the problem, it could be dismissed as being a result of having an alcoholic for a father. However, that wasn't the way it worked out. Some of the ones who had the problem had parents who didn't and two of Buddie's children did not.

As Buddie's granddaughter, Nancy Candler Nutter, explains it, "Alcohol was one of the big undoings among the grandchildren. It was the drug of choice, it was available, it was the 'in' thing during Prohibition. It became the 'cool' thing to do. All the really smart people were smoking and drinking. Young people who inherit a lot of money and don't have to work, tend to find all these things to do that are absolutely worthless."

Drinking contributed to the early death of Buddie's daughter, Martha, but it was the circumstances surrounding her death and burial that created a mystery back home.

Martha and Helen were fraternal twins, and no two people looked less like sisters than those two. It was a cruel twist of fate. Martha was tall, blond, and had a perfect figure. Helen was short, stocky, and looked just like her father. Their parents would dress them alike, send them to the same schools, and give them joint parties. The parties and the schools are understandable, but not dressing them alike. They were compared by everyone. Both girls had a creative flair that outshone their siblings and probably most of their cousins. Martha was the artistic one; she could paint, draw, do any kind of fancy needlework.

Mettelen Thompson Moore remembers her. "Aunt Martha was a trip. She could be more fun. We [Mettelen and her husband Jack] had moved to Panama City. We had been down there I guess a year and a half. Aunt Martha called and said she wanted to come down and visit, would it be all right? I said that of course it would be.

"So she said she would be down on the train the next

week and for us to meet her. Well, Martha hadn't hung up good before mother called and asked, 'Did she call you?' I said, 'Yes.' 'Did she want to stay with you?' And I said, 'Yes.' 'Mettelen, you don't know what you're getting yourself into,' mother warned me.

"Anyway, that next Wednesday, the train got in around 6 or 6:30. Jack and I went to the train station. She was one of maybe three to get off, and the last one at that. She had all kinds of luggage, with this porter behind her carrying all kinds of heavy suitcases. She had this huge hatbox. At that time she had the wildest red hair you will ever see. She had on a white suit with a red bouffant blouse and red shoes. She got off talking as loud as she could to the porter, 'This poor thing, it's his last trip. He can't take it anymore. After me, nobody could take it.' And carrying on like that.

"Anyway, she entertained everybody there at the train station until we could get her luggage and so forth to the car. We went on to the house. We had a two-bedroom, one-bath house. She began to unload all of these clothes. She said, 'I know I brought too much, but I have to have a new outfit for every day. Now what do we have planned for tonight?' I said, 'Well, we can go down to the yacht club and eat if you want to.' She said, 'That will be fine. Who do I know at the yacht club?' I said, 'Well, you know the black fellow that's in charge, because PaPa used to come down here.' Martha said, 'That's marvelous. That's marvelous.' She just went on and on with all this personality.

"We went down to the yacht club that night, and we had dinner. Of course, she meets everybody there and knows everybody by their first names. There was this one young fellow there, rather tall and nice looking. She turns on the jukebox and has him dancing before the night's over and has him invited over to my house the next evening for dinner or whatever. So I checked to make sure he was not married, because we didn't know him.

"She was down there a week and a half, and there wasn't a dull moment. She would come in and say something like, 'We're going to have pheasant under glass and wild rice. So I'd say, "Where in the world — this is Panama City, Florida — where in the world are we going to get a pheasant, much less any glass to put it under?' And she'd say, 'well, we'll just make something up.'

"She would say, 'What am I going to wear tonight? I think I'm going to wear my black dress. Therefore, I've got to go to the drugstore, because I'm going to be a blond tonight.' And that was the way she was. During the week and a half she was there, she colored her hair at least five times. Changed her hair — she was red, she was brunette, she was blond, she was streaked. If you weren't there, you would have walked in the door and wondered who your new houseguest was. She would just go to the drugstore and get whatever it was and here we'd go. Of course, women dyed their hair back then and often changed the color, but she did more often than anyone else. She was a trip. We entertained more in that week and a half than we entertained in the three years we were in Panama City.

"She would go out and meet these people and bring them back to our house. We'd have to serve them refreshments. One-Eyed Joes was her favorite drink to make. I bet I bought six dozen eggs during that week and a half. We'd come back after partying that night, and she would make One-eyed Joes, fry bacon, and so on. Jack and I were just in a whirlwind. Our friends thought it was wonderful. We had more fun that visit."

But Martha's life was not always a party although she worked hard to make it one. Her first marriage ended in divorce. She had picked out Dr. Jesse York; her family and friends liked him. Her father actually approved of him. However, their first clue that perhaps this wasn't the dream match of the century came shortly after the wedding when Dr. York's family had the bills for their clothes that they had purchased for the wedding festivities sent to Buddie and Florence. (Florence sent them back to the stores with a note saying that they had the wrong address. But with freeloading in-laws like that, Martha was in for a rough ride.)

She married a second time, to Tom Callaway, of Covington, Georgia. Everybody liked Tom, too. He fit right in and he was crazy about Martha. But they had an up-and-down marriage. They had a lot in common, including alcoholism. All their friends and relatives were surprised when they announced they were moving to Cuba! "Why Cuba?" people asked. And Martha would laugh and say, "Well, rum is just a nickel a glass." It seemed eccentric, but Martha and Tom were eccentric. Off they went to the Isle of Pines.

In May, 1961, Tom sent word to Atlanta that Martha had fallen and broken a leg. She was in the hospital. The next thing anyone knew, she was dead. She had developed pneumonia, and her body was so weak from the alcohol poisoning that she was unable to fight off the virus. The newspapers would say that she died of "complications from a broken leg." Martha was only forty-nine. It was a sad time made even sadder when the Cuban government suddenly refused to release the body.

Tommy Thompson takes up the narration of this story: "Of course, Aunt Martha got into the drinking really after PaPa died. She died really more from that than from anything else down at the Isle of Pines.

"We like to have never got her out of there. The Cubans didn't want to release her body. I think the two thousand dollars that Aunt Florence was told to pay was nothing more than a political bribe. It was something about the body had to stay there to be examined and checked, all nonsense.

"A lot of people didn't know this, but Tom Callaway was working for the United States government down there as a spy. This was part of the problem of getting her body out of there, because it became pretty well known that Tom was not down there as just a lark. I thought it was pretty funny when Aunt Martha and Tom all of a sudden moved to the Isle of Pines, Cuba. What the hell would you want to go down there for?

"I also was asked to come visit them down there, which I never did. When Tom got back, he didn't talk about it an awful lot. A good friend of mine, George Montgomery, whose people used to own a line of Coca-Cola bottling plants, was somewhat active, not with the government but in an anti-espionage type thing. He and Tom were friends, and George asked me one time, 'You didn't know your uncle was working for the government down there as an espionage agent?' I said, 'Hell, no, I didn't know that, George.' George could *habla español* as good as the Cubans could. I don't know whether Tom was talking to George here or George would talk to Tom, but anyway, it was a known thing, in their crowd. That's the way I really got it confirmed because Tom would not talk about it.

"I think that had more to do with not getting Aunt Martha's body out of Cuba. I think they were kind of holding her as ransom for Tom to confess what he had been up to. Of course, this was during Castro's early reign down there, and it was a peculiar situation. I never did find out all I wanted to find out about that. Tom came back here and lived here. He remarried, and then died not long afterwards."

Tragically, Martha's sister Helen would survive her by only three years. Helen could sing, play the piano by ear, and was a natural comic. Unfortunately, when she expressed a desire to try her talents in the theater, Buddie said "no." She also had an uncanny ability in math. Her cousins remember how odd it seemed to them that Martha was so good at English and reading, but Helen didn't seem to be able to read well. However, anything with numbers, she could handle, almost like an adding machine. Also an alcoholic, Helen, like her first cousin, Walter, Jr., burned to death, at her home.

Buddie's oldest son, John Howard Candler, typified the grandchildren's Gatsby-esque lives. He had good points — his *joie de vivre,* and his young, exuberant personality and lifestyle. The pain and tragedy caused by his death at a young age hit the whole family hard. However, this tragedy also highlighted that the family had a major problem it would need to solve — they were out of control in the way they were using their wealth. As a result, with a few exceptions, the next generation would draw inward and come to be very conservative.

John Howard Candler, is a classic example of all that was right about the Candler grandchildren and what, in some cases, went wrong. He had one early strike against him. Born just nine months after the death of little Asa III, he became the child on whom his parents focused their hopes and dreams; they doted on him and worried about him. His grandparents, as well, were rather taken with him.

All the Candler grandsons had the same burden that

their own fathers had had. They became the surrogates of their fathers. Each of the boys, Howard, Buddie, Walter, and William put a lot of pressure on their boys to be what the fathers wanted them to be. They had to go to Emory, they had to learn the father's business; there was little encouragement for the grandsons to seek their own identity and John was no exception.

Like his own father, John went to school with the girls until he was old enough to enter the University School for boys. At fifteen, he entered Emory. They gave him his own car so he could drive to college, after dropping his little brother, Sam, off at his school. John had the ability to do the college work, but not the maturity to handle college life. Added to that, his own home life was chaotic; his father's drinking and carousing was affecting the entire family. For John, this period in his life would be like something from one of F. Scott Fitzgerald's novels. Howard, Jr., and Bill Owens would survive it, perhaps because they had more stable homes or were stronger people.

John was friendly, outgoing, and liked people. He made friends easily. He was inclined to be reflective and to express his thoughts in a conversation. He would listen and exchange ideas; he loved to debate. He could write poetry, sing, and loved the theater as his grandmother Lucy had. He was willing to get up and perform in front of any group. He was a lot of fun.

John's college days were filled with lots of activities; however, he did not seem to have put his studies at the top of his priority list. Parties, dates, gambling, raising money for Emory, and being in love took up a lot of his time. He was not alone. Edgar Chambers, John Hurt, and Howard, Jr., were his boon companions in those years and certainly did their share of cavorting. Howard, Jr., and John Candler appear to have had the worst case of teenage love of the foursome. Howard, Jr., had a terrific crush on Ruth Ozburn and John had fallen for "Lib" Brandon. They filled their time together talking about the girls, commiserating over disappointments such as not getting a letter from Lib or Ruth having a date with someone else.

These two cousins were more like brothers, and they

were very supportive of each other's schemes. Howard and John would scout out the competition by driving by Ruth's on a regular basis and then work out an offense plan for Howard. John had a long-distance problem. Lib had been exiled back to Virginia by the Brandons in an effort to discourage the romance. How could John justify a trip to Richmond? He found his answer at the Emory Glee Club. John had a beautiful, trained tenor voice and enjoyed his participation in the glee club. When the director announced that the club would be taking a tour on behalf of the college and would travel to Virginia; an opportunity presented itself. The Glee Club wasn't going to Richmond, only to Danville and Charlottesville, but with Howard's help — he sent a fake telegram stating that John was urgently needed on family business in Richmond — John got to see Lib.

Howard, Jr., went on to finish Emory and to work for his father. John did not. John was expelled once from Emory, got back in, got his grades up, then dropped Emory and entered law school at the University of Virginia. He didn't want to be a lawyer, but the University of Virginia was closer to Lib, and her family felt law school was a necessary requirement for all young men. He later dropped law school. But, he did get his girl, just as Howard, Jr., got Miss Ozburn.

One of the problems John had, in addition to his father's alcoholism and his mother's long illness and early death, was a lack of focus. He had several talents but he never fully developed any of them. He had a beautiful singing voice. All of his cousins have recalled how John would stand at every family gathering and sing the *Vesti La Giubba* from Pagliacci. He was able to do the academic work necessary for a professional career. He could debate and negotiate for fun and for profit. But he never picked one thing to concentrate on. He flew, but he never became a pilot like his cousins, William Owens, Jr., and Henry Heinz, Jr.

John would typify Asa's grandchildren who drowned in the bottle. He struggled with it, he tried to quit, but he never succeeded. He did find that his talent for spotting sharp deals in real estate and negotiating, earned him a very good living. He was successful at that, but it was a hollow success.

John developed the first strip shopping center in the

Southeast, Briarcliff Plaza on Ponce de Leon Avenue in Atlanta. He had seen a similar development in either Texas or California in the early 1930s, and was convinced that it was the way to go. He saw that the American public would become more and more dependent on their automobiles, and this type of shopping facility would be the answer to their new lifestyles. He was right. Before his death, he would see success with his developments of grocery store and drug-store anchors coupled with additional retail space serving the motoring public.

What drove him to drink when he had so much to live for? What kind of drunk was he? What did his family think of him, his problem, and its cause and effect? Some family members shed their light on these questions.

Louise Owens (Lucy II's daughter-in-law): "John had a great personality, but, I think, also sort of an inferiority complex. Maybe it was all of them thinking they had to live up to something they couldn't — like more was expected of them than they could ever do. It's like Bill, my husband, went to Emory. Of course, it was because the family wanted him to go there. That was not where he wanted to go. He would have been better off at Georgia Tech where he could study something mechanical, something to do with his hands. They made him go to Emory, and by his second year there, he begged them to let him go to flying school. But by then, John had introduced him to flying and taken him up in a plane. He had gone out to the airport and taken flying lessons. John, after he got his pilot's license, was on the governor's staff. He and Gene Talmadge were great friends."

Caroline Candler Hunt (the Bishop's granddaughter): "I'll tell you what he told my father [Charles Candler]. Papa had asked, 'John, why do you drink like this after you lived with that at home the way you have?' He answered, 'If I analyze it myself, I'm getting even with my father.'"

Eugenia Candler Wilson (Walter's daughter): "[John] had automobiles, a dealership, real unusual ones. He sold one, I know, to Papa. He was a nice boy, a good boy. We all enjoyed him. Everybody loved him. He threw his life away, but I tell you, he was the dickens. When Lib died, he went nutty. He loved that little girl. She was a dear."

Laura Candler Chambers (Buddie's daughter): "Papa knew about John, and it just killed him. Just killed him. I almost was tempted to say, 'Well, you deserve it.' I shouldn't have, but I thought it. Papa grieved. He really grieved after that, for John. He really did.

"Papa told me, 'You know, for every quart of liquor you drink, they have made another quart? You'll never empty the bottle. Not until you say, "I quit." You're looking at somebody who knows all about it, because I quit,' and he did. When he quit, he quit for good. But he couldn't help John. He just grieved over John. He really did."

Asa G. Candler V (John's son) recounts the following stories: "Bill Ward was one of my daddy's best friends and a lawyer, and they lived next door to us at the corner or Briarcliff and North Decatur. They were contemporaries. Drinking buddies. Big friends.

"In the early 30s, my daddy had an airplane. They heard that Augustus Busch was starting an airline, and they were going to need airplanes, so my daddy wanted to sell his airplane, which was a single engine thing.

"He and Bill Ward flew the thing up to St. Louis to sell Augustus Busch his airplane. This is Ward telling the story. They had a pilot, I think it was Beeler Blevins, who ran the airport one time. This is probably 1932. Daddy's about twenty-seven, or twenty-six. This Augie Busch was there. So they go out there and they see Augie Busch, and he looks at the airplane, and Busch says, 'Well, boys. Don't believe I need your airplane.' He had a cane, you know. He took his cane, according to Ward, and poked the exhaust stacks. He thrust little holes in the exhaust stacks and he said, 'Before you go, let me have my mechanics put some new exhaust stacks on this plane so you'll get home.' Which they promptly did.

"Ward said he showed them all through the Busch beer factory, and they were three sheets in the wind taking off... Ward was sitting in the back seat, and my dad was sitting in the copilot's seat. He was drunk as a lord. So he wrote a little note and handed it to the pilot. And Ward was sitting back there wondering what the hell was going on, so he leaned forward and looked at the note, and the note said, 'Loop it.'

"He was a great storyteller, Ward was. They came on back. They didn't get to sell the airplane, but they got totally plastered and had a great time.

"The next thing you know, five or six years later, World War II is going, so my dad goes and tries to sign up and be a pilot and they said, no you're too old. That was a blow.

"In 1939, he was thirty-four years old. They didn't want him. Uncle Brad [Lancaster] said he was going to be the gunner and Daddy would be the pilot, and they would shoot down all the Germans.

"I'll say it was tough. You know what a chronic drunk is, don't you? That's what he was. The tough thing was he was just a charming guy when he was sober. But when he had a drink, he would get passed-out drunk and stay that way for weeks. Just passed-out drunk.

"When he came to, he'd be looking for the bottle to take another deep swig and go back down. We had to force food into him almost to get nourishment. He would go weeks.

"I remember him when my mother was alive. She got Uncle Brad to come and get him and put him in a hotel room and stay with him until he decided — and only he decided — when he had had enough. It might be two weeks, three weeks, but whatever it was, and then one day he'd quit. He would clean up and come home. It didn't register when I was a little bitty boy that he was that bad an alcoholic, because I didn't see anything else. She used to sort of insulate us from it. But after she died, of course it got worse. He, in his defense, and this was weak, but in his defense, he knew soon after they married that she had cancer.

"They told him that she could live about seven years. And in that period of time they had four children. So you knew how it could end — every time she got a cold, or something, it might be it. You get a little sick, something like that. Then after seven, eight, nine, ten years, you think, well, they were wrong. Toward the end, they were telling us it was arthritis.

"Well, they could have told me it was cancer. They could have told me whooping cough — cancer meant zero to me, but they told us arthritis. I was coming up on twelve years old. Hell, arthritis was a worse word than cancer. I had never heard of cancer. It could have been a chewing gum, far as I knew. I didn't know anything. But they thought that if they told us it was cancer, it would have a meaning. It might have to Nancy, but I doubt it. She was fourteen. Maybe it would have, but I don't know.

"In the end, he had that care, and that was a problem. Of course, that's a crutch. When you've got somebody sick, you ought to do the best you can to make them comfortable, not go get drunk. I think he had the genes for alcoholism, too."

Nancy Candler Nutter adds: "After mother died, Daddy told me that she had had cancer. He wanted us to know what the truth was, but he also told me not to mention it to anyone else. It was just for us to know because people thought it was contagious. He wanted me to know that it wasn't, but some people just didn't know any better."

Howard, Jr., was quiet like his father. He became Howard, Sr.'s right hand in everything. Unlike John, Howard, Jr., typified the ten grandchildren that did not have difficulties with alcohol. He worked hard, he played hard. Howard, Jr., also flew airplanes; he and John were both in the Civil Air Patrol. Howard stuck with it; John's drinking forced him to give it up. Howard sat on many of the same boards of directors that Howard, Sr., had served on. Howard, Jr., found his release in hunting and farming. It was Howard, Jr., who brought Bradley Lancaster into the Candler fold. Howard, Jr., and some friends had gotten up a hunting club and found this fellow down in Greenville, Georgia, to keep and train their dogs — Bradley Lancaster. Howard thought Brad was great and was sure that John would, also. He got them together, possibly hoping that John would get more involved with hunting and less with drinking.

Asa G. Candler V says: "That's how my daddy and Brad got together, and they just hit it off. Hell, Uncle Brad was a character. My daddy was an expert at debating. They loved to argue about politics. They loved it.

"I was with Uncle Brad and Daddy a lot. I just listened. They'd be arguing about Roosevelt, whether he was good or bad. Railroad freight rates were another hot topic of daddy's — Northern businesses charged a Southerner more to send

324 THE REAL ONES: The First Family of Coca-Cola®

a carload of anything from here to Chicago than they would charge people in Chicago to send a carload of stuff down to Atlanta. So there was discrimination in freight rates. Ellis Arnold was the governor who started a lawsuit against the railroads and got that corrected. But people talked about it a lot. I was born in 1931, and there were still discriminatory laws like that up until in the forties and fifties.

"Today, all those industries are moving out of the miserable towns up there that have snow six feet deep in the winter and they're going to Florida, the south of Georgia, and New Orleans. We are coming into our own again.

"But, back to Uncle Brad. My daddy met Brad through this hunting club that he joined because of Howard Jr. Uncle Brad kept the dogs. They leased land down at Camilla, Georgia, and they'd go down there on weekends during the hunting season and hunt. It was just one of those deals where a bunch of guys get up a hunting club.

"So Daddy went out and bought a shotgun and all the paraphernalia he needed to be a sportsman. I was four years old, this was 1935. After the shopping trip, we went home to Briarcliff Road and Uncle Brad came over. He was such a character! Let me tell you about Uncle Brad: We got into mother's car, that old Dodge she had, and started for Greenville down the old road. It took nearly an hour and a half. We got about halfway down there, and the guy in front of us was so drunk he was weaving from side to side.

"Interesting enough, Bradley didn't have a drink in his life. We got behind a guy that was drunk. So we finally get by, and we get down to the next town, stop, and Uncle Bradley somehow or another pulls this guy over. He said, 'Hell, he's going to kill himself or somebody else.' He stopped and waved this guy down somehow or other. He says, 'Hello, neighbor, how're you doing, neighbor?' and reached in there and got the keys. He got somebody from around there to drive the man home. That's the kind of guy Uncle Brad was. A lot of people would have just kept on going, minding their own business.

"Another thing that'll show you about Bradley. He used to drive the school bus for the county. And the black children didn't get to ride on a school bus. It bothered Uncle Brad, if it was raining, to see those little kids out in that. So, he'd speed up and deliver the white children and turn that bus around and go pick those little kids up and take 'em home. That's the kind of guy Uncle Brad was.

"Anyway, we finally got to Greenville, When I got out of the car, I was surrounded by all those bird dogs. I remember I was looking at them eye to eye. I was a little guy and we were nose to nose. I remember Cha-cha (Uncle Bradley's wife) coming out, how sweet she was.

"We went in the house, and I remember I slept in a bed at the foot of their bed, a little bed. And [Brad] said, 'OK, Bud, in the morning when you wake up, you just reach up there and pull my toe, and that'll wake me up. I remember they had a clock that went tick-tock, tick-tock. They had the thing forever, and it went tick-tock, tick-tock. It made you sleep at night, you know.

"I did, I woke up early the next morning and reached up and grabbed him by the toe and pulled the thing. Then we all got up and had breakfast. He said it was dawn. He was an early-rising man. They got up and got breakfast going and all that. I remember they got Frank, Jr., over [Frank Tigner, Jr.—Cha-cha's nephew who lived next door], and he was six, and we shot the .22 rifle. Later on that day, he drove me home. I just spent the one night.

"Ever since then, in the summer, I'd go down and spend a week. Thanksgiving, I'd go down, too. The next summer I spent two weeks. And on and on and on. Everybody else would be going to camp, I'd be going to Greenville. I'll never forget it. It was fun.

"John and Bradley really hit it off. But their joint interest was politics, not hunting. So, Bradley and Howard, Jr., would go hunting, but John and Bradley would go 'politicking.'"

John and Brad, along with many Georgians, were Dixiecrats and rabid supporters of Eugene 'Gene' Talmadge. They loved the give-and-take of politics and served Gene's campaigns. This included John being on the governor's staff while Gene was governor, flying Gene places he needed to go, and delivering the votes, which included going and picking up people and driving them to the polls and, if necessary, getting them a fifth of liquor after they voted. The importance of the turnout had to do with Georgia's county unit system.

John and Brad loved to talk about the value of the "county unit system."

Alton Roberts, Jr. [Aunt Florence's nephew]: "Because they [rural voters] supported Talmadge, Talmadge had the ability to win the rural vote and people with influence in Atlanta. Roll those two together, you could whip them all.

"Back then, we were in the fifth congressional district, and we were three counties. Fulton had six county units. DeKalb had six and Rockdale two. Rockdale and DeKalb always got the congressman they wanted. They wouldn't let Fulton County have one. The thing is, maybe Fulton County could go three to one for somebody, but Rockdale was just, back then, maybe five hundred votes. If the man running took those five hundred votes, he got Rockdale's county unit; that plus DeKalb's could beat Fulton. That man that went to Rockdale and DeKalb, won the county unit system.

"John loved to talk about the county unit system. It was a game to him. He and Bradley Lancaster were big buddies. I remember Bradley. All I remember, he wore suspenders like Gene Talmadge did. Gene Talmadge wore bright, red suspenders. That was his trademark.

For John, politics became almost an avocation. He loved it. He delighted in debating his country club friends in Atlanta over Talmadge and FDR. Oddly enough, John supported both men; however, Talmadge and FDR couldn't stand each other. Most of John's city friends couldn't stand either candidate. It was fun and challenging to John. He would later tell his daughter that one of his regrets was that he came to politics late in life, after he had already destroyed himself with liquor. Had he found the challenge earlier, he might have pursued it differently.

But politics did not hold any fascination for Howard, Jr. He enjoyed his farm and his hunting, and he enjoyed his friendship with Bradley. Bradley was a cutup, he could play a joke well, and he could also take a joke. As Howard, Jr.'s, son, Samuel Ozburn Candler relates, the Candlers liked to play tricks, too. All in good, clean fun.

"Well, it was on one of the fishing trips we had over to the islands. They went many, many times. They would take the boat over. Bradley would be on these trips, very often. They were out fishing, and I think Daddy took us up, he was with the boat captain. The lines, you know, you put the poles in the socket, and the line has the bait tied to it, off the side. You're not sitting there holding the pole, you're sitting there talking, and the pole's sitting in the socket.

"Once they pulled a trick on Uncle Brad by tying a noose around the line and putting this bucket on it. When the bucket hit the water, the boat moving forward would pull the bucket, and just pull the line almost right off, like a tremendous fish had taken the hook, if we grabbed the line. They all hollered to Brad to catch this pole. He grabbed the pole, and as long as the boat kept moving forward a little bit, the line just kept going off this pole — and he'd get that thing, and crank it in, and by the time he really had it cranked in, they'd motion the boat captain to go forward — it's about to get tangled up. He'd go forward, and the bucket would go *zooop*! and it would run back out like it did. He must have fought it for an hour. He finally got that bucket up. Brad saw that bucket, and he got so mad.

"He was had. They never did let him forget about the bucket. But they were always cooking up some sort of scheme.

"Brad liked to flirt with the ladies. He flirted a lot, maybe too much. Some of the group, one time, decided to give him a dose of his own medicine. They had stopped somewhere to eat and, as usual, Brad was flirting with the waitress. So, Brad excused himself and went to the bathroom. The waitress seemed like a good-natured person, so they called her over and explained that Brad was harmless, but he really did this all the time and they felt he needed a lesson, would she be willing to help? She agreed. So, old Brad comes back to the table and starts up flirting again. This time, she takes him up on it. Just flirts back and pats him, and maybe started to sit on his lap. Well, it nearly scared him to death. He jumped up and the chair fell backward, and Brad ran out from there to the first door open he could find. Turns out, he ended up in the women's bathroom and locked himself in. He wouldn't come out. They laughed over that, so often. But he deserved it."

Howard, Jr., led the life his father had encouraged him to lead. He set a good example, but was he really content? Did he ever get the chance to be all the things he wanted to be? We know that his cousin John did not. Perhaps Howard, Jr., as well, felt stifled by his father's aspirations for him. He married his sweetheart, Ruth Ozburn. They married young, grew up and grew apart. But, unlike others, both had a strong commitment to their family. They did not end their marriage until all of their children had grown and left home — and Howard, Sr., had died. They knew that he would never have been able to accept divorce within his family.

One of John Howard Candler's buddies was Edgar Chambers, Jr. Along with John Hurt, and Howard, Jr., Edgar was frequently in the company of John. More than likely, he had already fallen for John's next younger sister, Laura, so it wasn't hard for John to persuade Edgar to come on over and join in whatever was going on at Briarcliff. Edgar quickly became a fixture in the lives of the Candlers.

John and Edgar were loyal Emory students. John, like most of the Candler's, had a feeling for the college that went beyond the average student loyalty. The Candlers believed that Emory was an asset to the city of Atlanta and to Georgia and they supported her at every opportunity.

Edgar finished Emory's undergraduate and law schools, then went to work for Haas-Gambrell and Gardner in Atlanta. One of his accounts as a young lawyer was his father-in-law, Buddie. Florence Candler would later tell how after Buddie gave his zoo to the city of Atlanta and had sold the elephants that the city couldn't house to a circus, Edgar faced the unpleasant task of having to collect the note on the elephants. The circus was behind in their payments. Edgar came by Briarcliff to confer with Buddie prior to his flying to where the circus was located. Florence's parting comment to Edgar, (out of earshot of Buddie) was, "Edgar, whatever you do, *don't* repossess those elephants." That's the closest she ever came to giving her real feelings on the subject of zoo animals in the front yard.

As Walter's daughter, Eugenia Candler Wilson, explained, it can be very useful to have a large and very clannish family. If it hadn't been for her cousin Laura marrying Edgar Chambers, Eugenia might not have gotten to meet her future husband.

"I was over by Emory and walking home to Lullwater when Edgar drove by and offered me a ride. I wouldn't have gotten in the car with just anyone, but he was Laura's husband, so it was okay. Edgar had to drop some papers off down in the village, and we were sitting in the car waiting for something when I saw this good-looking creature crossing the road up ahead. I don't know what got into me, but I just blurted out, 'That's the man I'm going to marry.' Edgar looked at me and said, 'Eugenia, do you know that fellow?' 'No,' I said, 'but I'm going to marry him, I just know it.'

"About this time, the boy crossed the road near us and headed into Emory Village. Well, all of sudden, Edgar decides he needs some cigarettes and tells me to wait in the car, he'll be right back. Edgar Chambers wasn't gone a minute before he was back on my side of the car with that young man. He said, 'Eugenia, I'd like you to meet John Something or Other, he's a fraternity brother of mine.' I didn't hear another word. I was too surprised or embarrassed to say much. But I did remember saying something to the effect that it was nice to meet him, and I hoped I would see him again. Maybe I even mentioned we were having a party that weekend and would he like to come and meet some folks, and he said to send him an invitation. Well, that's what I wanted to hear. I just had one problem, I couldn't remember his name! And, I was already so embarrassed, I wasn't about to call up Cousin Edgar and admit it.

"So what was I to do? I fretted about it and then decided, that I'd tell Papa that maybe we ought to include all the boys down at the Kappa Alpha house since so many of them were new and might want to come out and meet some folks. Well, Papa thought that was great, like all the men in the family, he'd been a Kappa Alpha; before long, he thought it was his idea! So I just mailed an invitation to the entire fraternity and hoped that young man would show up on Saturday night.

"I stood in the doorway with Papa and we greeted all the guests as they came in. I kept watching and straining my neck to look down the drive. He wasn't out there. It got later and he still hadn't showed. Don't you know he was the last boy to come to that party. When he introduced himself, 'John Wilson,' I just thought — what a hard name to remember!

"We visited around with other people and mostly with each other, and I knew by the end of the party, we had an understanding. Papa didn't think too much of that. Thought we were too young, I was anyway. He made us wait. John went off to the Orient with the bank. He was in international banking after he got out of school.

"When he came back, we were determined to marry. So, I told John he'd have to go talk to the Bishop about it and all."

John Holtzendorff Wilson added his version of that meeting, "Well, the Bishop was very nice to me. He asked me about my work, my family, what my plans were. He was elderly by then. He made me feel welcome and said, 'Well, you seem like a fine young man and suitable for one of my great-nieces. And he married us out at Glenn Memorial Church. The funny thing was, he forgot the ring part of the ceremony, he just pronounced us man and wife."

Eugenia adds, "Yes, I'm walking down the aisle waving my finger saying where's my ring, where's my ring? All my cousins are giggling. So Edgar or someone got hold of Uncle Warren after the ceremony and asked him about the ring."

John: "And do you know what he said? This just shows you how quick witted the Bishop was. He said, 'well you seem like a nice young man with good prospects, but I didn't feel you had much right now and probably couldn't afford a ring, so I just didn't bring it up. Wouldn't want to embarrass you in front of all those people.' He had a quick comeback for everything.'

"But I did get my ring," added Eugenia.

Later on, after living in the Orient for several years, John and Eugenia would return to the U.S. (just before war broke out with Japan where they had been living) and John would go to work for Coca-Cola Export and watch it grow into the major business it is today. He retired from the company in the late 1960s.

Of Asa, Sr's grandsons, only one of the boys would actually work for the drink he made possible. While Howard, Jr., would eventually follow his father onto the board of directors of The Coca-Cola Company, he did not ever actually work for the company.

Walter's son, Asa IV, however, did go to work for Coca-Cola. Asa IV arranged to move away from Atlanta and thus avoid the unrelenting publicity that so plagued many of his cousins. He led his own quiet existence and yet remained within the fold. He loyally worked for and retired from the company his grandfather had founded.

And what of the rest of the Real Ones? What are they doing today?

Asa G. Candler, Sr.'s, kith and kin are spread across the country; some even live abroad part of the time. Some of his brother Milton's descendants followed their patriarch's lead and entered Georgia politics. Two of their more prominent members were his son, Charles Murphey Candler who served in the U.S. Congress, and his grandson, Scott Candler, Sr., affectionately known as "Mr. DeKalb." Scott literally ran and managed DeKalb County for better than sixteen years where he was DeKalb County's commissioner of Roads and Revenues. Scott was the moving force behind his county's industrial and economic development. This stubborn Candler prepared his county to handle the explosive growth that resulted from its proximity to metro Atlanta. He was the father of the county's water system, and the man who almost single-handedly readied DeKalb County for the later half of the twentieth century.

Zeke's son, Zeke, Jr., served in the U.S. Congress for over twenty-two years. Zeke had another son and a grandson who worked for The Coca-Cola Company all their lives. The Bishop, like Asa, has a large number of descendants whose careers run the gamut. His son Charles became prominent in the wholesale grocery business and banking circles while maintaining an active role in Methodist affairs.

The Judge's descendants have continued to field smart and aggressive lawyers with each successive generation.

They also keep up active roles in the National Guard.

Not everyone lived happily ever after, and that was just as true among Asa's brothers' descendants as it was for some of Asa's own. The plague of alcoholism was not confined to only Asa's grandchildren or their children, but cut across the family tree. Also, each of the brothers seem to have had at least one child or grandchild that did not ever get with the family's program of hard work, commitment to family, and service to the community.

The inherited love of self-promotion runs deep in Candler veins. Sometimes it comes up in unexpected and not-so-positive ways. It was Milton's son, Sam, who introduced Buddie to the fine art of gambling in California, among other activities. Sam later abandoned his wife and children to lead the life of an eccentric in San Francisco, where he claimed fame as a chess player.

Asa, Sr., set up his nephew John Curtright Candler, the Bishop's son, in several positions and jobs, but he could never make it work. These two plus others were mavericks and eccentrics, not unlike their cousins Buddie and even Walter. It worried their fathers, it worried their Uncle Asa, and yet there was no more they could do about it than they could stop the ones who chose to drink. The disappointment of members who chose a different and sometimes low road has not been confined to the second or even the third generations. It just crops up. One great-grandson of Asa G. Candler, Sr., even served time in prison for bank fraud.

The families who still have money — most of them — continue to build on it in all the usual ways. William's grandchildren and great-grandchildren continue to manage his vast ranch in Florida, and one great-grandson works for Coca-Cola. Many of Asa's grandchildren and great-grandchildren have farms out from the cities. Walter's descendants have farms but do not raise horses. Some of Howard's raise cattle and sometimes horses.

Many of Asa's descendants are independent business owners. A lot of them are in insurance and law. Many have developed their natural tendency towards hype and promotion into careers in advertising and public relations. There are numerous teachers, some ministers, writers, and decorators. Others have various and sundry kinds of businesses.

Those that own businesses are typically independent small business owners. Perhaps the largest number of Asa Sr.'s descendants pursue real estate, following in this family tradition. John Howard Candler's legacy to his children of real estate speculation has been carried on to a great degree by his son, Asa Griggs Candler V, and a number of John's grandchildren. John developed the first modern shopping center with off street parking in the Southeastern United States. At the time, his developments were unusual and innovative. One of his developments, the Briarcliff Plaza in Atlanta, remains in the family today.

From the time of Asa, Sr., real estate has been a Candler calling. The current Candler Development Company was founded in 1975, but its origins began at the turn of this century with the many successful speculations and real estate developments that Asa, Sr. did so well.

Asa V was graduated from Emory University in 1952 and served in the Air National Guard as a pilot. He started his career with the Adair Realty and Loan Company, one of Atlanta's oldest sales firms. After five years of "learning the ropes," he started his own firm with his brother-in-law, Robert S. Griffith. Candler and Griffith Company developed, owned, and leased office buildings, shopping centers, and apartments. By 1975, Asa V decided that he would concentrate his efforts in developing strip centers, primarily in the Florida and Georgia markets. Over the past fourteen years, the Candler Development Company has developed twenty-five shopping centers, most of them anchored by Publix Super Markets.

His three sons, Asa G. Candler VI, William Rackley Candler, and Richard Brandon Candler, run this business with him and their prospects for the next few years look exceptionally good as the shopping center business continues its growth in the Georgia market.

Another of John Candler's grandsons, Robert Sherrill Griffith, III, is in partnership with Griffith Associates, which specializes in the management and development of apartments, office complexes, and shopping centers.

The coauthor of this book — Elizabeth Candler Graham,
Asa Candler, Sr.'s, great-great-granddaughter — owns and
runs Graham Investments, a real estate company specializing in the North and South Carolina markets, as well as
eastern Tennessee. Her very successful firm specializes in
the sale, management, and division of large tracts of land, as
well as the sale and management of investment properties.

Like many other Candlers, Elizabeth is a graduate of
Emory. Her interests outside of real estate include geneal-
ogy and history (as you may have already guessed by the
very existence of this book). She is a member also of the
National Society of the Daughters of the American Revolution, Edward Buncombe Chapter.

Two of Asa's descendants would hold a place of particular pride for him. It would, no doubt, please him that after so
many years and with more than four hundred descendants,
he finally has a doctor in his family. One of Howard, Sr.'s
great-grandsons has achieved that distinction and is a
pediatrician. The other great-great-grandson who would
surely tickle Asa's sense of irony and pride is Edgar Chambers IV with his 7-UP connections and concoctions and who,
as we saw earlier, developed Diet 7-Up With Nutrasweet.

How many of the family are still shareholders of The
Coca Cola Company? Many. Some still have some of the
original stock that was issued, and at least one family
member said, "there's no way we can get rid of it, because
capital gains would eat us up. So we just give it to children,
grandchildren, and charitable institutions that catch our
interest."

The Candlers remain interested in The Coca-Cola Company for its tradition, as well as its dividends. They generally serve Coca-Cola to their guests and usually from the
original 6.5 ounce bottles of Classic Coke. They are proud of
Asa's company, its product, and their extended family's part
in the history of that company. At present, no members of
the Candler family are on the board of directors of The Coca-
Cola Company.

# Postscript

**M**oney does not protect you from tragedy or sorrow; sometimes, it can increase your exposure to the risk. Asa's family — The Real Ones — have learned about being a target. They understand that success such as his frequently generates unwanted and unwarranted publicity. It brings with it a lack of privacy. Wealthy people are often subject to negative press resulting more from jealousy than any action of theirs. And, as was the case for some of Asa's grandchildren and great-grandchildren security becomes an issue, along with the inevitable gigolos and gold diggers that come courting. But those are external nuisances that can be dealt with; of greater concern is the issue of coming to grips with life in the shadow of someone else's achievements. Many successful people have children and grandchildren who have difficulty with this. There is always the feeling of not being able to top papa; of being defeated before you even start and for some, the comparison can be crushing.

It is often perceived that the great national purpose in the United States is to make money. When the incentive for that is taken away, it can have a devastating effect on the descendants. Because they lack the "hunger factor" they do not have the same drive to succeed. In some cases this results in people who lack focus; they drift following totally effete pursuits.

The flip side of that same coin is that having been freed from the need to work in order to eat, some can pursue talents that have little to do with monetary rewards. It is a gift to be able to pursue one's own interests. And, most rewarding of all, it allows them to be able to give their time, their energy, and their money to worthwhile projects.

Asa's descendants for the most part have opted for low profile lives. They have learned from the excesses of the past that great wealth has both a good and a bad side to it. Asa's great success did impact on his children and most particularly on his grandchildren who probably had the hardest time with it. The fourth and fifth generations seem to have accepted the challenge. They are the most ardent capitalists since Asa's generation and thoroughly enjoy the give and take of the marketplace as Asa did.

Just as they have had to deal with the notoriety of Asa's success and wealth, they are learning to deal with the other inherited traits or tendencies. Some of the Candlers still have Asa's thin lips and blue eyes and most can be stubborn. The diabetes that plagued the Judge in his later years also attacked Lucy II and Lucy III. Several in the family have been diagnosed with dyslexia. The Candler "melancholia" continues to appear from time to time and may well have been the underlying cause of so much of the alcoholism within the family. But these are exceptions, rather than the rule. Now that the family members are aware of the possibilities, they can watch for and handle the problems if they show.

For the most part, the Candlers have found that what makes for the happiest lives is not money or notoriety but the same values that Asa and his brothers espoused. The Real Ones are quietly active in their various churches, civic, and charitable organizations. They give a great deal to their communities, most often anonymously or with little fanfare. And when they get together, which they still love to do, they talk about their hobbies and their families.

The last large gathering of the clan was in May 1986 when Coca-Cola celebrated its hundredth anniversary. Coca-Cola celebrated this centennial year in style. The city of Atlanta hosted a week long celebration for its hometown success. The city was in a holiday mood; special events were scheduled, parades held, and parties given. People associated with The Coca-Cola Company were in Atlanta from all over the world to help celebrate that anniversary in their soft drink's hometown. The Candlers celebrated, too. Asa Griggs Candler V, his wife June, and their sons hosted a spur-of-the-moment family reunion, which included trying to track down long-lost cousins across the nation. The elegant affair was held at Callan Castle, Asa and Lucy's old home in Inman Park which had been beautifully renovated, and at the time, was available for parties. They celebrated being a family. There was much laughing, joking, hugging, and kissing. Maybe the Candlers are still a little clannish, but they are also a lot of fun.

The Candlers came from far and wide to toast the soft drink and the kinship that binds them. For them, it is a part of their legacy from Asa which he so plainly wrote in his will:

"To my household, my children and to their children and the generations that follow, I bequeath my good name as it has come to me from an honorable and honest ancestry. My chief aim in life has been to help and not hurt my fellow man... May they be as faithful and true to their and our God is my prayer."

# Bibliography

## Books:

Atlanta City Directories: 1875-1945.

Bauman, Mark K. *Warren Akin Candler: The Conservative as Idealist*. Metuchen, NJ: Scarecrow Press, Inc., 1981.

Bonner, James C. *Georgia's Last Frontier: The Development of Carroll County*. Athens, GA: University of Georgia Press, 1971.

Boone, Don. *Alternatives to Alcoholism's Grand Conspiracy*. Asheville, NC: WorldComm Press, 1992.

Boylston, Elise Reid. *Atlanta: Its Lore, Legends, and Laughter*. Doraville, GA: Foote & Davies, 1968.

Braden, Betsy and Paul Hagan. *A Dream Takes Flight: Hartsfield Atlanta International Airport and Aviation in Atlanta*. Athens, GA: University of Georgia Press, 1989.

Bryant, James C. *Capital City Club: The First One Hundred Years, 1883-1983*. Atlanta: Privately Printed, 1991.

Bullock, Henry Morton. *A History of Emory University*. Atlanta: Cherokee Publishing Company, 1972.

Candler, Allen Daniel. *William Candler of Georgia: His Ancestry and Progeny*. Atlanta: Foote and Davis, 1896.

Candler, Charles Howard. *Asa Griggs Candler*. Atlanta: Emory University Press, 1950.

Candler, F.S. "Asa Griggs Candler, Jr." in *The National Cyclopaedia of American Biography*. New York: James T. White & Company, 1965.

Cash, Wilbur J. *The Mind of the South*. New York: Alfred A. Knopf, 1941.

Coulter, E. Merton. *The Confederate States of America*, Volume VII of *History of the South*. Baton Rouge: Louisiana State University Press, 1950.

Coulter, E. Merton. *The South During Reconstruction, 1865-1877*, Volume VIII of *History of the South*. Baton Rouge: Louisiana State University Press, 1947.

Davis, Glenn. *Childhood and History in America*. New York: Psychohistory Press, 1976.

Davis, Lance E. *The Growth of Industrial Enterprise, 1860-1914*, #3289 of *Economic Forces in American History*. Atlanta: Scott, Foresman, and Company, 1964.

DeMause, Lloyd, ed. *The New Psychohistory*. New York: Psychohistory Press, 1975.

Dennett, John Richard. *The South As It Is 1865-1866*. Athens, GA: University of Georgia Press, 1986.

Donald, David, ed. *Why The North Won The Civil War*. Baton Rouge: Louisiana State University Press, 1960.

Elam Franklin Dempsey, ed. *Wit and Wisdom of Warren Akin Candler*. Nashville, TN: Publishing House of the Methodist Episcopal Church, South, 1922.

Garrett, Franklin M. *Atlanta and Environs: A Chronicle of Its People and Events, Volume I.* Athens, GA: University of Georgia Press, 1988.
Garrett, Franklin M. *Atlanta and Environs: A Chronicle of Its People and Events, Volume II.* Athens, GA: University of Georgia Press, 1988.
Garrison, Webb. *The Legacy of Atlanta: A Short History.* Atlanta: Peachtree Publishers, Ltd., 1987.
Hahn, Steven. *The Roots of Southern Populism: Yeoman Farmers and the Transformation of the Georgia Upcountry, 1850-1890.* New York: Oxford University Press, 1983.
Hester, Robert L. *The Coca-Cola Cocaine Connection.* Gainesville, FL: Khoka Productions, Inc., 1987.
Jenkins, James S. *Murder in Atlanta!.* Atlanta: Cherokee Publishing Company, 1981.
Kahn, E.J., Jr. *The Big Drink.* New York: Random House, 1960.
Knight, Lucian Lamar. *Georgia's Landmarks, Memorials, and Legends, Volume I.* Atlanta: Byrd Printing Company, 1913.
Knight, Lucian Lamar. *Georgia's Landmarks, Memorials, and Legends, Volume II.* Atlanta: Byrd Printing Company, 1913.
Lapham, Lewis H. *Money and Class in America.* New York: Weidenfeld & Nicolson, 1988.
Lawrence, Harold. *The Tucker Band.* Milledgeville, GA: Boyd Publishing Company, 1992.
Lovejoy, Paul E. *Caravans of Kola: The Hausa Kola Trade 1700-1900.* Zaria, Nigeria: Ahmadu Bello University Press Ltd., 1980.
Martin, Harold H. *Three Strong Pillars: The Story of the Trust Company of Georgia.* Atlanta: Trust Company of Georgia, 1974.
Martin, Harold H. *Atlanta and Environs, A Chronicle of Its People and Events, Volume III.* Athens, GA: University of Georgia Press, 1987.
Morison, Samuel Eliot, Henry Steele Commager, and William E. Leuchtenburg. *The Growth of the American Republic, Volume I.* New York: Oxford University Press, 1969.
Morison, Samuel Eliot, Henry Steele Commager, and William E. Leuchtenburg. *The Growth of the American Republic, Volume II.* New York: Oxford University Press, 1969.
Munsey, Cecil. *The Illustrated Guide to the Collectibles of Coca-Cola.* New York: Hawthorn Books, Inc., 1972.
Murphy, Gregory. Ed. *Builders of Georgia.* Atlanta: Privately Printed by Gregory Murphy, 1941.
Oliver, Thomas. *The Real Coke, The Real Story.* New York: Random House, 1986.
Palazzini, Fiora Steinbach. *Coca-Cola Superstar.* Milan: Idealibri, 1986.
Pierce, Alfred M. *Giant Against The Sky: The Life of Bishop Warren Aiken Candler.* New York: Abingdon-Cokesbury Press, 1948.
Pollard, Sidney. *Wealth & Poverty: An Economic History of the Twentieth Century.* New York: Oxford University Press, 1990.
Preston, Howard L. *Automobile Age Atlanta.* Athens, GA: University of Georgia Press, 1979.
Rice, Grantland. *The Bobby Jones Story.* Atlanta: Tupper & Love, Inc., 1953.
Rogers, Ernest. *Peachtree Parade.* Atlanta: Tupper & Love, Inc.,1956.
Roper, John Herbert. *C. Vann Woodward Southerner.* Athens, GA: University of Georgia Press, 1987.
Rowland, Sanders and Bob Terrell. *Papa Coke.* Asheville, NC: Bright Mountain Books, 1986.
Rubinstein, W.D. *Wealth and the Wealthy in the Modern World.* New York: St. Martin's

Press, Inc., 1980.
Sanders, George, Helen Sanders, and Ralph Roberts. *The Pride Guide to Autographs, Second Edition*. Radnor, PA: Wallace-Homestead Book Company, 1991.
Shelton, Morris. *"Mr. DeKalb"*. Atlanta: Dickson's, Inc., 1971.
Simkins, Francis Butler and Charles Pierce Roland. *A History of the South*. New York: Alfred A. Knopf, Inc., 1972.
Soper, David Wesley, ed. *These Found The Way*. Philadelphia: Westminster Press, 1951.
Southern Historical Association. *Memoirs of Georgia, Volume I*. Atlanta: Southern Historical Association, 1895.
Southern Historical Association. *Memoirs of Georgia, Volume II*. Atlanta: Southern Historical Association, 1895.
Stadiem, William. *A Class By Themselves: The Untold Story of the Great Southern Families*. New York: Crown Publishers, Inc., 1980.
*Story of the Trust Company of Georgia, Atlanta: On Its 60th Anniversary*. Atlanta: Foote & Davies, Inc., 1951.
*The Coca-Cola Company: An Illustrated Profile of a Worldwide Company*. Atlanta: Privately Printed, 1974.
Tindall, George Brown. *The Emergence of the New South, 1913-1945*, Volume X of *History of the South*. Baton Rouge: Louisiana State University Press, 1967.
U.S. Census 1850: Carroll County, GA.
U.S. Census 1850: Slave Schedules, Carroll County, GA.
U.S. Census 1860: Carroll County, GA.
U.S. Census 1860: Slave Schedules, Carroll County, GA.
U.S. Census 1870: Carroll County, GA.
Watters, Pat. *Coca-Cola: An Illustrated History*. New York: Doubleday & Company, Inc., 1978.
Wells, Della Wager. *The First Hundred Years: A Centennial History of King & Spalding*. Atlanta: Privately Printed by King & Spalding, 1985.
White, George. *Statistics of the State of Georgia*. Savannah, GA: W. Thorne Williams, 1849.
Wiley, Bell Irvin and Hirst D. Milhollen. *Embattled Confederates*. New York: Harper & Row, 1964.
Willard, J.J., ed. *The Coca-Cola Bottler* (1909-1929). Hickory, NC.
Woodward, C. Vann. *The Burden of Southern History*. Baton Rouge: Louisiana State University Press, 1968.
Woodward, C. Vann. *Origins of the New South: 1877-1913*. Volume IX of *History of t the South*. Baton Rouge: Louisiana State University Press, 1971.

## Newspapers:

*Atlanta Constitution*
*Atlanta Georgian*
*Atlanta Journal*
*New York Times*
*The Hartwell Sun*
*The Sun*
*The Wall Street Journal*

## Unpublished Materials

Brandon, Nancy Hughes. Letters to Mary Hughes LeSeur (1943-1958), collection of the author.

Brandon, Nancy Hughes. Letters to Nancy Candler (1929-1936); letter to Elizabeth Louise Brandon Candler, courtesy of Nancy Candler Nutter.

Brandon, Nancy Hughes. Scrapbooks prepared for Helen Candler (1933-1958), courtesy of Helen Candler Griffith.

Brandon, Nancy Hughes. Scrapbooks prepared for Nancy Candler (1929-1958), courtesy of Nancy Candler Nutter.

Briarcliff Scrapbook. Courtesy of the DeKalb Addiction Center, Atlanta, GA.

Candler, Asa Griggs, Jr. Family movies 1928-1950, courtesy of Asa Griggs Candler, V.

Candler, Asa Griggs. Letters to "Bootsie" Candler (1921), courtesy of Marion Candler Ruffner.

Candler, Asa Griggs Papers. Archives Department, The Coca-Cola Company. Atlanta, GA.

Candler, Asa Griggs Papers. Special Collections Department, Robert W. Woodruff Library, Emory University.

Candler, Charles Howard. "Thirty-Three Years With Coca-Cola", courtesy of the Archives Department, The Coca-Cola Company, Atlanta, GA.

Candler, Charles Howard. Letters to Samuel Ozburn Candler, courtesy of Samuel Ozburn Candler.

Candler, Charles Howard Papers, Special Collections Department, Robert W. Woodruff Library, Emory University.

Candler, Charles Howard Papers. Archives Department, The Coca-Cola Company, Atlanta, GA.

Candler, Claire Clement. Family tree chart of descendants of Asa Griggs Candler (1985), collection of the author.

Candler, Daniel B. "Personal Recollections of the Early Days of The Coca-Cola Company," Archives Department, The Coca-Cola Company, Atlanta, GA.

Candler, Flora Glenn. Candler family genealogical data, courtesy of Catherine Candler Warren.

Candler, Florence Stephenson. Files on Florence Stephenson Candler and other Candler family members, courtesy of Rachel Hamlin Still.

Candler, Florence Stephenson. Letters to Nancy Candler (1948-1949), courtesy of Nancy Candler Nutter.

Candler, Florence Stephenson. Letters to the author (1963-1975), collection of the author.

Candler, John Howard. Letter to Asa Griggs Candler, Jr. 1929 re: death and burial of Asa Griggs Candler, Sr., collection of the author.

Candler, John Howard. Daily Journal 1924, courtesy of Helen Candler Griffith.

Candler, John Howard. Daily Journals 1925, 1926, 1927, courtesy of Asa Griggs Candler, V.

Candler, John Howard. Letters to Elizabeth Louise Brandon (1925-27); letters to Nancy Hughes Brandon (1927-1939), courtesy of Helen Candler Griffith.

Candler, John Howard. Letters to Mary Hughes LeSeur (1943-46), collection of the author.

Candler, Walter Turner Papers. Letters from Lucy Elizabeth Howard Candler to Walter Turner Candler (1904-1907); letters from Asa Griggs Candler, Sr. to Walter Turner Candler (1904-1907); letter from Charles Howard Candler (February 1905); letters from Mary Candler to Grandmother Bigham (1922), courtesy of Robert Anderson Edmondson, III.

Candler, Walter Turner Papers. Special Collections Department, Robert W. Woodruff Library, Emory University.

Candler, Warren Aiken Papers. Special Collections Department, Robert W. Woodruff Library, Emory University.

Candler Family Papers. Special Collections Department, Robert W. Woodruff Library,

Emory University.
Candler Memorial Room Inventory. Special Collections, Robert W. Woodruff Library, Emory University.
Chambers, Laura Candler. Letters to the author (1991), collection of the author.
Curtright Family Papers, Georgia Department of Archives and History, Atlanta, GA.
Edmondson, Mary Candler. Personal scrapbooks and memorabilia, courtesy of Robert Anderson Edmondson, III.
Emory University Alumni Records, Atlanta, GA.
Graham, Elizabeth Candler. Personal Journal (1967-1974), property of the author.
Graham, William Wayne. Letters to Louise Wetherby Graham (1951-1952), collection of the author.
Heinz, Henry Charles and Lucy Candler. Family movies (1922-1941), courtesy of Henry Charles Heinz, Jr.
Ruffner, Marion Candler. Personal scrapbooks and memorabilia, courtesy of Marion Candler Ruffner.
Salem Campground Annual Meeting Programs, re: Asa Griggs Candler, Jr. and Charles Candler, courtesy of Robert Hewlett Elliott, Jr.
Salem College Alumni Records, Winston-Salem, NC.
Thompson, Lucy Magill Candler. Personal scrapbooks and memorabilia, courtesy of Mettelen Thompson Moore.
Vann, Elizabeth Candler Owens. Wedding scrapbook and memorabilia, courtesy of Mr. and Mrs. William Davies Owens, Jr.
Willard, Sam. Personal Recollections of the Early Days of The Coca-Cola Company. Archives Department, The Coca-Cola Company, Atlanta, GA.
Wilson, Eugenia Candler. Personal scrapbooks and memorabilia, courtesy of Eugenia Candler Wilson.
Wilson, Ruth Nolen. "John Henry Magill" scrapbook prepared for Elizabeth C. Graham; article "John Henry Magill" prepared for the inauguration of the John Henry Magill Chapter #853, Children of the Confederacy, Conroe, Texas (1989), collection of the author.

## Court Papers

Asa G. Candler, Inc. vs. Hirsch, M.L. #94093 Fulton County records.
Byfield, Sarah vs. Candler, Walter T. #3604 DeKalb County, GA records.
Byfield (C.K.) vs. Candler, et al. #4096 DeKalb County, GA records.
Candler, Asa G. vs. Mae L. Candler, PreA/60607 (1924), Fulton County, GA records.
Candler, Asa G., Jr. vs. The Coca-Cola Company, et al, Muscogee County, GA records.
Candler, Walter T. vs. Byfield, C.K. PreA/53503 (1922-1925), Fulton County, GA records.
Criminal judgment dockets 1905-1924. DeKalb County, GA records.
DeBouchel vs. Candler, (1923-1924) U.S. District Court, Atlanta, GA.
DeKalb County, GA court records.
Divorce motion/decree: Marion Penland Candler vs. Walter Turner Candler. DeKalb County, GA records,
Divorce motion/decree: Marion Penland Candler vs. Walter Turner Candler. Fulton County, GA records.
Fulton County, GA court records.
Guardianship records, Minute Books (Antoinette C. Candler). DeKalb County, GA records.
Guardianship records, 1947-1954 (children of John Howard Candler, Sr.). Fulton County, GA records.

Land Records 1890-1950, DeKalb County, GA records.
Land Records 1890-1950, Fulton County, GA records.
Marriage Records (Colored) (1921-1939), DeKalb County, GA records.
Marriage Records (White) 1905-1955, DeKalb County, GA records.
Probate records, DeKalb County, GA.
Probate records, Fulton County, GA.
Suit by Asa Griggs Candler, Jr. and wife for custody of children of John Howard
    Candler, Sr. Fulton County, GA records.
Suit by Mae Little Candler against the estate of Asa Griggs Candler, Sr. 1933-1936.
    DeKalb County, GA records.
Wills: Asa Griggs Candler, Sr., Charles Howard Candler, Sr., Asa Griggs Candler, Jr.,
    Walter Turner Candler, Sr., William Candler, Sr., Elizabeth Louise Brandon Candler,
    John Howard Candler, Sr., Florence Stephenson Candler, Morris Brandon, Sr., Henry
    Charles Heinz, Sr., John Slaughter Candler, Sr.